LILAWATI

LILAWATI

OR

A TREATISE

ON

Arithmetic and Geometry

BHASCARA ACHARYA

TRANSLATED FROM THE ORIGINAL SANSCRIT

JOHN TAYLOR, M. D.

GYAN

Published by

Gyan Publishing House
5, Ansari Road
Daryaganj, New Delhi-110002
Phone: 011-47034999, 9811692060
E-mail: books@gyanbooks.com

Distribution Network
gyanbooks.com
India, USA, Canada, UK, Australia, France

ISBN : 978-81-212-9516-1 (PB)
First Published, 1816

2nd Impression 2023

Printed at: Gyan Press, Delhi.

LILAWATI
Translator: JOHN TAYLOR

LILAWATI:

OR

A TREATISE

ON

Arithmetic and Geometry

BY

BHASCARA ACHARYA,

TRANSLATED FROM THE ORIGINAL SANSCRIT

BY

JOHN TAYLOR, M. D.

OF THE HON'BLE EAST INDIA COMPANY'S BOMBAY MEDICAL ESTABLISHMENT.

1816.

TO

THE RIGHT HONORABLE FRANCIS,

EARL OF MOIRA, BARON RAWDON IN IRELAND,

&c. &c. &c. K. G.

GOVERNOR GENERAL OF INDIA,

&c. &c. &c.

THE FOLLOWING WORK,

Illustrative of the Mathematical Science of the Hindus,

IS MOST RESPECTFULLY DEDICATED

BY

HIS OBEDIENT AND HUMBLE SERVANT,

JOHN TAYLOR.

Extract from the Minutes of the Proceedings of the Literary Society of Bombay, 27th June 1815.

Mr. Erskine read to the Society a Translation by Dr. Taylor from the Original Sanscrit, of the Lilawati, a Treatise on Hindu Arithmetic and Geometry.

The above being a Work which has been frequently called for by the learned in Europe, and it being desirable for the sake of accuracy, that it should be printed under the eye of the Translator, it is resolved that the printing of the Work shall be immediately undertaken at the expense of the Society under Dr. Taylor's superintendance; and that their thanks be returned to him for his valuable labors.

ERRATA.

Introduction page 5, line 7, *for* Mecleod *read* Macleod.

——————— page 17, line 2 *for* 6 × 13, *read* 9 × 10.

Page 7 Line 33 *for* 317 28 *read* 17 28.

10 Line 6 *for* 12 *read* 20.

13 Line 3 *for* by double the sum of this last figure, *read* by double this last figure.

do. note c *for* 7890 *read* 7690 and *for* 861 *read* 661.

Page 16 line 27 *dele* the words " adding the unit if there be one to the preceding quosient figure."

Page 27 *dele* the first line.

The following remark, which with many other explanatory remarks, was furnished me by Lieutenants Macleod and Tate, on the rule for summation of tranposed numbers page 135, was omitted to be inserted in its proper place.

The truth of this rule is evident, for if the whole of the transposed numbers be set down, and added together, the sum of all the vestical columns of units, tens, &c. will be equal to each other, and will each amount to the sum of the given digits, multiplied by the number of transpositions, and divided by the number of these digits; consequently, each column being thus separately summed up, and set down one place forward, the amount of these sums will give the sum of the whole of the transposed numbers.

CONTENTS

INTRODUCTION

PART I.

ARITHMETIC

Tables of Money, Weights, &c: 1
Of Addition and Subtraction, ... 6
— *Multiplication,* 7
— *Division,* 11
— *the Square,* 13
——*Square Root,* 15
——*Cube,* 17
——*Cube Root,* 20
— *Fractions,* 24
— *the Effect of Cipher,* 29
— *Inversion,* 31
— *an Assumed Number,* 32
— *Multiplier of the Root,* 37
Rule of Three Quantities, ... 41
—— *Five, &c. Quantities,* 43
Of Barter, ... 46
— *Mixed Quantities,* 47
— *Buying and Selling,* 51
— *Computing Gold,* 54
— *Permutations,* 57
— *Progressions,* 59

CHAPTER II.

SECTION I.

Of Circles 94

SECTION II.

Of Ponds, ... 99

SECTION III.

Of the Bricks or Stones in a Wall, ... 101

SECTION IV.

Of Cutting Timbers, &c. 101

SECTION V.

Of Heaps, ... 103

SECTION VI.

Of Shadows, ... 104

PART III.

SECTION I.

Of the Kutaka, ... 111

SECTION II.

Of the Sthira or Fixed Kutaka, ... 122

SECTION III.

Of the Sanslista Kutaka, ... 129

PART IV.

Of Transpositions, ... 135

APPENDIX, ... 141

INTRODUCTION.

BHASCARA ACHARYA, the author of the following treatise, was born at Biddur, a city in the Deccan, in the year of Salivahana 1036, which corresponds with the year 1114 of the Christian era.* He wrote several astronomical and mathematical works, the most celebrated of which are the Lilawati, Bija Gannita, and Siromani. The two first, which relate to Arithmetic, Geometry, and Algebra, appear to have superseded entirely the more ancient treatises on these subjects, no other being in use, or, so far as we know, having even been seen, by astronomers of the present day.

The Bija Gannita treats of Algebra. It was translated into Persian in 1634 by Ata Allah Rashidi;† and from this version an account of the work has been published lately by Edward Strachey Esq. of the Bengal civil service, in what is termed "partly literal translation and partly abstract," accompanied with learned notes and illustrations.

The Siromani is a treatise on Astronomy. As it explains the science in a fuller and more perspicuous manner than the ancient and celebrated work called the Surya Siddhanta, it has a high repute among astronomers of the Deccan, and is often the only work which they peruse. It is divided into two *Adya*, or parts, named the *Gola Adya*, that which regards the globular form of the earth, and the *Gannita Adya*, that which relates to astronomical computations.

---

* As. Res. vol. 9. p. 351.

† Strachey's Bija Gannita, preface p. 4.

The Lilawati exhibits a regular, well connected, and, considering the period in which it was written, a profound system of arithmetic; and also contains many useful propositions in geometry and mensuration. It is the first work which is studied by Hindu astronomers, or rather astrologers; for in this country these two professions are always conjoined, and in general the former is considered subservient to the latter. The rules are written in verse in a very concise and even elliptical style, and possess in no slight degree the characteristic obscurity of Sanscrit compositions on science and philosophy.

By directions of the Emperor Acbar, whose liberal promotion of literature and science added glory to his conquests, it was translated into Persian in 1587 by Fyzi, the brother of Abu Fazil the Emperor's secretary. I procured a copy of this version from Mulla Firoz, a learned Parsi, who has studied with much success the astronomical system of the Arabians. Fyzi informs us that in making his translation he had the "assistance of men learned in the science, particularly of astrologers in the Deccan". His translation possesses that general accuracy which might be expected from a person of Fyzi's talents and knowledge, aided by such eminent mathematicians as his own situation, or the influence of his Royal Patron, could obtain. It is, however, often very obscure, and in several places there are considerable omissions, especially towards the end of the arithmetic, and in the geometrical operations which immediately precede the chapter on circles. The chapters on indeterminate problems and on transpositions are altogether omitted. Besides, the style is not only much more diffuse than what necessarily arises from the difference of the Persian and Sanscrit idioms, but the manner also of delivering the rules, and of detailing the operations, generally varies in a very considerable degree from that of the original text. This, indeed, is so remarkable as to induce a suspicion, that Fyzi contented himself with writing down the verbal explanation afforded by his assistants.

In the library of my very learned and estimable friend William Erskine Esq. there is a translation of the Lilawati into the language of Marwar which I have examined. It is of a date so late as 1762, and probably was made for the use of the Jaina priests, many of whom profess astrology. In consequence of the close affinity between the Marwari and Sanscrit languages, the translation is in general very literal, and also retains all the technical terms employed in the original. In several chapters, however, there are important omissions, and the indeterminate problems and transpositions are left out altogether.

A curious account of the occasion of writing the Lilawati is given by Fyzi in the preface to his translation. The story he relates has not been confirmed to me by any native of this country, nor have I observed it mentioned by any Hindu author; but as it may amuse the reader, I shall here transcribe a translation of it made by Mr. Strachey, and published in Hutton's mathematical tracts.

" It is said that the composing the Lilawati was occasioned by the following circumstance. Lilawati was the name of the author's (Bhascara's) daughter, concerning whom it appeared, from the qualities of the Ascendant at her birth, that she was destined to pass her life unmarried, and to remain without children. The father ascertained a lucky hour for contracting her in marriage, that she might be firmly connected, and have children. It is said that when that hour approached, he brought his daughter and his intended son near him. He left the hour cup on the vessel of water, and kept in attendance a time-knowing astrologer, in order that when the cup should subside in the water, those two precious jewels should be united. But, as the intended arrangement was not according to destiny, it happened that the girl, from a curiosity natural to children, looked into the cup, to observe the water coming in at the hole; when by chance a pearl separated from her bridal dress, fell into the cup, and, rolling down to the hole, stopped the influx of the water. So the astrologer waited in expectation of the promised hour. When the operation of the cup had thus been delayed beyond all moderate time, the father was in consternation, and examining, he found that a small pearl had stopped the course of the water, and that the long-expected hour was passed. In short, the father, thus disappointed, said to his unfortunate daughter, I will write a book of your name, which shall remain to the latest times—for a good name is a second life, and the ground-work of eternal existence."

My object in the following translation is to furnish an authentic document, which, by exhibiting not only the actual degree of mathematical knowledge possessed by the Hindus in the 12th century, but also, by shewing their modes and principles of operation, may lead to a fair conculusion regarding their pretensions to originality in this department of science. When it is considered that a translation of the present work has been long a desideratum, and that an unsuccessful attempt to translate it was made by that excellent mathematician Mr. Burrow, it will readily be supposed that considerable difficulties must have occurred in the course of this undertaking. It is probable, indeed, that I should have failed entirely, had not most material assistance been derived from three commentaries which I had the good fortune to obtain. Two of these were procured for me at Nagpore by the kind exertions of George Sotheby Esq. assistant to the British Resident at that place. It will be seen that ample use has been made of these commentaries. The method of operating in the examples is, in almost every instance, illustrated from them at full length. I reckon it also a great advantage to have possessed three different copies of the original text. One of these copies was written in Guzerat in Samvut 1729, which corresponds with the Christian year 1673. This being the copy from which I have translated, it has been sent to England in order to be placed in the Library of the Hon'ble East India Company. The other two copies were written in the Deccan. Their dates are not put down, but they are evidently not so old as the copy from Guzerat. The rules and examples of the Lilawati are also contained in two of the commentaries; so that I have had an opportunity of consulting actually five copies of the original work; and all these correspond with a degree of accuracy which I have rarely found to exist in different copies of Sanscrit books. The chief difference consists in the transposition of a few of the rules; and in the copy from Guzerat there are several *kshepaka*, or interpolated rules, which are not contained in the two other copies.

Tho' the opportunities now adverted to were favourable to the success of the undertaking, I am still not so sanguine as to imagine that this translation will fully satisfy the wishes and expectations of mathematicians in Europe. Some will perhaps be of opinion, that the examples, besides being drawn out at length from the commentaries, ought also to have been put down in the mathematical language of the western world. It did not, however, appear to me that, in regard to many of the examples, this was peculiarly requisite after the illustration afforded by the notes from the commentaries. Tho' neither brief nor elegant, these notes shew the different steps of each operation in a manner pretty clear and intelligible, so that no mathematician, it is imagined, will experience any difficulty or trouble in comprehending the rules or examples; and therefore they can occasion no trouble to any person who is disposed to translate them into the mathematical language to which he has been accustomed. Being chiefly desirous of presenting to the reader the views of the Hindu author, and the train of thought and of operation in the original, without any desire of accommodating them to the technical phraseology of European science, which in some instances might have led the mind into another series of ideas rendered familiar to it by long habit; I may perhaps have appeared sometimes to have carried this conformity to an excess scarcely justified by the idom of our language. But to any one who lays aside his preconceived habits of thinking on these subjects, and who takes up the work as a Scholar, and allows his mind to be led by the author's train of thought, this can occasion no difficulty. Illustrations, however, of such rules as were considered most curious and important, will be found in the notes. For most of these illustrations, many of which will be found extremely ingenious and elegant, I am indebted to the kind assistance of my young friends Lieutenants Mecleod, and Tate of the Engineers. It adds in no small degree to my obligation to these gentlemen, that their observations were written during the short intervals of leisure allowed them from the very laborious official duties in which they were engaged. I have only cause to regret that I had not the benefit of their assistance at an earlier period of the undertaking.

A defect of much more importance than what I have just noticed, will be discerned in the want of historical notes, comparing the mathematical knowledge displayed in the Lilawati with that which existed in Europe at the same period; and also comparing the Hindu rules and modes of operation with those of the Grecian school and of modern Europe. Such a comparison, however, even had the translator's qualifications rendered him competent to undertake it, could not have been accomplished with much success in this part of the world, where most of the works which ought to have been consulted cannot be obtained. Besides, any attempt of this nature, by a person even the best qualified, must be very imperfect until the astronomical and mathematical knowledge of the Hindus be more fully laid open to our view, by accurate translations of the principal works on these subjects. But whenever a work of so much curiosity and interest in the history of mathematical science shall be undertaken, it is perhaps not presuming too far to say, that the present small publication will be found a curious and valuable document.

Tho' I have aimed at rendering this version as literal as possible, still it is considerably more diffuse than the original text. The compact brevity of Sanscrit is incompatible perhaps with the idiom of the English language; but besides this, the rules in the Lilawati are delivered in a style so very elliptical and obscure, that often they would have been quite unintelligible had not the meaning been expanded in the translation. The two books on the *Kutaka*, or indeterminate problems, and on transpositions, being seldom studied, are peculiarly dark and doubtful. Before the rules could be comprehended, it was necessary, in most of the cases, to go over the examples, as they are exhibited both in the text and in the commentaries. Greater freedom, therefore, has been used in translating these chapters than in any other part of the work.

With the exception of the Sanscrit technical terms which have been retained, the words printed in *italics* are not in the original. In the geometrical operations it will be observed that by root is always meant the square root.

The statements, positions of the figures, and modes of operation, are given in the translation of the text precisely as they are exhibited in the original; and tho' this exact, or rather servile imitation, may sometimes cause a little perplexity to the reader, it corresponds with the rule which I mentioned to have laid down to myself in the translation; and is an evil of less magnitude than that of adopting methods which might lead to misinterpretation, and to erroneous conclusions.

In the notes taken from the commentaries I have also usually given the exact modes of expression, and of putting down the results. At the same time, in order to exhibit the operation in a shorter space, I have occasionally employed the marks used in European treatises. But it should be recollected that all these marks are foreign to the Hindu system. I shall have occasion to notice immediately, that the only mark employed by the Hindus, is that of minus.

The arithmetical operations of the *Hindus* are performed on a board about 12 inches long and 8 broad. A white ground being first formed with a kind of pipe clay, the board is covered with sand, or *gulal*, which is flour died of a purple colour. The forms of the figures or letters are traced with a wooden style, which displacing the sand or coloured flour, leaves the white ground exposed. By drawing the finger over the sand, these forms are easily obliterated, and the board is prepared for receiving new impressions. This is a matter of great convenience; for as the figures, in order to be distinct, must be written large, the board cannot contain the individual steps of even a short calculation. Hence the practice is to obliterate, in succession, the intermediate results, so that when the operation is finished, the general result only stands on the board.

The Hindu methods of operating in the four fundamental rules of addition, subtraction, multiplication, and division, are detailed at some length in the notes; but as these operations are not found in books, and can be learned only by seeing the processes gone through, a few more illustrations in this place may not be deemed superfluous.

In ADDITION they usually begin at the column on the right hand and proceed towards the left, in the same manner as is done in Europe. There is, however, another method, named inverse or retrograde, which is performed by beginning at the column on the left hand, and proceeding towards the right. According to this method the column of figures on the left hand is first added up, and the result put down beneath. The next column is then added up, and the units being put down, the tens are carried to the preceding result, which is blotted out, and the new result is set down in its place. The following example will illustrate this mode of operation.

3527685
9278316
5316925
8437207
4925624
―――――
29352667
3148578

The result of the operation, however, does not stand in this manner on the board; but, as each preceding result is rubbed out, and the new product put down in its place, the total amount stands thus;

31485787

To prove addition, a line is drawn below the uppermost number, or above the lowermost, which is then supposed to be cut off, and the rest of the numbers being added up, the uppermost line, or the lowermost, as the case may be, is added to the sum; and if the total amount correspond with that found by the first addition, the operation is considered correct.

The Hindus seem to be entirely ignorant of the method of proving addition by rejecting the nines; a fact which is deserving of notice, because as this method is familiar to those who follow the Arabian system, it shews how slow the Hindus are to borrow from their neighbours, even after a long period of free and unreserved communication.

Subtraction is performed either from right to left, or from left to right, the less number in both cases, being placed above the greater. In subtracting from right to left, when the number in the minuend is less than the one above it in the subtrahend, ten is borrowed upon the next minuend figure (which represents tens, hundreds, &c. according to its place); and this operation is denoted by a perpendicular stroke placed opposite the figure upon which the ten is borrowed; the subtrahend figure being then subtracted from the borrowed ten, and the remainder added to the figure in the minuend, the result is put down in the line below; after which, one is added to the preceding figure in the subtrahend, and the same process is repeated as before.*

EXAMPLE.

263543
7652432

7388889

The operation is thus expressed in words; 3 cannot be subtracted from 2, therefore borrow 10 upon the next minuend figure 3 (which here represents tens); then subtract 3 from 10, and there remains 7; 7 and 2 are 9, put down 9 below the minuend, and carry or add 1 to the subtrahend figure 4; this makes 5; then say 5 cannot be subtracted from 3, therefore borrow ten upon the next minuend figure 4, and subtract 5 from 10, there remains 5, which added to 3 makes 8; put this down below the minuend; and thus proceed thro' all the figures. This method differs from ours in placing the subtrahend above the minuend, and in subtracting the subtrahend figure from the borrowed 10, and adding the remainder to the minuend figure, instead of adding the borrowed 10 to the minuend figure, and subtracting the subtrahend figure from the sum.

As the method of subtracting from left to right is explained in the note p. 7. it will be sufficient in this place merely to give an example by way of illustration.

EXAMPLE.

16747358
42353437

26616189
25 0 07

25606079

Which is thus expressed in words: 1 from 4, there remains 3; 6 cannot be subtracted from 2, therefore take 10 from the preceding remainder 3 (which represents tens, hundreds, &c. according to its place) and adding it to the subtrahend figure 2, say 6 from 12, there remains 6; and thus proceed thro' all figures.

---

* In note D p. 6 and 7, a mistake has occurred in stating this mode of subtraction; but it will be easily corrected by looking at the operation given above.

Under the head of MULTIPLICATION, the first thing which probably will be noticed, is the want of a multiplication table. The table given in European treatises, is considered of high antiquity, being generally ascribed to Pythagoras, who is supposed by some to have studied arithmetic in India. The omission of such a table in the Lilawati, may have arisen from that work being designed not for children, but for grown up persons who have received the rudiments of education at school, where several very extensive multiplication tables are taught.

No less than five methods of multiplication are given in the text, and the commentaries add one or two more; but the most common method is that comprehended under the first rule. It is performed in the following manner:

Write down the multiplicand, and below it the multiplier, so that the first figure on the right of the multiplier shall be immediately below the last figure on the left of the multiplicand; and multiply this last figure on the left by all the figures of the multiplier; then having put down the products according to their places above the multiplicand, move the multiplier forward one place, and multiply the second figure of the multiplicand in the same manner as before; thus continuing to repeat the operation until all the figures in the multiplicand are gone through.

EXAMPLE.

131
2150
100112
126298
25508624
multiplicand .... 52436 .... 28000824 product.
multiplier 534
534
534
534
534

The individual results, however, are not set down in this manner, but the tens in each succeeding product are carried to the preceeding one, which is then rubbed out, and the new result is set down in its place. At the end of the operation, therefore, the whole product stands in one line, with the multiplier under it; thus

28000824
534

The obliterated figures, and the new results, may be presented in the following manner:

00
128
6971
81111
15860
72156
101112
670450
126258
25588681

multiplicand .. 52436 ...... 28000824 product
multiplier .. 534

The figures that are not crossed out form the product.

Though this method must appear very complicated and confused to an European arithmetician, it is the one which is most generally practised by the Jyotishis, or astronomers; and when we recollect that their manner of writing on the board does not admit of the individual steps being exhibited together, the above method, notwithstanding its apparent perplexity, may perhaps be considered the easiest, and most simple, which could be adopted under these circumstances. To perceive this, it is only necessary to attempt the multiplication of the above sum by proceeding from right to left, according to the European mode; at the same time blotting out each individual product in succession, and bringing the tens from the succeeding product to form a new result, in the place of the preceeding one, and thus exhibiting at once the whole product, without the intermediate operations.

It may be considered a coincidence worthy of notice, that the Greeks performed multiplication from left to right, probably for the same reasons which still influence Hindu arithmeticians.

The only method which the Hindus have of proving multiplication is by division. They seem entirely unacquainted with the method of proving it by casting the nines out of the sum of the figures in each of the factors, a method, however, which is given in Arabian treatises, and is denominated *tarazu*, or the balance.

As the method of performing DIVISION is pretty fully explained in a note page 11 and 12, the reader is referred to it for information. The divisor is usually placed below the dividend; and the quotient is set down indifferently on any part of the board which is considered most convenient.

In the original work of Bhascara Acharya, it will be observed that no marks are employed to denote addition, multiplication, or division; neither are there any to denote the roots or powers of numbers. The only mark employed is that of minus. It is a small circle or dot placed over the figure which is to be subtracted, thus $\overset{\circ}{6}$ or $\dot{6}$. This sign is very generally employed throughout India, and also in other parts of Asia. In the common books of accounts kept by the inhabitants of Guzerat and of the Mahratta country, items which are discharged, or considered struck out, are usually denoted by a circle placed opposite to them, or drawn around the figures; and this serves instead of an erasure, or any other remark. For instance, to denote that the item

4 yards of cloth .... Rs. 40

is discharged or struck out, it would be marked in this manner

• 4 yards of cloth .... Rs. 40

or thus,

4 yards of cloth .... Rs. (40)

This mode of intimating that any thing is struck out or annulled, appears also to be employed by some Tartar nations. Du Halde, treating of the Tartarian language, informs us, that "if a word is redundant or ill placed, instead of blotting it out, an oval is drawn round it; but should it afterwards on reflection appear to be a good word, two ovals or *oo* are placed at the side of it to signify that it ought to stand."*

In Sanscrit the word *shunya* signifies a circle, cipher, or vacuity; and the Arabs, on receiving the numeral notation from India, translated it by the word *syfr*, which, in their language, also means emptiness, vacuity, or nothing. The Arabic word *syfr*, it is well known, has been adopted into the European languages; and ciphers, or cyphering, are terms frequently used to denote arithmetic in general, probably on account of the important part which the *shunya*, *syfr*, or cipher, performs in that science.

It is stated by a learned Reviewer of the Bija Gannita, that the Hindus denote

---

* Du Halde vol. 4. p. 205.

plus or addition by two parallel perpendicular lines. I suspect however, that this remark is incorrect. It is indeed an usual practice to place one or two such lines between numbers that are to be added; but this seems merely with a view of separating the numbers; for the same mark is used in a statement of numbers which require to be subtracted or multiplied. The following examples of addition and multiplication are taken from a copy of the Bija Gannita in my possession.

Required the remainder of two plus subtracted from three plus; of two minus subtracted from three minus; of two minus subtracted from three plus; of two plus subtracted from three minus?

Statement.—3 || 2. $\overset{\circ}{3}$ || $\overset{\circ}{2}$.   3 || $\overset{\circ}{2}$. $\overset{\circ}{3}$ || 2.

What is the product of two plus multiplied by three plus; of two minus multiplied by three minus; and of two plus multiplied by three minus?

Statement.—3 || 2. $\overset{\circ}{3}$ || $\overset{\circ}{2}$.   2 || $\overset{\circ}{3}$.

In translating the second rule contained in page 63 of the following treatise, Fyzi directs that an *alamut*, or sign of multiplication, be put down; and on this authority Dr. Hutton supposes that the Hindus had a mark for multiplication. In this instance, however, as is remarked in the note p. 65, Fyzi has mistaken the sense of the original. The words in the rule are, " write down multiplier," which the commentators expound by directing to " write down *the word* multiplier;" and accordingly, in performing the operation, the commentators have written the word multiplier, or its initial letter, in the different places where it is required to be set down.

Mr. Strachey says that the Hindus mark division as we do " by a horizontal line drawn between the dividend and divisor, the lower quantity being the divisor." In making this observation he was probably misled either by Hindus who were conversant with the European system of notation, or by the Persian translator Fyzi, who, instead of adhering to the modes exhibited in the original, generally performs the operations in the manner practised by the Arabians. On looking at the Hindu method of performing division, it will be observed that the divisor is placed under the dividend, but without any horizontal line between them. It will also be remarked that no line is used, even in fractions, to separate the numerator and denominator; they are put down simply the one below the other, and the reader has to find out from the question, or operation, whether the figures, thus set down, be a fraction or two integers.

As mixed numbers are exhibited in a fractional form in several of the statements, they have been printed in smaller figures than the whole numbers for the sake of distinctness, tho' no such difference is observed in the original. Take for example the statement in page 44.

4	16
3	5
100	125
26	2
15	0

Here $\frac{4}{3}$ are the improper fraction of $1\frac{1}{3}$; $\frac{16}{3}$ the improper fraction of $5\frac{1}{3}$; $\frac{10}{3}$, the improper fraction of $3\frac{1}{3}$; and $\frac{125}{2}$ the improper fraction of $62\frac{1}{2}$. A cipher is put at the bottom of the right hand column to make the number of terms equal to that in the other column.

The mode of adding the numerator of the fraction to the denominator, and of subtracting it, which occurs in page 26, shews the exact form in which the operation is done on the board; but as it differs from our method of putting down the same operation, it may be necessary to notice that

$$\begin{matrix} \frac{1}{3}+1=4 & & \frac{1}{3} \quad 3+1=4 \\ \frac{1}{8}-1=7 & \text{denote} & \frac{1}{8} \quad 8-1=7 \end{matrix}$$

Again, in pages 30 and 34, $\frac{1}{2} - 1 = \frac{1}{3}$, is the Hindu method of notation, but we would put it down $\frac{1}{2+1} = \frac{1}{3}$.

Also $\frac{1}{2} - 1 = 1$ $\quad \frac{2}{9} - 2 = 7$ $\quad \frac{1}{4} - 1 = 3$ $\quad \frac{6}{10} - 6 = 4$, denote what we would express thus,

$$\frac{1}{2}\ \ 2-1=1 \qquad \frac{9}{2}\ \ 9-2=7 \qquad \frac{1}{4}\ \ 4-1=3 \qquad \frac{6}{10}\ \ 10-6=4.$$

After this explanation of the manner in which the Hindus perform the rules of arithmetic, it will not perhaps be considered altogether irrelevant or unimportant to shew the different modes followed by the Arabians in performing the same rules. A very brief account of the arithmetical knowledge of the Arabians will also be subjoined, as it may afford matter for curious comparison, and even lead to interesting conclusions.

I have consulted several arithmetical treatises in the Persian language, but in the subsequent remarks, I shall cite only the Risala Hisab, and the Khalasat-ul-

Hisab, which are the two oldest works I have seen, and are also the best known, and of the highest authority.

The Risala Hisab is a short treatise on arithmetic and geometry, written in Persian by Kazi Zadeh al Rumi, surnamed Ali Kushchi, who was one of the celebrated astronomers employed in the 14th century by Ulug Beg, to draw out the astronomical tables which bear this Prince's name.*

The Khalasat-ul-hisab is in the Arabic language, and was composed by Baha-ud-din, who was born at Balbec in 1575, and died at Ispahan in 1653.† It is reckoned a work of great authority, and has been printed lately under the auspices of the College at Calcutta, along with a translation into Persian. An abstract of its contents, furnished by Mr. Edward Strachey, will be found in the second vol. of Hutton's mathematical tracts.

Ali Kushchi's treatise gives one method only of performing ADDITION, and it is the same which is followed in Europe. But, besides the rule for this method, Baha-ud-din's work contains a rule for adding and subtracting from left to right, as is practised by the Hindus. This rule is illustrated by three examples, which are thus put down:

EXAMPLE

ADDITION.

5	3	7	3	2
	4	4	7	9
		1	0	5
5	7	9	0	6
	8	0	1	

5	2	5	3	7
2	7	9	4	2
7	9	4	7	9
8	0			

EXAMPLE

SUBTRACTION.

9	2	6	3
6	2	7	4
3	0	9	9
2	9	8	

* D'Herbolet. Bib. Orient. Art. Ulug Beg and Zig.

† Hutton's Mathematical Tracts, Vol. 2. p. 180.

The lower horizontal line is called *Khuti Mahi*, or the obliterating line, because it is supposed to obliterate the result which stands above it. This method corresponds in principle with that adopted by the Hindus, who, however, do not exhibit all the results at once, but efface the preceding result, and put down in its place the one obtained by adding the tens of the succeeding column.

MULTIPLICATION occupies a long chapter both in Ali Kushchi's work, and that of Buha-ud-din. The latter author's remarkable definitions of multiplication and division are noticed by Mr. Strachey in Hutton's tracts. Ali Kushchi does not define division, but his definition of multiplication is the same which is given by Baha-ud-din: "Multiplication is the producing a third number, such as shall bear the same "ratio to one factor, as the other factor bears to unity." And on the margin there is written this example. "$3 \times 4 = 12$. $3 : 12 :: 1 : 4$. For as 1 is the $\frac{1}{4}$ of "4, so is 3 the $\frac{1}{4}$ of 12. And $4 : 12 :: 1 : 3$. For as 1 is the $\frac{1}{3}$ of 3, so is "4 the $\frac{1}{3}$ of 12."

Ali Kushchi also delivers a rule which Mr. Strachey has translated from the Khalasat-ul-hisab, and which, as he observes, "exhibits an application of something resembling the indices of Logarithms." The rule is this: "As to the multiplication of even tens, hundreds, &c. into one another, multiply the two factors together without any regard to their places, (that is, as if they were units) and write down the product. Then add the numbers of the ranks together, and subtract 1 from the sum; the remainder is the number of the rank of the product.—Example; if I wish to multiply 20 by 400, I multiply the significant figure of 20 by the significant figure of 400, the product is 8. I then add together the numbers of the places of the two factors, the sum is 5; from this I subtract 1, the remainder is 4, which is the number of the rank of the product. The product, therefore is 8000.*"

The first sort of multiplication mentioned is that of a single figure by a single fi-

---

* This rule will answer generally when the product of the significant figures does not exceed an unit; or, when the product exceeds an unit, if it be reckoned only as one digit or place.

gure, and is exhibited in the Khalasat-ul-Hisab by the following table:

								2
						3	4	2
					4	9	6	3
				5	16	12	8	4
			6	25	20	15	10	5
		7	36	30	24	18	12	6
	8	49	42	35	28	21	14	7
9	64	56	48	40	32	24	16	8
81	72	63	54	45	36	27	18	9

The Risala Hisab gives the table in this form:

9	8	7	6	5	4	3	2	1	
9	8	7	6	5	4	3	2	1	1
18	16	14	12	10	8	6	4	2	2
27	24	21	18	15	12	9	6	3	3
36	32	28	24	20	16	12	8	4	4
45	40	35	30	25	20	15	10	5	5
54	48	42	36	30	24	18	12	6	6
63	56	49	42	35	28	21	14	7	7
72	64	56	48	40	32	24	16	8	8
81	72	63	54	45	36	27	18	9	9

After this there follow several ingenious modes of multiplication, of which the following may be taken as a specimen:

1. Multiply one of the factors by ten, and also by the number by which ten differs from the other factor; and subtract the one product from the other.

Example.—Multiply 8 by 9.

$$6 \times 13 - (9 \times \overline{10 - 8}) = 72.$$

2. Add together the two factors and subtract ten from the sum; multiply the remainder by ten, and to the product add that of the two numbers by which ten differs from each of the factors.

Example.—Multiply 7 by 8.

$$\overline{8 + 7 - 10} \times 10 + (\overline{10 - 7} \times \overline{10 - 8}) = 56$$

Of multiplying units by any number between 10 *and* 20.

3. Add together the two factors, and subtract ten from the sum; multiply the remainder by ten, and from the product subtract that of the two numbers by which each of the factors differs from ten.

Example.—Multiply 8 by 14.

$$\overline{8 + 14 - 10} \times 10 - (\overline{14 - 10} \times \overline{10 - 8}) = 112.$$

Of multiplying together factors from 10 *to* 20.

4. Add the units of one of the factors to the whole of the other factor, and multiply the sum by ten; to the product add that of the two numbers by which the factors differ from ten.

Example.—Multiply 12 by 13.

$$\overline{12 + 3} \times 10 + (\overline{12 - 10} \times \overline{13 - 10}) = 156.$$

Where a whole number is multiplied by 5, *or* 50, *or* 500.

5. Multiply half of the multiplicand by 10, if the multiplier be 5; or by 100, if the multiplier be 50; or by 1000, if the multiplier be 500; and if a fraction result in halving the multiplicand, then on account of this fraction, take half of whatever number was taken to multiply half of the multiplicand; that is, in the first case take 5; in the second 50; and in the third 500.

Example.—Multiply 16 by 5.

$$\frac{16}{2} \times \frac{10}{1} = 80$$

Example of 2d case.—Multiply 17 by 50.

$$17 \div 2 = 8\tfrac{1}{2}.$$
$$8 \times 100 + 50 = 850.$$

Of multiplying numbers from 10 *to* 20 *by numbers from* 20 *to* 100.

6. Multiply the unit of the less factor by the tens of the greater; add the product to the greater factor, and multiply the sum by ten; to the product add that of the units of the two factors.

Example.—Multiply 12 by 26.

$$(2 \times 2 + 26) \times 10 + (2 \times 6) = 312.$$

Where any whole number is multiplied by 15, *or* 150, *or* 1500.

7. To the multiplicand add half of itself, and multiply the sum by 10 in the first case, by 100 in the second, and by 1000 in the third case. If a fraction result, take on account of it half of whatever may have been taken on account of the whole number; that is in the first case take 5, in the second 50, and in the third 500.

Example.—Multiply 24 by 15.

$$\overline{24 + \tfrac{24}{2}} \times 10 = 360.$$

Example.—Multiply 25 by 150.

$$25 + \tfrac{25}{2} = 37\tfrac{1}{2}.$$
$$37 \times 100 + 50 = 3750.$$

To multiply together any number between 20 *and* 100, *where the digits in the place of tens are the same.*

8. Add the units of one of the factors to the whole of the other factor; multiply the sum by the tens of one of the factors, and having multiplied the product by ten, to this last product add the product of the units in the two factors.

Example.—Multiply 23 by 25.

$$\overline{23 + 5} \times 2 \times 10 + \overline{3 \times 5} = 575.$$

To multiply any number between 20 *and* 100, *where the digits in the place of tens are different.*

9. Multiply the tens of the less factor by the whole of the greater factor; then

multiply the units of the less factor by the tens of the greater factor, and add this latter product to the former one; multiply the sum by 10; and to this product add the product of the units of the two factors.

Example.—Multiply 23 by 34.

$$\overline{2 \times 34 + 3 \times 3} \times 10 + \overline{3 \times 4} = 782.$$

10. Add together the two factors, and multiply half of the sum into itself; then taking half of the difference of the two factors, multiply it into itself; and subtract this last product from the former one; the remainder is the product of the two factors.

Example.—Multiply 24 by 36.

$$\left(\frac{24 + 36}{2}\right)^2 - \left(\frac{36 - 24}{2}\right)^2 = 864$$

Such modes of multiplication, however, are never adopted in practice, and are considered merely an ingenious and amusing display of the properties of numbers.

When each of the factors consists of several figures, multiplication is performed by the figurate process which is called *Shabakh.* In Ali Kushchi's work the operation proceeds from left to right, according to the Hindu mode.

The rule is as follows: Draw a square figure, and divide it into a number of small squares equal to the product of the number of places in the two factors; then divide each of these small squares into two triangles, and place the figures of the multiplicand over each square in their proper order, and the figures of the multiplier down the left side of the square in the same manner. Then, agreeably to the succeeding example, multiply the thousands in the multiplicand first by the hundreds, then by the tens, and lastly by the units, in the multiplier, and put down each product in the triangular spaces opposite to the multiplier, the units being placed in the lower triangle, and the tens in the upper one. After multiplying the thousands in the multiplicand by all the figures in the multiplier, proceed to multiply the hundreds, tens, &c. setting down the results in the manner above directed. When all the figures in the multiplicand are multiplied, sum up the diagonal lines of figures.

EXAMPLE.

Multiplicand.

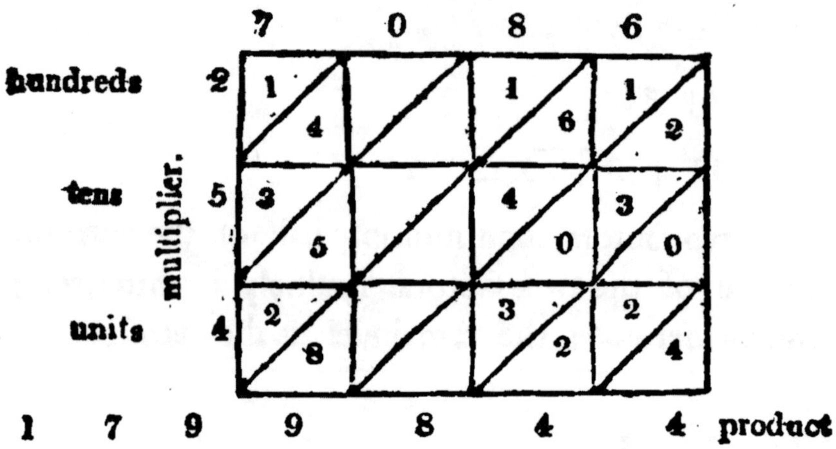

The mode of operation is thus;

2 × 6 12
5 × 6 30
4 × 6 24
2 × 8 16
5 × 8 40
4 × 8 32
2 × 7 14
35
28

1799844

The Khalasat-ul-Hisab, however, directs the operation to be performed from right to left, multiplying the units in the multiplicand first by the units, then by the tens, and lastly by the hundreds in the multiplier; thus,

4 × 6 24
4 × 8 32
4 × 7 28
5 × 6 30
5 × 8 40
5 × 7 35
2 × 6 12
2 × 8 16
2 × 7 14

1799844

An example of this method is given in Hutton's tracts, and this learned mathematician remarks, that it has some resemblance to the operation by Napier's bones.

This figurate mode of operation has been communicated to the Hindus, who frequently teach it in their schools, but it is neither contained in Sanscrit works, nor practised by the astronomers who follow only the rules of the shashters.

DIVISION is exhibited both in the Risala-Hisab and Khalasat-ul-Hisab, in the following manner:

Draw such a number of parallel lines as shall form as many compartments as there are places in the dividend; and then draw a horizontal line which shall join together each of the perpendicular lines: Write the dividend under the horizontal line at the top, placing one figure between each two perpendicular lines; and then set down the divisor so that its last place, reckoning from the right, shall correspond with the last place of the dividend, at the same time leaving such a space between them as will be sufficient to contain the whole operation: Find how often the first figure on the left of the divisor is contained in the corresponding figure of the dividend, and after multiplying this figure in the divisor by the number thus found, subtract the product from the dividend, and drawing a line beneath, write down the remainder; then multiply the next figure of the divisor by the quotient obtained, and put down the result one place forward. Having proceeded thus until all the figures of the divisor are multiplied by the first quotient, find a second quotient, and then proceed as before.

This is the method most commonly practised, but there is also another which is performed in the following manner:

Multiply each figure in the divisor by the number of times that the last figure in the divisor is contained in the last figure of the dividend, and subtract the products from the dividend, on taking down one of its figures successively: write down the last remainder in a line with the remaining figures of the dividend, and remove the whole one place backward towards the left; then find how often the last figure in the divisor is contained in the last figure or figures of the dividend, and repeat the former process; proceeding in this manner until the whole dividend is divided.

EXAMPLE 1st METHOD.

Divide 680045

by 255

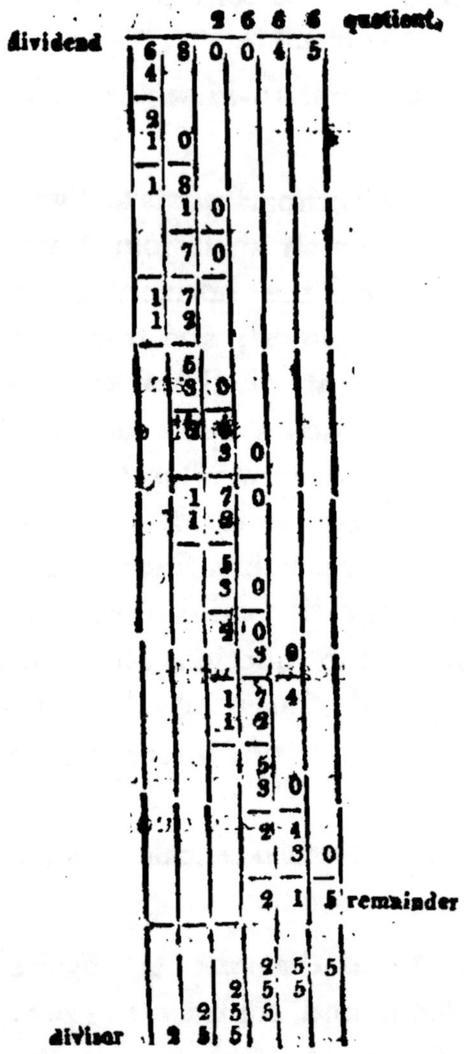

EXAMPLE 2d METHOD.

Divide 680045

by 255

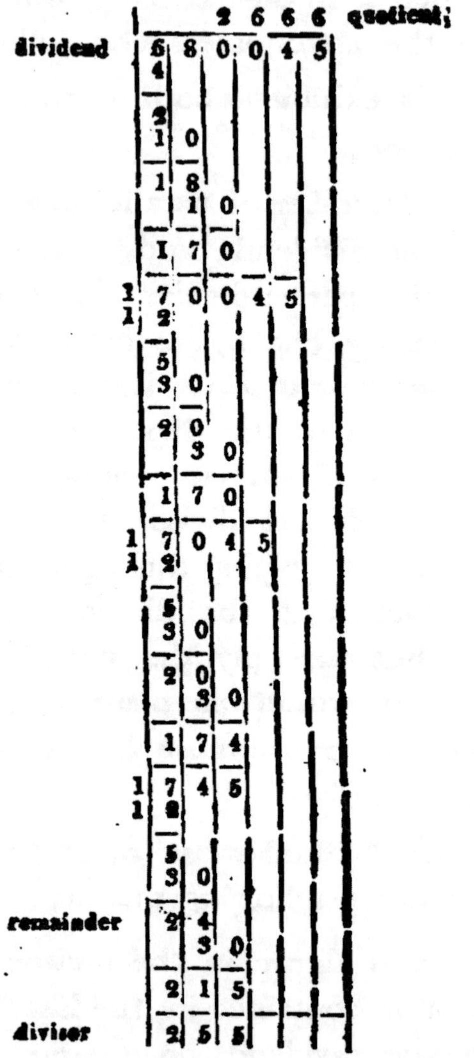

After treating of these four fundamental rules, Ali Kushchi and Buha-ud-din give the method of extracting the square root. The former author in the first place delivers a rule for finding the nearest root of a number whose root is a surd. The rule is not clearly expressed, but I apprehend that the following is its meaning:

Subtract from the number whose root is a surd the nearest square number below it; and make the remainder the numerator of double the root of the nearest square plus an unit: Then the root of the nearest square together with this fraction, is the nearest root of the number whose root is a surd; that is, if the mixed number formed by the root of the square and the fraction be multiplied into itself, the product will not be the assumed number whose root is required, but something less. Example; suppose you require the square root of ten, then from this number subtract 9, which is the nearest square, there remains one; call this the numerator of double the root of the nearest square plus one, which is 7; then $3\frac{1}{7}$ is the nearest root of 10; that is, if $3\frac{1}{7}$ be multiplied into itself, the product is $9\frac{6}{7}$ and $\frac{1}{7}$ of $\frac{1}{7}$, which is less than 10 by $\frac{6}{7}$ of $\frac{1}{7}$.—The Persian translator of the Khalasat-ul-Hisab adds, that some arithmeticians after subtracting the nearest square from the number whose root is required, make the remainder the numerator of double the root of the nearest square without adding an unit. In this case, if the nearest root obtained be multiplied into itself, the product will be more by a fraction than the number whose root is required. According to this rule the square root of 10 would be $3\frac{1}{6}$, which being multiplied into itself, gives 10 and $\frac{1}{6}$ of $\frac{1}{6}$, which is $\frac{1}{6}$ of $\frac{1}{6}$ less than $\frac{6}{7}$ of $\frac{1}{7}$. He states, however, that this rule is not general; and he instances that it will not answer for the number 3.

In extracting the square root the mode of proceeding is as follows; taking for example the number 128172.

	3		5		8	root
1	2	8	1	7	2	
	9					
	3					
	3	0				
		8				
		2	5			
		5	6			
		5	6	6	4	
					8	remainder
			7	1	7	
			7	0	8	
		6	5			
	3					

Put a mark over the units, hundreds, tens of thousands; that is, over each uneven figure. Find a number greater than an unit, such that when multiplied by itself the product may be subtracted from the last period on the left; the number is

3; write 3 above the left hand mark, and also at the bottom of the diagram; multiply the upper 3 by the lower one, and write the product 9 below the number whose root is required, so that it shall be opposite the multiplier, and subtract it from 12, the remainder is 3; write this below the minuend and subtrahend, and draw a horizontal line; then add the upper 3 to the lower 3, and, after drawing a horizontal line above the 3 at the bottom of the diagram, set down 6 the result one place forward to the right, in the compartment opposite to which there is no mark: Then find a number greater then one in the same manner as before; it is 5; write this above the mark preceding the last one, and also at the bottom of the diagram on the right of the figure 6; multiply 5 by 6 the product is 30; write this below the number whose root is required, so that the units place shall be opposite the multiplier; subtract 30 from 38 the opposite number, the remainder is 8; write this below the minuend and subtrahend; then multiply the upper 5 by the 5 in the lower part of the diagram, the product is 25; write this down, placing the units opposite the multiplier, and subtract it from its opposite number which is 81, the remainder is 56; write this below the minuend and subtrahend, and draw a horizontal line; then add the upper 5 to 65 in the lower line, the result is 70; and having drawn a horizontal line above 65, which is in the lower part of the diagram, carry the said 70 one place forward on the right, so that the units place may be in that compartment opposite to which there is no mark: Then find another number greater than one in the same manner as before; 8 is obtained; write this above the first mark on the right, and also at the under part of the figure on the right of 70; then multiply this 8 by the 7 in the lower line, and having put down the product 56 below the number whose root is required, so that its units place shall be opposite the subtrahend, subtract it from its opposite number, which is also 56, nothing remains; draw a horizontal line below, and multiply 8 into the cypher, the result is cipher; then multiply this 8 by the 8 in the under line, the product is 64; write this below the number whose root is required, so that the units may be opposite the multiplier, and subtract it from the opposite number which is 72; there remains 8. The root of the number therefore is a surd. In order to find the nearest root, add the figure which stands above the first mark, that is 8, and also add an unit, to the number in the lower line; the sum 717 is the denominator, and the remainder 8 is the numerator of this number 717, which is double the root of the nearest square plus an unit. The nearest square root, therefore, of 128172 is 358 $\frac{8}{717}$.

The extraction of the cube root is not contained in the Risala-Hisab or Khalasat-nl-Hisab. Nujm-ud-din says that it was omitted on account of its difficulty, and he supplies this defect at the end of a short treatise on algebra, subjoined to the edition of the latter work published at Calcutta. His rule is as follows:

Draw a *judwel*, or figure, as in division, and in the extraction of the square root, dividing it by three horizontal lines, and leaving a sufficient space between them for the operation. Call the first of these lines *makaab*, or cube line; the second *mal*, or product line, and the third *zila*, or side line; and write in order, under the first horizontal line, the number whose root is sought. Then mark with a dot the first, fourth, seventh, &c. places, to the end of the number, passing over two places each time. Then find a number greater than units such, that if it be placed above the last mark, and also below it, opposite thereto at the bottom in the zila line, and the upper figure be multiplied by the lower one, and the product written down in the *mal* line, so that its units may be opposite the units of the number placed in the *zila* line, and its tens on its left; and after this, if the upper number be multiplied by the numbers placed in the *mal* line, and the product put down below the *makaab* line in the same manner as before—that then the subtraction of this product from the number opposite to it in the *kaab* line, or from that number together with what is on the left, shall be possible: Then when such a number is found, perform the operation in the manner above mentioned; and after subtracting the last product from the number in the *kaab* line, *write* down the remainder in the same numeral place, below a horizonatal line: Then in order to the succeeding operation, add the upper figure to the lower figure situated in the *zila* line, and write the result beneath the lower figure, separating them by a horizontal line; then multiply the upper figure by this result, and add the product to whatever is in the *mal* line, and set down the result in the same numeral place below a horizontal line; after this write the sum of the products, one place to the right in the same *mal* line; and in like manner add to the upper figure the sum of the upper and lower figures which is written in the *zila* line below the horizontal line, and having drawn a horizontal line, in order to the succeeding operation, set down the result in that zila line, two places towards the right. Then seek another greater number such, that if it be written above the mark preceding the former one, and also below it, in the *zila* line opposite to the said mark, and the upper figure be multiplied by whatever is in the *zila* line, and the product increased by whatever is opposite to it in the *mal* line; and after this if the upper figure be multiplied into what, ever is in the *mal* line—that the subtraction of all the products from the remaining numbers opposite to them in the *makaab* line shall be possible : Then when such other number is found, perform the operation according as before directed, and after subtracting, write the remainders in the *makaab* line below the horizontal line ; and in order to the succeeding operation write down according to the form in the *mal* line and the *zila* line, in the manner formerly mentioned. And if a number such as above mentioned is not found, write a cipher in its place above the mark, and also write it below in the *zila* line, and observe the usual form in the *mal* line and *zila* line, without multiplying. Then seek a number such as above mentioned, in order to write it above each mark that there may be, until the operation be finished at the first mark. Whenever you bring the preceding operation to this place, the work is done ; and if no remainder be left the cube root is a rational number.

But if any thing remain the cube root is a surd, and the number above the *judwel*, together with the remainder or fraction, is the nearest cube root. The manner of finding the denominator of the fraction is this : having performed on the right hand side whatever operation is done in the *mal* line and *zila* line, add an unit to the number in the *zila* line, and add the result to what is in the *mal* line. This last result is the denominator of the fraction. The nearest cube root therefore of 94818826 is $456\frac{10}{625177}$.

Example.—Required the cube root of 94818826?

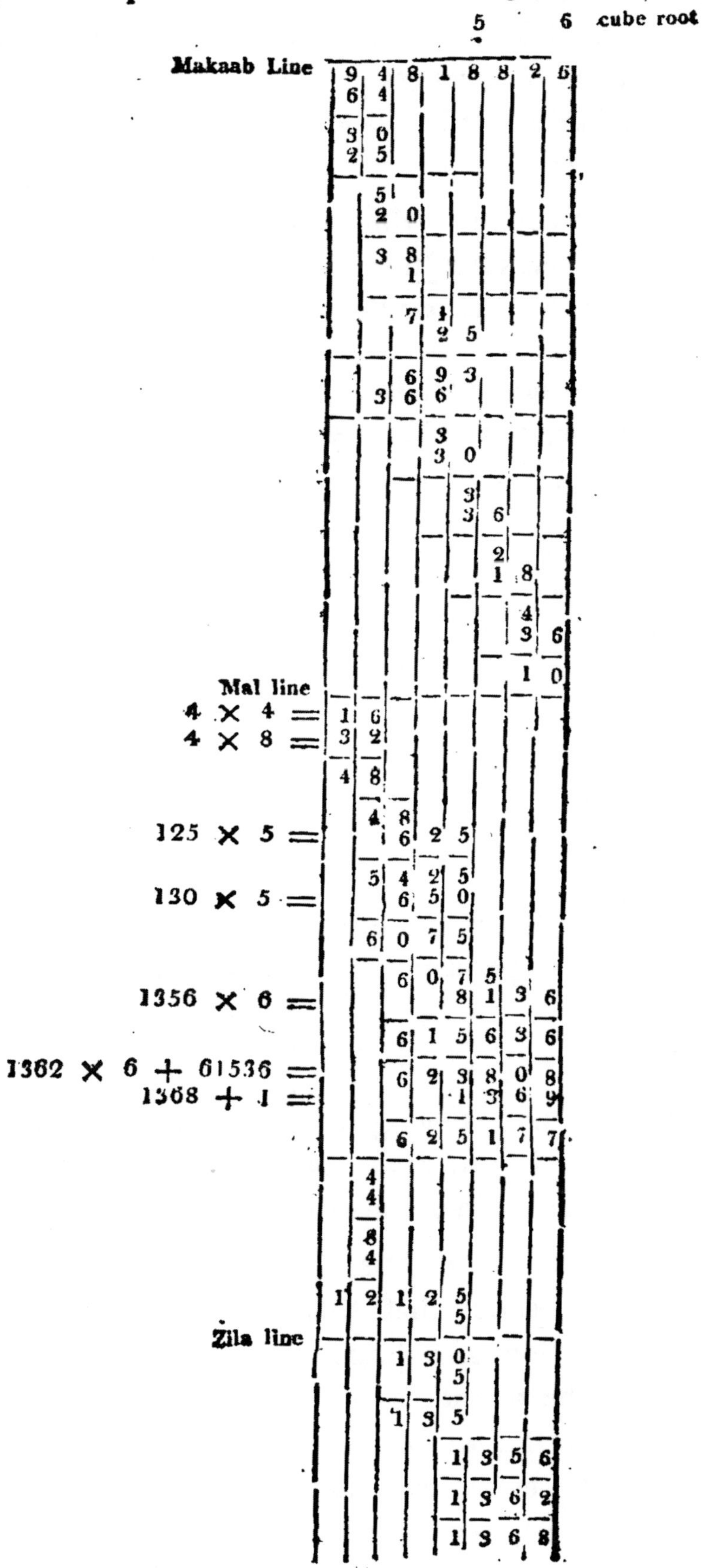

These rules for extracting the square and cube roots are much more prolix and confused than those contained in the Lilawati; for though the mode of extracting the square root is expressed with greater conciseness in the original Arabic than in the Persian translation which I have followed, still it is by no means so concise and clear as that which Bhascara delivers for performing the same operation.

In the Khalasat-ul-hisab the extraction of the square root is succeeded by a long chapter on fractions, which, however, does not seem to contain any thing that requires particular notice. The fraction is written below the integer in the manner of the Hindus; thus $\begin{array}{c}1\\2\\3\end{array}$, denotes one and two thirds. When there is no integer, its place is pointed out by a cipher, which the Arabians write like a dot, and place above the numerator of the fraction, thus $\begin{array}{c}\cdot\\2\\5\end{array}$ two fifths.

Compound fractions are written in three different ways. First, the secondary fraction is written above the primary one; or, secondly, opposite to it on the right hand, with the word من of, between it and the primary fraction; or, thirdly, it is separated from the primary fraction by a horizontal line; thus,

$$\begin{array}{c}\cdot\\1\\2\\5\\6\end{array} \qquad\qquad \begin{array}{c}5\\6\end{array}\ \text{of}\ \begin{array}{c}1\\2\end{array} \qquad\qquad \begin{array}{c}\cdot\\1\\2\\\hline 5\\6\end{array}$$

denote one half of five sixths. Two or more fractions are joined by the conjunction *and*, or are denoted by a perpendicular line drawn between them. Thus,

$$\begin{array}{c}\cdot\\3\\4\end{array}\ \text{and}\ \begin{array}{c}\cdot\\2\\5\end{array} \qquad\qquad \begin{array}{c|c}\cdot&\cdot\\3&2\\4&5\end{array}$$

express two fifths and three fourths. Owing to the Arabian practice of writing from left to right, the positions of the fractions connected by the words *of*, or *and*, are the reverse of what would be given in our treatises.

The third Chapter of the Khalasat ul-Hisab treats of proportion, or the Rule of Three. In the first place, it is stated that this rule shews the method of finding an unknown number by the operation of a fourth proportional such, that the ratio of the first number shall be to the second, as the ratio of the third is to the fourth; that is, if the first be the half of the second, the third also shall be the half of the fourth; and the fourth shall be such, that the product of the extremes shall be equal to the product of the middle terms. The rule is then given as follows;

When one of the two extremes, the first and fourth terms, is unknown, divide the product of the middle terms by the known extreme. And when one of the two middle terms, the second and third, is unknown, divide the product of the extremes by the known middle term. In the first case, the quotient will be the unknown extreme required, and in the second, the quotient will be the unknown middle term required.

The Persian translator observes that this is the rule most commonly used; but he also gives another, which is thus expressed:

When one of the extremes is unknown, divide one of the known middle terms by the known extreme, and multiply the quotient by the other middle term; the product is the unknown extreme required. When one of the middle terms is unknown, divide one of the known extremes by the known middle term, and multiply the quotient by the other extreme; the product is the unknown middle term required.

Chapter fourth shews the manner of finding an unknown quantity by the process of errors. It is performed thus: Assume any unknown number you please, and calling it the first assumed number, operate upon it according to the conditions of the question. If the result come out agreeably to the question, the said assumed number is the number demanded. If, on the contrary, the result contain an error, that is, if it be more or less than the required number, call the quantity of excess or deficiency, the first error. After this assume any other number you please, and calling it the second assumed number, operate upon it according to the conditions of the question. If the result come out conformably to the question, the number demanded is obtained. If on the contrary, it contain an error, that is, come out more or less than the required number, call the quantity of excess or deficiency, the second error. Thus four numbers are obtained; the first assumed number, and the first error; the second assumed number, and the second error. After this, multiply the first assumed number by the second error, and call the product the first ascertained number; and multiply the second assumed number by the second error, and call the product the second ascertained number; if both the errors be alike, that is, if both be greater than the required number, or less than it, divide the difference between the two ascertained numbers, by the difference between the two errors; but if the two errors be unlike, that is, if the one be greater, and the other less, than the required number, divide the sum of the ascertained numbers by the sum of the errors; the product in each of the two cases will be the number demanded.

Chapter fifth treats of what is named either *tuhlil*, resolution, or *taakas*, inversion. It is precisely the same which is given in the Lilawati under the title of Inversion. The following is a literal version of the rule:

" The process in this case is to operate in a reverse manner to whatever is stated in the question. If the question require doubling, halve; if it require addition, subtract; if it require multiplication, divide; and if it require the extraction of the square root, multiply the number into itself; or if the question require the reverse of all this, then operate in a manner reverse to the conditions of the question. Thus begin at the end of the question, and proceed in this reverse manner until the answer is obtained."

Dr. Hutton justly observes that the word algebra, which is compounded of *al*, the, and *jebr*, contortion, contumacy, consolidation, appears to have been derived from this mode of transposing the terms. The words *vyasta* and *vilom*, which are employed in the Lilawati, also signify inversion.

The arithmetical part of the Khalasat-al-Hisab finishes with the rule of inversion. This, however, is considerably more than what is contained in Ali Kuschi's work, which does not go farther than the extraction of the square root; but afterwards proceeds to explain the sexagesimal numeration. As this system is still used by Arabians in their astronomical calculations, the following brief account of it will perhaps not be unacceptable to the reader.

In the sexagesimal system numbers are represented by the letters of the alphabet, which is divided, tho' not regularly according to the order of the letters, into 9 units ا ب ج د ه و ز ح ط; into 9 tens ي ك ل م ن س ع ف ص; and into 9 hundreds ق ر ش ت ث خ ذ ض ظ; and غ which expresses 1000. The compound numbers are formed by uniting the units with these round numbers; as in the following table:

يا	11	كا	21	لا	31	ما	41
يب	12	كب	22	لب	32	مب	42
يج	13	كج	23	لج	33	مج	43
يد	14	كد	24	لد	34	مد	44
يه	15	كه	25	له	35	مه	45
يو	16	كو	26	لو	36	مو	46
يز	17	كز	27	لز	37	مز	47
يح	18	كح	28	لح	38	مح	48
يط	19	كط	29	لط	39	مط	49

And so on with the rest.

Several of the letters, when employed to express numbers, undergo a small alteration in their form. The *dal*, for instance, is written in a form which resembles the figure 4 in the decimal notation. The double letters also, which express compound numbers, are, in many cases, so considerably changed, as to retain little affinity to their original make.

The reader may recollect that the Hebrew numerals are expressed by dividing the letters of the Alphabet into three classes, the first nine letters representing 9 units, the next nine letters 9 tens, and the four last letters the numbers 100, 200, 300, 400. The final *kaph*, *mem*, *nun*, *pe*, and *jaddi*, were employed to express 500, 600, 700, 800, 900. Though the Arabian arrangement of the alphabet differs from the Hebrew, the Arabians express the 9 units, 9 tens, and also 100, 200, 300, 400, by the same letters which denote these numbers in Hebrew.

The Greeks also expressed numbers by a tripartite division of the alphabet, with the addition of the figures called *episemon*, *koppa*, and *sanpi*; and it will be observed, on comparing them, that as far as 80, the letters which correspond with those of the Hebrew and Arabian alphabets, have the same numeral power.

When expressed by the letters of the alphabet, numbers are written from right to left, whereas the numeral characters are written from left to right, a fact which, as has frequently been remarked, would afford a strong presumption that the decimal notation was received by the Arabians from a foreign people, were not this universally admitted by themselves.

Excepting the figures 1, 5, and perhaps 4, the Arabians have adopted the numeral figures of the Hindus with very slight alteration of form. The arabic letter ا aleph, which denotes 1 in the alphabetical notation, has exactly the same form as the figure ١ in the decimal scale. In the alphabetical notation, also, 5 is represented by the letter ه, which in the numeral figures, undergoes no farther change than in being a little more rounded, so as to have the appearance of a circle or cipher. The form of the figure ٤ differs in a very slight degree from that of the letter *dal* when it represents 4. It may be a question, however, whether this mode of writing the *dal* has not been adopted since the introduction of the Indian notation.

The examples of addition and subtraction are given in signs, degrees, minutes and seconds.

EXAMPLE.—ADDITION.

sec.	min.	deg.	signs
20	4	8	5
55	41	20	8
15	46	28	13

The process is the following. 20 + 55 = 75, which is one 60 and the remainder is 15; put down 15, and carry one to the next number 41. 41 + 1 + 4 = 46, which being less than 60 is put down; and so also are 20 + 8 = 28; and 8 + 5 = 13. The sum then is 13 signs, 28 deg. 46 min. 15 seconds.

EXAMPLE.—SUBTRACTION.

8	5	2
20	9	1
48	55	*

Say as 20 cannot be subtracted from 8, borrow one time 60 from the preceding number 5 (which represents 5 times 60); and 20 being subtracted from 68 there remains 48; then say as 9 cannot be subtracted from 4, one time 60 is borrowed from 2 (which represents twice 60), and there remains 55: then 1 from 1 and nothing remains.

Multiplication by the sexagesimal system is performed agreeably to the method exhibited in page 20, excepting that in the sexagesimal numeration the intersecting lines in the diagram are drawn from left to right, instead of from right to left; and, conformably to this, the products are put down and read from right to left, according to the manner of writing and reading among the Arabians. Another difference is, that in the sexagesimal diagram the number of sixties is put down in the upper triangle, and the remainder in the lower one, which is just the reverse of what is done in the decimal diagram; and in order to correspond with this mode of multiplication, the multiplier is put down on the right hand side. The sexagesimal diagram is drawn in this manner:

Multiplicand.

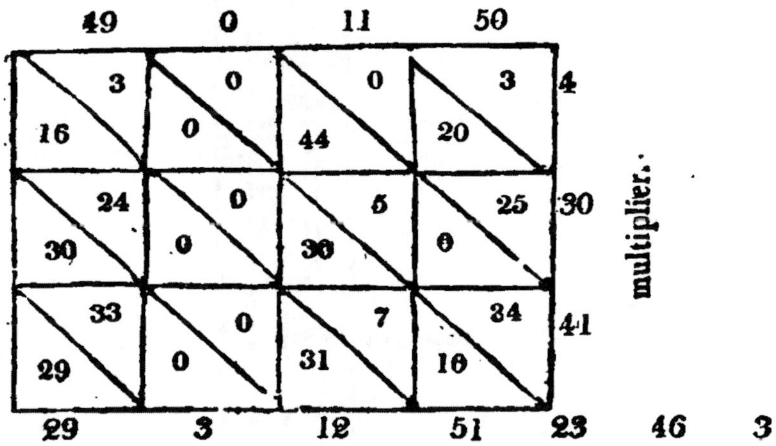

The operation is thus: say 4 times 50 = 200, this contains 3 times 60, and the remainder is 20; put down 3 in the upper triangle and 20 in the lower one; then say 4 times 11 = 44; put this down in the lower triangle; then 49 × 4 = 196 = 3 times 60, and the remainder is 16; proceed in this manner thro' the whole diagram. After the whole multiplication is gone through, sum up the products, beginning with the last on the left hand, and proceeding towards the right. The excess of sixties is carried to the succeeding number as the excess of tens is carried in common Arithmetic.

Division is performed in the sexagesimal system according to the method adopted by the Arabians in operating by the decimal scale, with this difference, that as the numbers are written from right to left, the operation is begun at the right, and proceeds towards the left.

Take the following example:

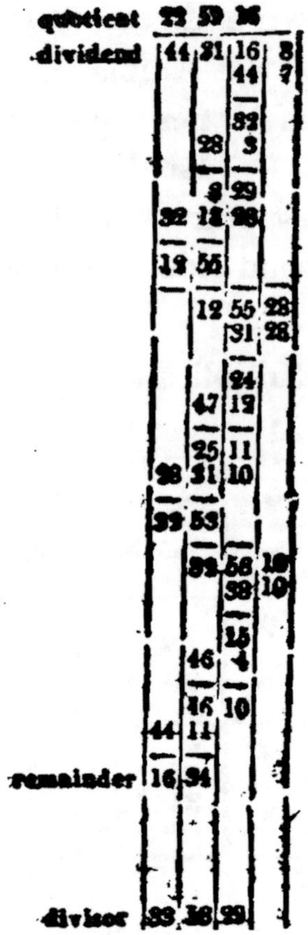

The process is this:

(16 × 29) ÷ 60 = 7. 44
(16 × 13) ÷ 60 = 3. 28
(16 × 32) ÷ 60 = 8. 32
(59 × 29) ÷ 60 = 28. 31
(59 × 13) ÷ 60 = 12. 47
(59 × 32) ÷ 60 = 31. 28
(22 × 29) ÷ 60 = 10. 38
(22 × 13) ÷ 60 = 4. 46
(22 × 32) ÷ 60 = 11. 44

After treating of arithmetic the Risala Hisab and the Khulasat-ul-Hisab proceed to geometry.

An abstract of the geometrical part of these works would, however, greatly exceed the bounds prescribed to these few cursory remarks; and it is besides rendered unnecessary, in consequence of the very excellent account which has been already furnished by Mr. Strachey, and published in the 2d vol. of Hutton's mathematical tracts.

Both treatises set out with definitions of a point, line, surface, solid, right, acute, and obtuse angles, circumference, radius, sector, &c. and both also make use of the alphabetical letters in demonstrating problems and propositions. These circumstances which point out the connection between the Grecian and Arabian geometry, have no resemblance to the plan of the Lilawati, in which no notice is taken of angles, but all the geometrical operations seem to be performed by the relations of the three sides in a right angled triangle.

It has been already remarked that the Arabians call the decimal scale of arithmetic, *Hindasi*, or Indian arithmetic; a circumstance which clearly indicates the source from which they consider this manner of notation to have been derived. This astonishing improvement in arithmetic being thus traced to India, it becomes a matter of curious enquiry, whether the decimal notation was discovered by the Hindus, or was received by them from a people who had made greater advances in the science of calculation. To determine this question with much degree of certainty we must wait for information regarding the state of mathematical science in those countries which border upon India, and which, from the near resemblance of their religious and philosophical tenets, appear to have had a free and large communication with it in every department of knowledge. It may be sufficient to observe here, that if the decimal notation did not originate in India, it must at least have existed there from time immemorial, for no traces whatever are to be found of an alphabetical notation. Several hundred years have elapsed since the numeral notation was adopted by the Arabians, and through them introduced among the nations of Europe; but neither in Europe nor Arabia has it yet altogether superseded the use of alphabetical characters to express numbers. Both Europeans and Arabians still occasionally employ letters for this purpose; and among the latter people, and such eastern nations as have adopted their science, it is considered elegant in noticing an event, to employ a word whose literal powers shall point out the date of its occurence; but I never met with any Hindu who was aware of this use of letters, except thro' Musselman intercourse; nor did I ever observe any thing like it in Sanscrit works, or in any books written in the colloquial dialects of this country. Objects indeed are employed to represent numbers, but letters never are. Thus, the earth, or moon signifies one; the eyes signify two; yug, and Vedas, four, and so forth: and these symbolical words are almost constantly used throughout the Lilawati.

Mr. Strachey's abstract of the Bija Gannita and this translation of the Lilawati, are no doubt important documents on the state of mathematics among the Hindus, but still they exhibit only an imperfect and partial view of the subject. Imperfect, however, as these specimens are, in no other nation of Asia has any work been found, which contains nearly the same degree of mathematical knowledge.

The Chinese, it is said, possess treatises on arithmetic and geometry; but as no translation, or even an abstract of the contents, of any work has yet been published in Europe, we are ignorant how far their knowledge of these subjects extends. All their ordinary arithmetical operations are performed by the mechanical contrivance of the swampan. No traces of algebra have been discovered among them; and although they pretend to high attainments in astronomical scienee, it is alledged by the best writers on China, that they are unable to calculate an eclipse with any degree of precision. From these facts it appears, that the Chinese are far behind the Hindus in point of mathematical knowledge.

In reference to the opinion which has been entertained by several men of eminence, that the high distinction of priority in mathematical improvement, may belong to the nations of upper Asia, it is sufficient to observe, that as none of the accounts with which we have been favoured of the extensive regions of Thibet, afford the least countenance to such an hypothesis, we may be allowed to maintain, that until works of superior antiquity to the Lilawati, and Bija Gannita, and containing a system of arithmetic and algebra equally extensive and complete, be discovered in other eastern countries, it is merely justice to allow that the honour of having invented the decimal notation belongs to the Hindus; and that by means of this wonderful improvement, they had made greater progress in mathematical science at least 700 years ago, than has yet been attained by any other nation in Asia.

That the Hindus are unable to comprehend the demonstrations of the rules employed in their present calculations, is an opinion not uncommon amongst the learned in Europe; and it has consequently been inferred, that they either were not the original discoverers of the rules which they now follow, or that mathematics must have degenerated amongst them to such a degree, that they are now unable to comprehend the fundamental principles of the science, as demonstrated and handed down by their ancestors.

Without entering into any enquiry regarding the foundation on which this opinion rests, it may be sufficient at present to remark, that I have received information of several works, some of which were composed in modern times, and which are said to contain demonstrations of the rules given in the Lilawati, Bija Ganita, and Surya Siddhanta; and though little confidence can be placed in such accounts, even when furnished by learned and respectable brahmans, yet, in the present instance, I am induced to give them some degree of credit, because the *Udaharna*, a work in my possession, contains demonstrations of many of the rules in the Lilawati; but unfortunately my copy is so incorrect and mutilated that no satisfactory use could be made of it.* The operations contained in this work corroborate the verbal information I have received, that the demonstrations, both in arithmetic and geometry are performed by means of algebra; and that the Hindus never appear to have known or practiced the Grecian mode of analysis.

Within these two hundred years, however, the mathematical and astronomical sciences appear to have been gradually declining among the Hindus. The Jyotishis of the present day are in general profoundly ignorant of every branch of mathematics. Inattentive to astronomy as a science, they devote themselves solely to the study of astrology, and possess no ambition to arrive at a higher degree of knowledge than what enables them to cast up a nativity, or to determine a lucky hour for marriages, and for performing the numerous ceremonies practised by their countrymen.

In Poona, which may now be regarded the seat and asylum of brahmanism, it is said that no more then 10 or 12 persons understand the Lilawati, or Bija Ganita; and tho' there are many professed Jyotishes in Bombay, I have not found one individual who understands almost a single page even of the Lilawati.

Among the brahmans the appellation of learned seems to be confined to grammarians, logicians, and metaphysical theologians; and those who devote themselves to any of these studies often exhibit a very fair proportion of ignorance on every other subject. Astronomy, in particular, as it relates to gross material objects, is considered beneath their notice, except as the means of developing the purposes of heaven. Those persons even who pursue the study of mathematics and astronomy, are in general very ill informed regarding the opinions of the scientific writers.

* Since writing this paragraph I have received from Poona several valuable and curious works, which I hope will throw much light on this subject, and on the general state of astronomy and mathematics among the Hindus.

Few are found who have read the whole of the Lilawati; for which this very cogent reason is assigned, that whoever actually goes through the whole work, is doomed to a deprivation of his mental faculties, or at least to perpetual proverty. This ridiculous belief proves that a knowledge of the Lilawati is now considered of no easy attainment.

The common people, and even learned brahmans who are unacquainted with mathematical studies, relate many absurd stories relating to the wonderful powers which are acquired by a knowledge of this work. It is supposed, for instance, that he who understands it, can, in the twinkling of an eye, tell the number of leaves on a tree, of blades of grass in a meadow, or the number of grains of sand on the sea shore. The Lilawati is in fact considered as a sort of magical production, the understanding of which endows the individual with powers and qualities that command both admiration and fear.

As the following passages, which are translated from the *Siddhanta Siromani*, are both curious in themselves, and shew how much the opinions of men of science differ from the absurd doctrines of the Puranas, I am induced to subjoin them, tho' they are not immediately connected with this work.

This globe which is formed of earth, air, water, space, and fire, and which is surrounded by the planets, stands firm in the midst of space by its own power, and has no support.

This globular shaped world has no support, but stands firm in space by its own power.

I shall now answer the objections which have been brought from its being affirmed in the Puranas that the world has a support.

If this world has a material support, then that support must have something else to support it, and this second support must also be supported, and so on; but at last something must be supposed to stand by its own power; and why should not this power be ascribed to this world, which is one of the eight visible forms of the deity.

As the sun and fire in their own nature possess heat, the moon coldness, water fluidity, stones hardness, and the air motion, so is the earth in its own nature immoveable; for different bodies possess different powers.

The earth has an attractive power, by which it draws towards itself any heavy body in the air, and which body has then the appearance of falling; but where could this earth fall which is surrounded only by space.

This attractive power of the earth shews why things situated at the lower part, or at the sides, do not fall from its surface.

The Boudhists observing the motion of the wheel of the constellations, concluded that the earth could have no support; but having never observed any heavy body stationary in empty space, they suppose that the earth is continually falling downwards, tho' this not perceived, as the motion of a ship is not perceived by the passengers. They imagine that there are two suns, two moons, two zodiacs, and that these rise at alternate corners. That is, they suppose that two suns, two moons, and 56 constellations move round Meru, which is four cornered, these planets rising at alternate corners.

To this opinion I object, that if the earth is continually falling downwards, an arrow, or any thing thrown into the air, could never reach it again. Should it be said that the descent of the earth is slow, I reply, that this is not the case, for the earth being the heaviest body, its descent would be more rapid than that of the arrow.

Neither can the earth be like a mirror, as they suppose. Were it so, why is not the sun, which is one hundred thousand yojan high, seen by men in the same manner as by the Gods* If the intervention of Meru causes night, why is not Meru itself seen? Besides, Meru lies north, whereas the sun rises to the southward of east; instead of which, if it rises when it comes to the side of Meru, it ought to rise north of east.

The level appearance which the earth presents to us is owing to its magnitude, for the 100th part of the circumference appears level; therefore as the sight of man extends only to a short distance, the earth appears to be a plain.

From Lunka, the commencement of latitude, to Ujein, is the 16th part of the earth's circumference.

People always suppose that they are uppermost, and that others are below them; that those on the sides stand horizontally, and those below with their heads downwards, as the shadow of a man is seen in water.

The earth's circumference is 4967 yojanas (4 coss); its diameter is 1581 $\frac{1}{24}$; the convex superficies 7853034 yojanas.

---

* That is, as seen at the north pole, where the Gods are said to reside.

LILAWATI.

SALUTATION to the elephant-headed Being who infuses joy into the minds of his worshippers, who delivers from every difficulty those that call upon him, and whose feet are reverenced by the gods.

The science of calculation which I teach delights the intelligent by its brevity, the clearness of its demonstrations, and its curious operations.

TABLE OF MONEY.[A]

20 Varataka[B]	1 Kakini
4 Kakini	1 Pana
16 Pana	1 Dramma
16 Dramma	1 Niska

TABLE OF WEIGHTS.

2 Barleycorns	1 Gunja[C]
3 Gunja	1 Valla
8 Valla	1 Dharana
2 Dharana	1 Gadyanaka

A weight equal to 14 valla is called dhataka.

[A] The titles of the Tables are not contained in the text, but are taken from the Commentary, in which also it is stated that the weights and measures of the Magadha country are adopted as the standard.

[B] Cowry or small shell which passes for money in several parts of India.—The seed of the lotus is also called Varataka.

[C] In the common dialects of India called Retti; Abrus precatorius.

ANOTHER TABLE OF WEIGHTS.

5 Gunja [A]	....	1 Masha
16 Masha	....	1 Karsha
4 Karsha	....	1 Pala

A Karsha of gold is denominated suvarna (gold) [B]

LAND MEASURE [C]

8 Diameters of a barley corn	....	1 Angula [D]
24 Angula	....	1 Hasta [E]
4 Hasta	....	1 Danda [F]
2000 Danda	....	1 Kros [G]
4 Kros	....	1 Yojana

ALSO

10 Hasta	....	1 Vansa [H]

[A] ANOTHER TABLE.

8 Gunja	....	1 Masha
12 Masha	....	1 Tola

ANOTHER TABLE.

10 Gunja	....	1 Masha
8 Masha	....	1 Tola

[B] Karsha as to metals in general signifies the weight which passes under this name;—but in reference to gold this weight is called either karsha or suvarna, i. e. gold.

[C] This is the title given in the commentaries ;—but the measures contained in the table are employed in long and cloth, as well as in square measure.

[D] Lit.—A finger ;—it corresponds nearly to an inch.

[E] Lit.—A cubit, or measure extending from the elbow to the tip of the middle finger. One of the commentators says that either gaz, or kara, i. e. cubit, is used for measuring cloth. Gaz is a Persian word and is usually translated yard.—The commentator who uses this word lived about 200 years ago.

[F] Lit.—A Staff;—rod, or pole.

[G] In the vernacular dialects pronounced coss.

[H] Lit.—A Bamboo,—Bambusa Arundinacea and other species.

Nivartana is a quadrangular field each of whose sides is bounded by 20 Vansa [A]

Ghanahasta, or solid cubit, is that which measures one hasta or cubit in breadth, in length, and in thickness, and which has twelve angles. [B] The shasters declare that the measure for grain, &c. called ghanahasta or solid cubit, is the kharika of the Magadha country.

GRAIN MEASURE.

16th of a Kharika [C]	......	1 Drona.
4th of a Drona	....	1 Adhaka.
4th of an Adhaka	....	1 Prast,ha.
4th of a Prast,ha	....	1 Kudava.

[A] The Rati Ratna mentions that this measure is by some named vigah, by others nivartana. The vigah or bigah is a measure of land used in several parts of India, especially in the province of Bengal. An author named Mishra gives a different meaning to this paragraph and the first part of the following one :---He says :—" 20 vansa make 1 nivartana. Kshetar, i. e. a quadrangular figure, or, literally, a field, is that which is bounded by four sides."—And here he is followed by Fyzee in his Persian Translation :—" 20 vans make 1 nivartana :—A space which comprehends four dast or cubits, so that one dast or cubit may be on each side, is called chetar or field."—The original will bear this interpretation, but the one I have given appears more probable and correct, and also agrees with that adopted by three commentators.

[B] Derived from ghana and hasta :—Ghana means cube ;—the literal meaning therefore is cubic cubit.—In this sense it is frequently employed in subsequent parts of this treatise ;—and sometimes also it is used in the same sense as ghana phal, which means simply cubic result or contents.

It does not at first appear evident what is meant by 12 angles ; for according to the definition ghanahasta is a cube, and consequently has 24 angles.—It must therefore be presumed that the definition relates only to a hollow cube open on one side for the purpose of a measure, and that the angles at the bottom alone are reckoned.

[C] ANOTHER TABLE.

72 Tanka	....	1 Seer, or.
$\frac{1}{40}$ Mana	....	1 Seer
$\frac{1}{20}$ or according to some $\frac{1}{16}$ of a Mana		1 Kharika

The Tables of Time, &c. not here specified, are generally known. A

A TABLE OF TIME.

60	Pala	1	Ghatika
60	Ghatika	1	Divasa or day,
30	Days	1	Masa or month
12	Months	1	Varasa or year.

TABLE OF DIVISIONS OF THE ZODIAC.

60	Vikala	1	Kala
60	Kala	1	Ansa
30	Ansa	1	Rasi or sign
12	Rasi	1	Bhagana, or period in which the sun moves thro' the 12 signs.

PART I.

CHAP. I.

REVERENCE to Ganesa who is beautiful as the pure purple lotos, and around whose neck the black curling snake winds itself in playful folds.

The places of numbers increase in value in a tenfold proportion.—Preceding authors, for practical purposes, have given them the following names:

Eka—dasa—shata—sahasra—ayuta—laksha—pryuta—kotya—arbuda—abja—kharva—nikharva—mahapadma—sankha—jaladhi—antya—madhya—parardha,

Which are thus put down in figures:— 1000000000000000000 [A]

[A] The Udaharna, or book of examples, states that the names of these eighteen places are put down on the authority of the Vedas; but it also adds that in some books there are names for 32 places.—The eighteen places and names may be thus put down:

Figure	Name	Value
1	Parardha	a hundred thousand billions
0	Madhya	ten thousand billions
0	Antya	a thousand billions
0	Jaladhi	a hundred billions
0	Sankha	ten billions
0	Mahapadma	a billion
0	Nikharva	a hundred thousand millions
0	Kharva	ten thousand millions
0	Abja	a thousand millions
0	Arbuda	a hundred millions
0	Kotya	ten millions
0	Pryuta	a million
0	Laksha	a hundred thousand
0	Ayuta	ten thousand
0	Sahasra	a thousand
0	Shata	a hundred
0	Dasa	ten
0	Eka	unit

Dr. Wilkins in his Shanscrit grammar has given the names of twenty-two places, several of which differ from the above. The order also in which some of them occur is different.

SECTION I.

OF ADDITION AND SUBTRACTION.

Figures are added from right to left, [A] or from left to right; [B] and also are subtracted from right to left, or from left to right, according to their places.

Example.—Tell me the sum of two, five, thirty-two, one hundred and ninety-three, eighteen, ten, and one hundred? Also what is the result if this sum be subtracted from ten thousand?

Statement.—*For Addition.*—2, 5, 32, 193, 18, 10, 100.—Added together the sum is 360. [C]

Statement —For Subtraction.—2, 5, 32, 193, 18, 10, 100.—The sum of these being subtracted from ten thousand, *the remainder* is 9640. [D]

[A] Krama.—This word literally signifies forwards or progression. Here it means that the operation is to be performed from right to left.

[B] Utkrama.—The literal signification is backwards or retrogression. It means here that the operation is to be performed from left to right. This is done by adding up the column of figures on the left hand and putting down the result beneath, then adding the next column and putting down the units, and carrying the tens to the preceding result, which is then blotted out and the new result written down in its place, and so on to any number of columns, as,

EXAMPLES.

2	3629	5735269
5	8134	3829683
32	5629	7258264
193	8765	1537636
18	———	———
10	24937	16239632
100	2615	1835085
———		6
240		
36		

[C] Com.—Place of units, 2,5,2,3,8,0,0 .... added 20
Place of tens 0,0,3,9,1,1,0 .... added 14
Place of hundreds 0,0,1,1,0,0,0 .... added 2

Total sum 360

[D] The lesser number is placed above the greater, units above units, tens above tens, &c.
In subtracting from right to left, if the figure in the upper line is greater than that below it, take 10 upon the preceding figure in that line, and mark it by a perpendicular stroke;

SECTION II.

OF MULTIPLICATION.

Multiply the last figure to the left of the multiplicand by the multiplier; then on

---

then subtract the upper figure from 10, and having added the remainder to the lower figure, and set down the result below, add one to the preceding upper figure over which the perpendicular stroke is placed, and subtract it thus increased from the one below it, proceeding as before if the upper figure is greater than the lower one. Example.

68387
243675

Thus say, 7 cannot be subtracted from 5, therefore 10 is taken upon 8; mark this figure by a perpendicular stroke, and subtract the upper figure 7 from 10; there remains 3; this remainder 3 added to the lower figure 5 makes 8; write down this number below the 5; then add 1 to the preceding upper figure 8 over which the perpendicular stroke stands; thus 1 added to 8 makes 9; as this upper figure 9 cannot be subtracted from 7 the figure below it, take 10 upon the preceding upper figure 3 and proceed as before: and so on thro' all the figures. The result of the operation is exhibited, thus;

68387
243675

175288

In order to subtract from left to right write down the subtrahend above the minuend as before directed; and if the subtrahend contains fewer places than the minuend, put ciphers above the remaining places of the minuend. Then write down below the minuend line the figures over which there are ciphers; and after subtracting the first upper figure on the left from the corresponding lower one, set down the remainder below it. If the upper figure is greater than the lower one, take ten from the preceding remainder, and adding it to the lower figure, subtract the upper figure from the lower one thus increased. Then blotting out the preceding remainder from which ten is taken, put down the reduced number in its place; and proceed in this manner thro' all the figures.. Example.

0068387
3243675

3185298
317 28

3175288

The former method of subtracting from right to left is considered the easiest, and accordingly is the one most commonly adopted.

moving forward the multiplier *one place*, multiply the next figure; A thus repeating the operation until all the figures of the multiplicand are multiplied: B or

Write down the multiplicand in as many different places as the multiplier may have been divided into parts, and by these parts multiply the multiplicand, and then sum up the products: C or

Multiply the multiplicand by any figure which divides the multiplier without leaving a remainder, and then multiply the product *so obtained* by the quotient *of the multiplier*: D or

---

A The last figure on the left hand is called *anta*, which signifies last or final; the figure preceding it is called *upantya*, or that which is next to the anta or final; all the other figures are called *adi*, which signifies first or antecedent.

In general however the figures are classed into *anta* and *adi*, i. e. final and antecedent, excluding the term *upantya*, or that which is next to the final; and in this arrangement the last figure on the left hand is considered the *anta*, final, and all the others *adi*, antecedent. But these terms being merely relative, the antecedent next to the final becomes itself the final when in the course of the operation the first *anta* or final is thrown out; hence each of the antecedent figures may in succession become the final.

B Take the example given in the text of 135 multiplied by 12. The operation according to this method is performed in the following manner:

```
135        135        135
12          12         12
----       ----       ----
12          36         60
 36
  60
----
1620
```

This is called *swarupa gunanam;* or multiplication by the multiplier itself as a factor.

```
C Thus,   135 × 4  ........  540
          135 × 8  ........ 1080
                --          ----
                12          1620
```

This is called *khanda gunanam;* or multiplication by component parts of the multiplier.

```
D Thus,   135 × 3  ........ 405
          405 × 4  ............... 1620
```

This is called *vibhaga gunanam*; or multiplication by submultiples of the multiplier.

Separate the figures of the multiplier into their different places; then multiply the multiplicand according to the places, and also sum up the products according to the places: [A] or

Multiply by the multiplier either increased or diminished by any number you choose; and add to the product or subtract from it, the product which results from multiplying the multiplicand by the number chosen. [B]

Example.—If thou art acquainted with the method of multiplying by the multiplier itself, or by component parts of the multiplier, or by submultiples of the multiplier, or by the places of the multiplier, then tell me my young girl whose tremulous eyes resemble those of a young fawn, what is the product of one hundred and thirty-five multiplied by twelve?

Statement.—Multiplicand 135:—Multiplier 12.

According to the rule, multiply the last figure to the left of the multiplicand by the multiplier, and so on; the result is 1620: or

Separate the multiplier into the parts, 4, 8; *and having put down the multiplicand in two places,* multiply separately by these parts of the multiplier, and add the products; the result is the same, 1620: or

Divide the multiplier by 3; the quotient is 4; then multiply the multiplicand by 3, and multiply the product by *the quotient* 4; this gives the same result, 1620: or

---

[A] Thus,

```
 135
 1.2
 ----
 135
  270
 ----
 1620
```

This is called *St,hana gunanam*; or multiplication according to the places.

[B] If the multiplicand is multiplied by the multiplier increased by an assumed number, then from the product obtained subtract the product of the multiplier by the assumed number. If the multiplicand is multiplied by the multiplier diminished by an assumed number, then to the product obtained add the product of the multiplicand by the assumed number; thus,

Example where the product is added		Example where the product is subtracted	
135 × 10	1350	135 × 20	2700
135 × 2	270	135 × 8	1080
	1620		1620

Separate the *figures of the* multiplier into their places 1, 2; then multiply *the multiplicand* by these figures separately according to their places, and also add the products according to their places; the result is the same, 1620: or

Multiply *the multiplicand* separately by the multiplier minus two which is 10, and also by 2, and add the products together; the result is the same, 1620. Or multiply *the multiplicand* by the multiplier plus 8, which is 12, and from the product subtract the product of the multiplicand multiplied by 8; the same result is found, 1620. [A]

[A] In the copy from which this translation is made there is also the following:

"Or, the multiplier being divided by 4, the quotient is 3; the multiplicand multiplied by 4 is 540; this multiplied by the quotient 3 gives the product 1620."—But this appears to be an interpolation, as it is not contained in the other copies. It is also misplaced, for it belongs to the third method.

Besides these different methods of multiplication, another method is adopted when the multiplier contains three or more figures. In that case, write down the two factors so that the first figure of the multiplier shall be below the last figure of the multiplicand reckoning from right to left. Then multiply the last figure of the multiplicand by all the figures of the multiplier beginning at the last figure to the left, as directed in the retrograde method of multiplication. After the last figure of the multiplicand is thus multiplied, throw it out, and on moving the multiplier forward one place, multiply the next figure in the multiplicand in the same manner as the former one, and thus proceed thro' all the figures of the multiplicand. The result of the different products added together is the whole product.

EXAMPLE.

Multiplicand 724635
Multiplier 829

The result is shewn, thus,

7 × 829	5803		724635
2 × 829	1658		829
4 × 829	3316		829
6 × 829	4974		829
3 × 829	2487		829
5 × 829	4145		829
	600722415		829

Multiplier moved forward one place successively after throwing out the figure of the multiplicand which has been multiplied.

The individual products are obtained by multiplying the multiplicand figure by each figure

SECTION III.

OF DIVISION.

In division the quotient is that number by which when the divisor is multiplied and the product subtracted from the dividend, beginning at the last figure on the left hand, no remainder is left [A]

---

of the multiplier separately, beginning with the last on the left hand; thus,

```
8 × 7 ........ 56
2 × 7 ........  14
9 × 7 ........   63
               ----
               5803
```

It may be proper to remark that the Hindus do not place the results of multiplication below each other as is done in Europe, but above each other in the following manner,

```
  63
 14
56
----
5803
```

For further illustration see the example in the preface.

[A] This is rather a definition or statement of the nature of division, than a rule shewing the manner in which the operation is done. No work indeed that I have consulted contains the rule of operation; and I suppose that in general the pupil learns it from the oral instructions of his master.—The following method is that which is commonly exhibited on the abacus or board:

Having placed the divisor below the dividend, find how often the divisor is contained in as many figures of the dividend as are just necessary, and place the number on one side calling it the quotient. Multiply the divisor by this quotient and set the product above the figures of the dividend above mentioned. Subtract this product from that part of the dividend above which it stands; then throwing out that part of the dividend, put down the remainder before the other figures of the dividend and repeat the former process on the new dividend thus formed. And

When it can be done, reduce the divisor and dividend by a common measure, and then divide; this will give the quotient.

Example.—Divide the product of the former example *given in multiplication*, taking the multiplier as a divisor.

Statement.—1620: this being divided *by the former multiplier* 12, the quotient obtained is the *former* multiplicand 135 : ^ or

Reduce both the dividend and divisor by three: We have, dividend 540; divisor 4. Or reduce by four: We have, dividend 405, divisor 3. These dividends being divided by their respective divisors, the same quotient is obtained, 135.

---

proceed in this manner until no dividend remains, or until the dividend is less than the divisor.

EXAMPLE.

	1614	......remainder which at the end of the operation stands in the dividend line, and the divisor having been moved forward one place in each case of division, stands below it; thus,
	6490	
	8104	
	9735	
	105454	
	22715	1614 ...... remainder
	2376954	3245 ...... divisor
	19470	
	21845954	
	6490	
dividend	86746954	quotient
divisor	3245	26732
	3245	
	3245	
	3245	
	3245	

• Statement.—$\frac{1620}{12}$. In this example the divisor being multiplied by one, and the product subtracted from the dividend, the quotient is 1, and the remainder is 420. Then move the divisor forward, thus, $\frac{420}{12}$; the divisor being then multiplied by three, and the product subtracted from the dividend, the quotient is 3, and the remainder is 60. Then move the divisor forward and repeat the operation. Com.

SECTION IV.

OF THE SQUARE.

A SQUARE is the product of any number multiplied by itself.[A] or

Put down the square of the last figure *which is on the left hand,* and multiply the preceding figures[B] by double the sum of this last figure, writing down the products according to their places; then blot out the last figure, and after moving the preceding figures[B] forward *one place,* repeat the process:[C] or

---

[A] Literally;—"The same number multiplied twice is called a square."—This is merely a definition. The different modes of operation are given in the three succeeding paragraphs of the text.

[B] Or figure if the number to be squared consists of two figures only. Take for example 67, and put the products above each other according to their places; thus,

```
           7 × 7  ................ 49
           7 × 12 ...............  84
           6 × 6  ...............  36        ........ 4489  square
Number to be squared ............. 67
                                    7
```

[C] This method is shewn according to the Hindu mode of operation in the following manner, taking for example the number 297. The products are written down and added together agreeably to the directions given in the rule of multiplication; thus,

```
                              1
                              82
                              3214
                              46889    .......... 88209  square
                              7880
                              861
                              82
Number to be squared ......... 297
                              97
                               7
```

[a] Divide the number into two parts, and after multiplying the product of these parts by two, add *to the last product* the sum of the squares of the parts; the result is the square *of the whole number*: [b] or

---

But the operation will perhaps be more clearly understood by shewing the results in the following manner:

2 × 2 4
97 × 4 388
9 × 9 81
7 × 18 126
7 × 7 49

88209

Gangadhar gives another method of performing the operation, viz. Having put down the square of the last figure, multiply the preceding figure by double the sum of the last figure; then square the said preceding figure, and after multiplying double the sum of the two last figures on the left hand by this preceding figure, square the next preceding figure:—thus

2 × 2 4
9 × 4 36
9 × 9 81
29 × 2 ... 58 × 7 ... 406
7 × 7 49

88209

But as this method is not conformable to the rule it is rejected by the other commentators.

[a] If a line be divided into any two parts the squares of the parts together with twice the rectangle contained by the parts are equal to the square of the whole line.

Euclid. B. 2. Pr. 4.

[b] Take for example 9; and divide it into the parts 4, 5; Then,

4 × 5 20   and   4 × 4 16
20 × 2 40   5 × 5 25

41 + 40 .... 81 square of 9.

Having diminished the quantity and also increased it by any number you choose, multiply the results together, and *to the product* add the square of the number chosen. The sum is the square of the quantity. [A]

Example.—What are the squares of 9, 14, 297, 10005?

Statement.—9, 14, 297, 10005. These being multiplied in succession, according to the rule, the squares obtained are 81, 196, 88209, 1000100025: or

Take the parts of nine, 4, 5; the product of these multiplied by two is 40; to this product add the sum of the squares of the parts; the result is 81, *the square of* 9. Or take the parts of fourteen, 6, 8; the product of these multiplied by two is 96; to this product add 100 the sum of the squares of the parts; the result is 196, *the square of* 14. The parts of fourteen, 4, 10, also give the square 196: or

The number 297 diminished by three is 294, and increased by three is 300. Then 294 and 300 being multiplied together, and the square of 3 added to the product, the result is 88209, which is the square of 297.

SECTION V.

OF THE SQUARE ROOT.

Subtract from the last uneven period [B] the *greatest* square *which it contains.* Set down double the *square* root in a *separate* line, and after dividing by it the next even period, subtract the square of the quotient from the next uneven period, and also set down double this quotient in the line: Then divide the next even period by the number in the line, and on subtracting the square of the quotient from the next uneven period, set down double this quotient in the line. Thus repeat the operation thro' all the figures. The half of the *separate or quotient* line is the root.

[A] If a straight line be bisected, and produced to any point, the rectangle contained by the whole line thus produced, and the part of it produced, together with the square of half the line bisected, is equal to the square of the straight line which is made up of the half and the part produced. Euclid B. 2. prop. 6.

[B] The figures in the first, third, fifth, &c. places, reckoning from the right, are called *visama* or uneven, and are marked by a perpendicular stroke. Those in the second, fourth, sixth, &c. places, are called *sama* or even, and are marked by a horizontal stroke. In the operation the period receives its name from the denomination of the first figure on the right hand. When the first figure on the right is uneven, the period is called uneven; when this first figure

Example.—What are the square roots of 4, 9, 81, 196, 88209, 100100025?—They are 2, 3, 9, 14, 297, 1005. [A]

---

is even, the period is called even. Thus in the subsequent example of extracting the square root of 88209, the numbers 48, 122, 410, 49, are respectively named even, uneven, even, uneven.

[A] The details of the operation are thus given in the commentary, taking for example 88209.

"Make the marks even and uneven. Here the last uneven figure is 8; from this subtract 4 which is the square of 2, and there remains of the square number 48209: Then multiply the root of 4 by 2, the product is 4; set this down in a separate line, and by it divide the next even period 48; the quotient is 9, and there remains *of the square* 12209; subtract 81 which is the square of the quotient 9 from the next uneven period 122; there remains *of the square* 4109: Then multiply the quotient 9 by 2; the product is 18, which being put down in the separate line below 4, *one place forward*, the sum is 58: By this number divide the next even period 410; the quotient is 7, and there remains *of the square* 49; from this uneven period subtract 49 which is the square of 7; no remainder is left: Then multiply the quotient 7 by 2, the product is 14; put this down in the separate line one place forward, and add together the different products in the separate line; their sum is 594, and the half of this is 297, which is the root of the square 88209."

The rule for extracting the square root will perhaps be more intelligible when expressed in the following terms:

Subtract from the last uneven period the greatest square in the said period, and write down double the root of this square in a separate line.

To the remainder bring down the next even figure for a dividend, which being divided by double the root, and the next uneven figure annexed to the remainder, subtract the square of the quotient from the period thus formed, and also write down double the quotient in the separate line one place forward, adding the unit if there be one to the preceding quotient figure.

To the last remainder bring down the next even figure for a dividend, which being divided as before by the number contained in the separate line, and the next uneven figure annexed to the remainder, subtract the square of the last quotient from the period thus formed, and then

SECTION VI.

OF THE CUBE

A CUBE is the product of any number multiplied twice by itself.[A] or

Put down the cube of the final *or last figure which is on the left hand,* and multiply the square of this final by the antecedent figure and by three. Then having multiplied the square of the antecedent figure by three and by the final, and also having cubed this antecedent figure, add up all *the results*[B] each one place forward, and their sum will be the cube. Then taking the two figures whose cube is found call them the final, and repeat the operation.[C]

---

write down double this quotient in the separate line. And thus repeat the process thro' all the figures.

Example 88209

		Separate Line
88209		
4	greatest square	
4) 48	even period divided by double the sum of the root, the quotient is 9	root 2 × 2 .... 4 quot. 9 × 2 18
36		58
122	uneven period	quot. 7 × 2 14
81	square of the quotient 9	594
58) 410	even period divided by the number contained in the separate line, the quotient is 7	The half of which is 297 the square root.
406		
49	uneven period	
49	square of the last quotient 7	

[A] Literally;—" The same number multiplied thrice is called a cube."

[B] The cube stands in the first place, and the other results or products follow in succession, each being put down one place before the other.

[C] This rule may be stated in the following manner:

Write down somewhere the cube of the last number which is on the left hand, and after

The operation for squaring or cubing *any number* may also be performed by beginning at the first figure on the right hand: [A] or

Multiply the number by its two component parts and also by three; then cube the two parts, and add the products.

---

multiplying the square of this last number by the next or preceding number and by three, put down the product one place forward from the cube. Then multiply the square of the said preceding number by three and by the last number, and also cube this preceding number, setting down each product one place forward. The products being added together according to their places, their sum is the cube of these two numbers. Then taking the figures whose cube is found, call them the final number, and the next figure the second number; and repeat the operation.

It will be observed that the whole series of figures is divided successively into two numbers, the figures whose cube is found being considered one number, and the succeeding figure the other number. Take for example 125679. After finding the cube of the sum formed by the final number 1 and its preceding number 2, these two figures are taken for one number which is called the final, and the next figure 5 is the other number. Also after finding the cube of the sum formed by the two numbers 12 and 5, these three figures are then taken for one number and their preceding figure for the other, and so on thro' all the figures.

[A] This sentence seems to come in as a note or remark.

In order to perform the operation of squaring or cubing according to this method, the Udaharna first directs the denominations of the figures to be changed, calling the final figure on the left hand the preceding or antecedent, and the preceding or antecedent figures, the final.

Then to produce the square of any number proceed agreeably to the rule in page 13. Take the example 297 given under that rule; thus,

	2
	29
	297
7 × 7	49
29 × 14	406
9 × 9	81
2 × 18	36
2 × 2	4
	88209

In order also to produce the cube of any number, proceed agreeably to the preceding rule in the text; observing in addition to what is there directed, that the products must be set down so that in adding up the whole each product shall be one place before its factor in the

Also, the cube of the root of a square being multiplied by itself, the product is the cube of that square.

Example.—What are the cubes of 9, 27, and 125?

Statement.—9, 27, 125. The cubes of these numbers in succession are 729, 19683, 1953125: [A]

---

number. Take for example the sum 2125; thus,

		2125
5^3	....	125
$5^2 \times 2 \times 3$	....	150
$2^2 \times 3 \times 5$	....	60
2^3	....	8
		15625
$25^2 \times 1 \times 3$	....	1875
$1^2 \times 3 \times 25$	....	75
1^3	....	1
		1953125
$125^2 \times 2 \times 3$	....	93750
$2^2 \times 3 \times 125$	....	1500
2^3	....	8
		9595703125

[A] According to the first rule the operation may be exhibited in the following manner, taking for example the sum 125.—Thus

1	cube of last figure on left hand
6	square of last figure multiplied by the preceding figure, and the product mutiplied by three
12	square of the said preceding figure multiplied by three, and the product mutiplied by one the last figure
8	cube of the preceding figure
1728	

Then calling 12 the final number, and 5 the preceding number, repeat the process: Thus

1728	cube of final number 12.
2160	square of the final number multiplied by the preceding number, and the product multiplied by three
900	square of the said preceding number multiplied by three, and the product multiplied by the final number
125	cube of the said preceding number
1953125	cube of 125.

Or, the number 9 being multiplied by its parts 4, 5, and also by 3, the product is 540; to this number add 189 which is the sum of the cubes of the parts; the result is 729, the cube of 9. [A] Or, the number 27 being multiplied by its parts 20, 7, and also by 3, the product is 11340; to this number add 8343 which is the sum of the cubes of the parts; the result is 19683, *the cube of* 27.

Or take the number 4. The cube of its root is 8, the square of which 64 is the cube of 4. Also the cube of the root of 9 is 27, the square of which 729 is the cube of 9.

SECTION VII.

OF THE CUBE ROOT.

The first place on the right hand is called *ghana* or cube; the two next places *aghana* or not cube. [B]

Subtract the cube contained in the final period from the said period; put down the root *of the cube* in a separate line, and after multiplying its square by three, divide the antecedent figure by the result, and write down the quotient in the separate line: Then multiply the square of the quotient by the preceding number *in that line* and by three, and after subtracting the product from the next antecedent figure cube the said quotient, and subtract the result from the next antecedent figure. Thus repeat the process thro' all the figures. The separate line contains the Cube Root.

The operation according to the remaining two methods will be readily understand by looking at the examples in the text.

[A] Thus,

9 × 4 .... 36 × 5 .... 180 × 3 540
4^3 64
5^3 125
189 189
729 cube of 9

[B] The ghana or cube place is marked by a perpendicular stroke; the aghana or not cube place by a horizontal stroke, as in the extraction of the square root; thus 19683.

Example.—What are the cube roots of 729, 19683, 1953125. The roots are 9, 27, 125.[A]

[A] The commentaries shew the operation in the following manner, taking for example 1953125 :

" Mark the cube place by a perpendicular stroke, and the not cube place by a horizontal stroke. In this example the cube contained in the final cube period is 1; subtract this number from the final, and no remainder is left; put down the root which is 1 in a separate line, and after multiplying its square by 3, divide the antecedent 9 by the product; the quotient is 2,* and the remainder is 3; put down the quotient in the separate line, thus 1,2; the square of the quotient 2 is 4; multiply this by 1 the preceding figure in the separate line, the product is 4, which being multiplied by 3, the product is 12; subtract this from the antecedent 35,† the remainder is 23; the cube of the quotient 2 is 8; subtract this from the antecedent 233, the remainder is 225. Again the square of the root 12 is 144, multiply this by 3, and by the product 432 divide the antecedent 2251; the quotient is 5, and the remainder is 91; put down the quotient in the separate line, thus 1,2,5; the square of the quotient 5 is 25, which being multiplied by the preceding number 12, the product is 300, and this again multiplied by 3, the product is 900; subtract this from the antecedent 912, the remainder is 12: the cube of the quotient 5 is 125, which being subtracted from the antecedent 125, no remainder is left."

The rule for extracting the cube root may also be expressed in the following terms.

Subtract from the last period on the left hand the greatest cube contained in that period, and set down its root in a separate line.

---

* In this division it is necessary that such a remainder be left as, with the antecedent figure annexed to it, will be equal to the square of the quotient multiplied by its preceding figure or figures in the line and by three; hence 3 is taken twice only in 9, for had it been taken three times, no remainder would have been left, and 5 the next antecedent figure is less than $2 \times 2 \times 1 \times 3$ ...... 12.

† The term antecedent denotes not only the antecedent figure, but also the number or period formed by annexing the antecedent figure to the number which remains after the preceding operation. Thus the antecedent figure 5 being annexed to 3, the number which remains after dividing 9, makes 35, which is denominated the antecedent. In the same manner the next antecedent figure 3 being annexed to 23, the number which remains when 12 is subtracted from 35, forms the antecedent number or period 233: and so on.

NOTE CONTINUED.

Annex the next figure to the remainder, and having divided this number by triple the square of the root, set down the quotient in the separate line.

Annex the next figure to the remainder, and from this number subtract the product of triple the square of the last quotient multiplied by the preceding figure or figures in the separate line.

Annex the next figure to the remainder, and from this number subtract the cube of the last quotient.

Repeat this operation thro' all the figures. The number in the separate or quotient line is the cube root.

Agreeably to this enunciation of the rule the operation is exhibited in the following manner:

Example	1953125
cube contained in first period	1
square of cube root multiplied by 3 is	3) 9 (2 quotient
	6
	35
square of the quotient 2 is 4; this multiplied by 3, and the product by 1, the preceding figure in the separate line, is	12
	233
cube of the quotient 2 is	8
square of the root 12 is 144; this multiplied by 3, is 432)	2251 (5
	2160
	912
square of last quotient 5 is 25; this multiplied by 3, and the product by 12, the preceding figures in separate line, is	900
	125
cube of last quotient 5 is	125
	**

Separate or Cube Root Line
125

NOTE CONTINUED.

The following example is selected merely for further illustration, and is not taken from the commentaries.

	Divisor	Working
		122615327232
4^3		64
$4^2 \times 3$	48)	586 (9
		432
		1541
$9^2 \times 3 \times 4$		972
		5695
9^3		729
$49^2 \times 3$	7203)	49663 (6
		43218
		64452
$6^2 \times 3 \times 49$		5292
		591607
6^3		216
$496^2 + 3$	738048)	5913912 (8
		5904384
		95283
$8^2 \times 3 \times 496$		95232
		512
8^3		512
		**

Separate or Cube Root Line
4968

CHAP. II.

SECTION I.

OF FRACTIONS

To reduce fractions to a common denominator.

Multiply reciprocally each numerator and its denominator by the other denominators: This will give *fractions having* a common denominator. or

Reduce the denominators by a common measure, and multiply each numerator and its denominator by the other *reduced* denominators.

Example.—Required the common denominator of 3 $\frac{1}{5}$ $\frac{1}{3}$;[A] and the sum of these fractions. Also required the common denominator of $\frac{1}{63}$ $\frac{1}{14}$; and the difference of these fractions.

Statement.—$\frac{3}{1}$ [B] $\frac{1}{5}$ $\frac{1}{3}$.—These fractions reduced to a common denominator are $\frac{45}{15}$ $\frac{3}{15}$ $\frac{5}{15}$.[C] The sum of the fractions is $\frac{53}{15}$.

Statement for 2d method. $\frac{1}{63}$ $\frac{1}{14}$. These being multiplied, *according to the first rule*, by the denominators divided by seven, the two *fractions reduced to a common* denominator are $\frac{2}{126}$ $\frac{9}{126}$. The difference *of the two fractions* is $\frac{7}{126}$.[D]

A The Hindus do not distinguish fractions by any mark, but merely write the numerator above the denominator. For the sake of distinctness I have employed the common fractional figures in the notes.

B The whole number is converted into a fraction by placing an unit for its denominator.

C Thus,

$$\frac{3}{1}\times\frac{5}{5}\times\frac{3}{3}=\frac{45}{15} \quad \Big| \quad \frac{1}{5}\times\frac{1}{1}\times\frac{3}{3}=\frac{3}{15} \quad \Big| \quad \frac{1}{3}\times\frac{1}{1}\times\frac{5}{5}=\frac{5}{15}$$

D Divide each of the denominators by 7; thus

$$\left.\begin{array}{l}63 \div 7 = 9\\ 14 \div 7 = 2\end{array}\right\}\text{ new denominators.}$$

Then multiply reciprocally the original numerator and denominator of one fraction by the reduced denominator of the other;

$$\frac{1}{63}\times\frac{2}{2}=\frac{2}{126} \quad \Big| \quad \frac{1}{14}\times\frac{9}{9}=\frac{9}{126}$$

then, $\frac{9}{126}-\frac{2}{126}=\frac{7}{126}$.

Compound Fractions.

Multiply the numerators by the numerators, and the denominators by the denominators. This gives the equivalent simple fraction [A] contained in the compound fractions.

Example.—A person gives to a poor man the $\frac{1}{4}$ of $\frac{1}{16}$ of $\frac{1}{5}$ of $\frac{3}{4}$ of $\frac{2}{3}$ of $\frac{1}{2}$ of a dramma; how many varatakas does the man receive?

Statement.—$\frac{1}{2}$ $\frac{2}{3}$ $\frac{3}{4}$ $\frac{1}{5}$ $\frac{1}{16}$ $\frac{1}{4}$. Simple fraction $\frac{1}{1280}$; so that the person gave one varataka.

Plus and Minus Fractions.

If the fraction of any quantity is plus, add the numerator to the product of the integer by the denominator; if it is minus, subtract the numerator *from the said product.*

When its own fraction is plus or minus, [B] that is, when it is to be added or subtracted, multiply the upper denominator by the denominator of the lower fraction: also multiply the *upper* numerator by the denominator of the lower fraction plus or minus its numerator. [C]

[A] As the original word signifies class or tribe, the term *general fraction* might perhaps be adopted.

[B] That is, when the fraction of a fraction is plus or minus.

[C] The first rule under this head teaches how to reduce a mixed quantity to an improper fraction.

The second rules gives the method of reducing fractions of a fraction, or compound fractions, to an equivalent simple one. In the commentaries the rule is thus stated; "Multiply the denominator of the upper fraction by the denominator of the lower fraction. Then add the numerator of the lower fraction to its own denominator, if the fraction is plus, or subtract it, if it is minus; and multiply the numerator of the upper fraction by the denominator of the lower fraction thus augmented or diminished by its own numerator. Again, multiply the denominator of the upper fraction by the denominator of the lower fraction, and so on; repeating the same process till you arrive at the upper-most fraction."

But the operation will perhaps be more easily understood by stating the rule thus:

Multiply the upper denominator by the denominators of the lower fractions. Also multiply the upper numerator by the denominators of the lower fractions plus their numerators, if the fractions are plus, or minus if the fractions are minus.—For illustration take the three examples which are given in the text; viz.

Example.—What are the equivalent fractions of two plus one fourth? Also of three minus one fourth? [A]

Statement.—$\begin{array}{c}2\\ \frac{1}{4}\end{array}$ | $\begin{array}{c}3\\ \dot{\frac{1}{4}}\end{array}$ Equivalent fractions $\frac{9}{4}$ | $\frac{11}{4}$ [B]

Example.—What is one fourth plus one third of itself, plus one half of the result? What are two thirds minus one eight of itself minus three sevenths of the remainder? What is one half minus one eight of itself plus nine sevenths of the remainder?

1st Example.—Add $\frac{1}{4}$ + $\frac{1}{3}$ of itself + $\frac{1}{2}$ of the result; thus, $\frac{1}{4} + \frac{\frac{1}{4}}{3} + \frac{\frac{1}{4}+\frac{\frac{1}{4}}{3}}{2}$

$$\frac{1 \times 4 \times 3}{4 \times 3 \times 2} = \frac{12}{24} = \frac{1}{2}$$

$$\frac{1}{3} + 1 = 4$$

$$\frac{1}{2} + 1 = 3$$

2d Example.—Subtract from $\frac{2}{3}$ $\frac{1}{8}$ of itself, and from the remainder $\frac{3}{7}$ of itself; thus,

$$\frac{2}{3} - \frac{\frac{2}{3}}{8} - \frac{\frac{2}{3}-\frac{\frac{2}{3}}{8}}{\frac{7}{3}}$$

$$\frac{2 \times 7 \times 4}{3 \times 8 + 7} = \frac{56}{168} = \frac{1}{3}$$

$$\frac{1}{8} - 1 = 7$$

$$\frac{3}{7} - 3 = 4$$

3d Example;—viz $\frac{1}{2} - \frac{\frac{1}{2}}{8} + \frac{\frac{1}{2}-\frac{\frac{1}{2}}{8}}{\frac{9}{7}}$

$$\frac{1 \times 7 \times 16}{2 \times 8 \times 7} = \frac{112}{112} =$$

$$\frac{1}{8} - 1 = 7$$

$$\frac{9}{7} + 9 = 16$$

[A] In the original the minus fraction is distinguished by a cipher placed above it; but as this might create some confusion in reading, I have here used a dot instead of the cipher.—It may be observed that in stating a mixed quantity the fraction is put below the integer; and further, that compound fractions are arranged in a line below each other, the highest fraction of the series being at the head.

[B] Example 1.—Plus fraction.

$\begin{array}{c}2\\ \frac{1}{4}\end{array}$ $2 \times 4 + 1 = 9$ numerator

$\frac{9}{4}$ equivalent fraction.

Example 2.—Minus fraction.

$\begin{array}{c}3\\ \dot{\frac{1}{4}}\end{array}$ $3 \times 4 - 1 = 11$ numerator.

$\frac{11}{4}$ equivalent fraction.

minus one eighth plus nine sevenths ?

Statement. $\begin{array}{c}1\\4\\1\\2\\1\\2\end{array}\Bigg|\begin{array}{c}2\\3\\\bullet\\1\\8\\3\\7\end{array}\Bigg|\begin{array}{c}1\\2\\\bullet\\1\\8\\9\\7\end{array}$ Equivalent fractions $\frac{1}{2}$ | $\frac{1}{3}$ | $\frac{9}{10}$

Addition and Subtraction of Fractions.

The addition of fractions which have a common denominator gives their sum ; the subtraction gives their difference.

When there is a quantity without a demominator, an unit must be assumed as its denominator. [A]

Example.—What is the sum of one fifth, one fourth, one third, one half, and one sixth added together ? And their sum being subtracted from three what is the remainder ?

Statement. $\frac{1}{5}$ $\frac{1}{4}$ $\frac{1}{3}$ $\frac{1}{2}$ $\frac{1}{6}$; their sum is $\frac{29}{20}$. And this subtracted from 3 leaves the remainder $\frac{31}{20}$. [B]

Multiplication of Fractions.

Divide the product of the numerators by that of the denominators ; the quotient is the product in the multiplication of fractions. [C]

Example.—What is *the product of* $2\frac{1}{3}$ multiplied by $2\frac{1}{7}$? And what is *the product of* $\frac{1}{2}$ multiplied by $\frac{1}{3}$?

[A] The commentaries in the first place direct compound fractions to be reduced to simple ones, and mixed numbers to improper fractions, according to the rule for plus and minus fractions. The text under one rule comprehends the two common rules for the addition and subtraction of fractions ; viz. add the numerators together in the case of addition, and subtract them in the case of subtraction.

[B] Example 1.—Add $\frac{1}{5}$ $\frac{1}{4}$ $\frac{1}{3}$ $\frac{1}{2}$ $\frac{1}{6}$.—These fractions when reduced to a common denominator, are $\frac{144}{720}$ $\frac{180}{720}$ $\frac{240}{720}$ $\frac{360}{720}$, $\frac{120}{720}$; the sum of the numerators added together is $\frac{1044}{720}$; and reduced by 36 the fraction is $\frac{29}{20}$.

Example 2.—Subtract $\frac{29}{20}$ from 3. Assume an unit for the denominator to 3 ; then

$$\frac{29}{20} \times 1 = 29 \;|\; \frac{3}{1} \times 20 = 60 - 29 = \frac{31}{20}$$

[C] The mixed numbers being first reduced to improper fractions according to the rule for plus and minus fractions.

These rules for extracting the square and cube roots are much more prolix and confused than those contained in the Lilawati; for though the mode of extracting the square root is expressed with greater conciseness in the original Arabic than in the Persian translation which I have followed, still it is by no means so concise and clear as that which Bhascara delivers for performing the same operation.

In the Khalasat-ul-hisab the extraction of the square root is succeeded by a long chapter on fractions, which, however, does not seem to contain any thing that requires particular notice. The fraction is written below the integer in the manner of the Hindus; thus $\begin{matrix}1\\2\\3\end{matrix}$, denotes one and two thirds. When there is no integer, its place is pointed out by a cipher, which the Arabians write like a dot, and place above the numerator of the fraction, thus $\begin{matrix}\cdot\\2\\5\end{matrix}$ two fifths.

Compound fractions are written in three different ways. First, the secondary fraction is written above the primary one; or, secondly, opposite to it on the right hand, with the word من of, between it and the primary fraction; or, thirdly, it is separated from the primary fraction by a horizontal line; thus,

$$\begin{matrix}\cdot\\1\\2\\5\\6\end{matrix} \qquad\qquad \begin{matrix}\cdot\\5\\6\end{matrix}\ \text{of}\ \begin{matrix}\cdot\\1\\2\end{matrix} \qquad\qquad \begin{matrix}\cdot\\1\\2\\\overline{5}\\6\end{matrix}$$

denote one half of five sixths. Two or more fractions are joined by the conjunction *and*, or are denoted by a perpendicular line drawn between them. Thus,

$$\begin{matrix}3\\4\end{matrix}\ \text{and}\ \begin{matrix}2\\5\end{matrix} \qquad\qquad \begin{matrix}\cdot\\3\\4\end{matrix}\ \Bigg|\ \begin{matrix}2\\5\end{matrix}$$

express two fifths and three fourths. Owing to the Arabian practice of writing from left to right, the positions of the fractions connected by the words *of*, or *and*, are the reverse of what would be given in our treatises.

The third Chapter of the Khalasat ul-Hisab treats of proportion, or the Rule of Three. In the first place, it is stated that this rule shews the method of finding an unknown number by the operation of a fourth proportional such, that the ratio of the first number shall be to the second, as the ratio of the third is to the fourth; that is, if the first be the half of the second, the third also shall be the half of the fourth; and the fourth shall be such, that the product of the extremes shall be equal to the product of the middle terms. The rule is then given as follows:

SECTION II.

OF THE EFFECT OF CIPHER.

When a number is added to cipher the result is that number. The square, &c. of cipher is cipher. A number divided by cipher has cipher for its divisor.[A] When a number is multiplied by cipher the product is cipher;[B] but in case any operation remain to be done, cipher is merely conceived to be the multiplier; for when cipher is the multiplier, and cipher also becomes the divisor, the number is considered unchanged.[C] Also *a number* is considered unchanged by the subtraction[D] or addition of cipher.

Example 1.—What is the result of 5 added to cipher? What are the square, square root, cube, and cube root of cipher? What *is the quotient if* 10 is divided by cipher?

[A] This I understand is a kind of technical phrase denoting that in such case the quotient is infinite. The following is the explanation given in the commentaries:

" A quantity divided by cipher is not changed, but obtains the denomination 'quantity with cipher for its divisor.' When a quantity acquires cipher for its divisor, the quotient is infinite; for the quotient is that number by which, when the divisor is multiplied, and the product subtracted from the dividend, no remainder is left. Hence in Algebra when cipher is the divisor, the quotient is considered infinite."

In the Udaharna it is observed, that " in proportion as the divisor is small, so is the quotient great; but the divisor when it is cipher being infinitely small, the quotient is therefore infinite."

The original word *ananta* signifies infinite or endless. It is an epithet applied to the Deity, space, &c.

[B] When a number is multiplied by cipher, the product is cipher, as cipher has no numerical value. Also when cipher is multiplied by any number, the product is cipher. *Com.*

[C] The words 'in case any operation remain,' mean that if cipher becomes the multiplier, and more operations remain to be done, cipher is to be considered the multiplier, without however performing the actual operation. The reason of this is, that after cipher has become the multiplier, should cipher in the subsequent operation also become the divisor, the number is unchanged and stands as it is; and as both the multiplier and divisor are ciphers, it is merely required to strike them out, and the work of multiplication and division is done. If, however, a the succeeding parts of the operation, cipher does not become the divisor, the expert arithmetician knows that a number which has cipher for its multiplier, will become cipher. *Com.*

[D] In Algebra, however, a number subtracted from cipher changes its denomination. Further properties of cipher will be learned from Algebra. *Com.*

Example 2.—Required such a number that being multiplied by cipher, and half of the result added *to the product*, this sum multiplied by three, and *this last product* divided by cipher, the result shall be 63 ?

Statement.—*For first example.*—0; its augment 5; square of cipher is 0; its root is 0. The multiplicand 5 multiplied by cipher becomes 0. The dividend 10 divided by cipher becomes $\frac{10}{0}$.

Statement.—*For second example.*—The number is unknown; the multiplier is 0; the augment is $\frac{1}{2}$; the multiplier is 3; the divisor is cipher; the known number is 63.—Then by the rule for an assumed number, which shall be afterwards given,[A] the quotient obtained is 14, the number required.[B]

This method of reckoning is of great utility in calculating the motions of the heavenly bodies.

[A] See page 32.

[B] Assume the number 4; then conceive* it multiplied by cipher, and add 2 which is one half of the assumed number; the result is 6; multiply this by 3, the product is 18, which being divided by cipher, the number remains the same, 18. The answer is then obtained by the rule for Three Numbers. Thus, if 18 gives 4, what will 63 give? Having made this statement, multiply 63 by 4, and divide the product by 18; the quotient is 14. *Com.*

That is, $\frac{\left(x \times o + \frac{x \times o}{2}\right)}{0} \times 3 = 63$. Or putting $a = o$, $\overline{ax + \frac{ax}{2}} \times \frac{3}{a} = 63$; the solution of which equation gives $x = 14$.

The same commentary also shews the question brought out by the rule of Inversion. See page 31. "First prepare the numbers according to the rule of Inversion. The known quantity is 63. Conceive this multiplied by cipher, which is the divisor changed to multiplier, and divided by 3, which is the multiplier changed to divisor; the quotient obtained is 21. Half of this is the augment, which however becomes one third, according to the rule "if there is a plus fraction, &c."† This plus fraction being changed to minus and subtracted from 21, the remainder is 14; and this being divided by cipher, which is the multiplier changed to divisor, the number remains the same, 14; for when a cipher is multiplier, and also divisor, the number is not changed."

Then follows this remark: "The rules for cipher, inversion, and assumed number, being of great use in calculating the motions of the planets, ought to be carefully studied."

---

* The process of multiplication must not be actually performed, because in the subsequent operation cipher becomes the divisor.

† See page 32. Then according to that rule $\frac{1}{2+1} = \frac{1}{3}$ and $\frac{1}{3}$ of 21 is 7, the plus fraction, which being changed to minus is sub tracted from 21.

SECTION III.

OF INVERSION.

Any quantity being known, in order to find the unknown quantity, make the divisor the multiplier, and the multiplier the divisor ; the square the square root, and the square root the square. Also make the negative affirmative, and the affirmative negative. If there is a plus fraction, add the numerator to the denominator, if a minus fraction, subtract it, for a denominator. The numerator remains unchanged. Then proceed with the subsequent operation in the inverse manner above directed.

Example.—A quantity is multiplied by three ; to the product there is added the fourth of itself multiplied by three ; and this last product is divided by seven ; the quotient minus one third of itself is squared, and fifty-two being subtracted from the square, to the square root of the remainder eight is added ; the sum is then divided by ten, and there is obtained the quotient two. What is the quantity ?

Statement.—Multiplier 3 ; augment $\frac{3}{4}$; [A] divisor 7 ; decrement $\frac{1}{3}$ square 0 ; [B] minus 52 ; root 0 ; plus 8 ; divisor 10 ; known number 2. [C] Then, according to the rule, the result obtained is the required quantity 28. [D]

A This represents one fourth multiplied by three.

B The square and square root not being known are denoted by 0.

C In another copy the statement is thus : " Quantity unknown : the multiplier is 3 ; to be added of the product $\frac{1}{4}$; divisor 7 ; *quantity to be* subtracted *from the quotient* $\frac{1}{3}$ of itself ; the square *of the remainder* is 0 ; *quantity to be* subtracted *from the square* is 52 ; *quantity to be* added to the square root *of the remainder* is 8 ; the divisor *of the result* is 10 ; the known number is 2. According to the rule the required number is found to be 28."

D The commentaries exhibit the operation in the following manner :

" Multiply the known quantity 2 by 10, the product is 20 ; from this subtract 8, the remainder is 12, the square of which is 144 ; this plus 52 is 196, the root of which is 14. The question then directs 14 to be reduced by $\frac{1}{3}$ of itself ; therefore according to the rule* " if the fraction is minus, &c." one half, or 7, is added to 14, and the result 21 being multiplied by 7, the product is 147. The condition of the question then requires that 147 be augmented by $\frac{3}{4}$ of itself ; therefore according to the rule † " if the fraction is plus," &c. one seventh,

---

* Rule.—If the fraction is minus, subtract the numerator from the denominator for a denominator ; therefore, $\frac{1}{3} - 1 = \frac{1}{2}$

† Rule.—If the fraction is plus, add the numerator to the denominator for a denominator ; therefore

$$\frac{1}{4} \times \frac{3}{1} = \frac{3}{4} + 3 = \frac{3}{7}$$

SECTION IV.

ASSUMED NUMBER.

Multiply or divide an assumed number, and subtract or add the fractions, according to the conditions of the question: by the result divide the product of the known number by the assumed. The quotient will be the number required.

Example.—A number is multiplied by 5; from the product is subtracted one third of itself, and the remainder is divided by 10; to the quotient is added $\frac{1}{2}$ $\frac{1}{3}$ $\frac{1}{4}$ of the assumed number, and the result is 68. What is the number?

Statement.—Multiplier 5; fraction to be subtracted $\frac{1}{3}$; divisor 10; plus fractions of assumed number [A] $\frac{1}{1}$ $\frac{1}{3}$ $\frac{1}{2}$ $\frac{1}{4}$; known number 68. In this example assume the number 3, and multiply it by 5, the product is 15, from which subtract one third of itself, *the remainder* is 10; divide this by ten, *the quotient* is 1; to which add the fractions of the assumed number, $\frac{1}{3}$ $\frac{1}{2}$ $\frac{1}{4}$, after reducing them to a common denominator; *the result* is $\frac{17}{4}$. By this divide 204, which is the product of the known number 68 by the assumed 3; the quotient obtained is 48. [B]

---

or 21, is multiplied by 3, and the product 63 being subtracted from 147, there remains 84; divide this by 3, the quotient is 28.————Proof, 28 × 3 = 84; to this add 63 which is three times the $\frac{1}{4}$ of 84; the result is 147; divide this by 7, the quotient is 21, from which subtract $\frac{1}{3}$ of itself; the remainder is 14. Then $\frac{(14^2-52)^{\frac{1}{2}}+8}{10} = \frac{\overline{144}^{\frac{1}{2}}+8}{10} = \frac{20}{10} = 2$ the known number."

The commentary then proceeds to make this remark: "This example cannot be performed by the rule for an assumed number, because it contains the root of a square. When there is a square, square root, cube, or cube root, the operation cannot be performed by an assumed number; but exclusive of square, square root, cube, and cube root, all other operations may be done by the rule of three quantities. Thus it is mentioned in the Siddhanta."

A The first is the assumed number represented by an unit, and converted into a fraction by placing another unit below it for a denominator.

B The commentaries exhibit the operation in this manner: "Multiply an assumed number 3 by 5, the product is 15; from this subtract one third of itself, the remainder is 10; divide this by 10, the quotient is 1: to this quotient add one half, one third, and one fourth of the assumed number; thus $\frac{1}{1}$ $\frac{3}{2}$ $\frac{3}{3}$ $\frac{3}{4}$, which reduced to a common denominator, are $\frac{24}{24}$ $\frac{36}{24}$ $\frac{18}{24}$ $\frac{24}{24}$, or, reduced to their lowest terms, are $\frac{4}{4}$ $\frac{6}{4}$ $\frac{3}{4}$ $\frac{4}{4}$, the sum of which is $\frac{17}{4}$: the known number 68 being

Thus as to every example where a number is required to be multiplied by any other number, or divided by it, and fractions to be added or subtracted, and a number is known—in that case operate upon an assumed number according to the conditions of the question, and by the result divide the product of the known number multiplied by the assumed. The quotient will be the number required.

Where a certain quantity is known.

Example.—One third of a collection of beautiful water-lilies is offered to Mahadev, one fifth to Huri, one sixth to the Sun, one fourth to Devi, and six which remain are presented to the spiritual teacher.—Required the whole number of water-lilies?

Statement.—$\frac{1}{3}$ $\frac{1}{5}$ $\frac{1}{6}$ $\frac{1}{4}$: known number 6. In this case after assuming a quantity, the result obtained is 120.[A]

Where there are remainders.

Example.—A traveller pays away one half at Pryag; from the remainder he pays two ninths at Benares; from the remainder he pays one fourth for customs, &c. from the remainder six tenths are paid at Gaya; and there remain 63 which he brings home. What was the original sum?

Statement.—$\frac{1}{2}$ $\frac{2}{9}$ $\frac{1}{4}$ $\frac{6}{10}$. Here the rule is, divide the product of the denominators minus their numerators by the product of the denominators; and by the quotient

---

multiplied by 3, the assumed, the product is 204; divide this by $\frac{17}{4}$, the quotient is 48, which is the number required.————Proof:—$48 \times 5 = 240$; from this subtract one third of itself, or 80, the remainder is 160; divide this by 10, the quotient is 16; to this quotient add a third, half, and fourth of 48, that is 15, 24, 12; the result is 68, which is the known quantity. *Com.*

[A] Having assumed one or an unit, reduce it along with the fractions to a common denominator. Thus $\frac{1}{1}$ $\frac{1}{3}$ $\frac{1}{5}$ $\frac{1}{6}$ $\frac{1}{4}$, reduced to a common denominator, and reduced to their lowest terms are $\frac{60}{60}$ $\frac{20}{60}$ $\frac{12}{60}$ $\frac{10}{60}$ $\frac{15}{60}$. The sum of the four last negative fractions, is $\frac{57}{60}$; subtract these from $\frac{60}{60}$, which is the assumed number converted into a fraction with the common denominator; the remainder is $\frac{3}{60}$: Then multiply the known number 6 by the assumed number 1, the product is 6, which being divided by the fraction $\frac{3}{60}$, the quotient is $\frac{360}{3} = 120$, which is the number of water-lilies.————Proof:—One third of 120 is 40; the fifth is 24, the sixth is 20, the fourth is 30; the known number is 6: then $40 + 24 + 20 + 30 + 6 = 120$. *Com.*

obtained," divide the product of the known quantity multiplied by the assumed: Thus,

The known number is 63. Let 1 or unit be the number assumed. Then subtract *each* fraction from the *preceding* remainder, according to the rule for minus fractions; the result is $\frac{7}{60}$; and the known number being multiplied by the assumed, and *the product* divided by $\frac{7}{60}$, *the quotient* is 540.[A] The answer may also be obtained by the Rule of Inversion.

Where there is the difference.

Example.—One fifth of a hive of bees flew to the Kadamba flower; one third flew to the Silandhara; three times the difference of these two numbers flew to an arbour; and one bee continued flying about, attracted on each side by the fragrant Ketaki and the Malati. What was the number of bees?

Statement.—$\frac{1}{5}$ $\frac{1}{3}$ $\frac{2}{5}$. The number of bees is 15.[B]

In the same manner other examples may be performed by the rule of an Assumed Number.

A Subtract the numerators from the denominators; thus,

$$\frac{1}{2} - 1 = 1 \qquad \frac{2}{9} - 2 = 7 \qquad \frac{1}{4} - 1 = 3 \qquad \frac{6}{10} - 6 = 4$$

Then, $1 \times 7 \times 3 \times 4 = 48$ product of denominators minus the numerators

$2 \times 9 \times 4 \times 10 = 720$ product of original denominators

Reduce $\frac{84}{720}$ by 12; the fraction obtained is $\frac{7}{60}$: then multiply the known number 63 by the assumed number 1, and divide the product by $\frac{7}{60}$; thus $\frac{60}{7} \times \frac{63}{1} = \frac{3780}{7} = 540$. *Com.*

In the *Udaharna* the operation is thus exhibited: "Assumed number 1; the half of which being subtracted, there remains $\frac{1}{2}$; two ninths of one half are $\frac{2}{18}$; subtract this from $\frac{1}{2}$, the remainder is $\frac{7}{18}$; from this subtract $\frac{1}{4}$ of itself or $\frac{7}{72}$, the remainder is $\frac{21}{72}$; from which subtract $\frac{6}{10}$ of itself or $\frac{126}{720}$; there remains $\frac{84}{720} = \frac{7}{60}$. By this fraction divide the product of the known quantity multiplied by the assumed; the quotient which results is 540, the number required.————Proof:—Half of 540 is 270; two ninths of 270 is 60, which being subtracted from 270 there remains 210; and the fourth of this, or $\frac{210}{4}$ being subtracted from 210, there remains $\frac{630}{4}$; six tenths of this remainder are $\frac{3780}{40}$, or, reduced by 20 is $\frac{189}{2}$; subtract this from $\frac{630}{4}$, there remains 63."

B Thus $\frac{1}{5}$ $\frac{1}{3}$ $\frac{2}{5}$, being reduced to a common denominator, *and the equivalent fraction* subtracted from the assumed number 1, the remainder is $\frac{5}{75} = \frac{1}{15}$:—Then the known number being multiplied by the assumed, and the product divided by $\frac{1}{15}$, the quotient obtained is 15. ————Proof:—Number of bees is 15; from which subtract one fifth of itself or 3, the

When there are the sum and difference.

Add the difference to the sum, and also subtract it from the sum; then the results halved will be the quantities.

Example.—The sum is 101, and the difference is 25. What are the two quantities?

Statement.—Sum, 101; difference, 25. The two quantities are 63, 38.

When there is the difference of the squares.

Divide the difference of the squares by the difference of the quantities; the quotient will be their sum. The quantities *themselves* are then found by the last rule.

Example.—What are those two quantities the difference of which is 8, and the difference of their squares is 400?

Statement.—Difference of quantities 8; difference of squares 400. The two quantities are found to be 21, 29.

Concerning Squares.

Multiply the square of an assumed number by eight, and subtract an unit from the product; divide half of the remainder by the assumed number; and the quotient will be one of the quantities: Add an unit to half the square of this quantity; and the result will be the other quantity: or

Divide an unit by the double of an assumed number, and add the assumed number to the quotient: the result is the first quantity: the second quantity is an unit. [a]

---

remainder is 12; from this subtract 5 which is one third of 15, the remainder is 7: The difference of 3 and 5 is 2; multiply this by 3, the product is 6, which being subtracted from the last remainder 7, there remains 1. *Com.*

[a] These problems belong to the class called Diophantine. This case may be solved in the following manner:

$$\left.\begin{array}{l} x^2+y^2-1=\square \\ x^2-y^2-1=\square \end{array}\right\}$$ to find the value of x and y in terms of any assumed number a.

2d Rule.—If $y=1$ then $x^2+1-1=\square$ or $x^2=\square$

and x^2-1-1 or $x^2-2=\square$ substituting $2a-x$ for the side of this square we have

$$x^2-2=4a^2-4ax+x^2$$

$$4ax=4a^2+2$$

$$x=\frac{2a^2+1}{2a} \text{ or (according to the rule) } =\frac{1}{2a}+a$$

The squares of the two quantities being added *together*, or subtracted *from each other*, and an unit subtracted *from the result*, there will remain a square.

Example.—What two quantities are those the squares of which being subtracted *from each other*, or added *together*, and an unit subtracted *from the result*, there will remain a root ? [A] Tell me this if thou art able to perform an operation which is difficult even to the Algebraist.

Statement.—In order to find the first quantity, let the number assumed be $\frac{1}{2}$; the square of which is $\frac{1}{4}$; this multiplied by eight, the product is $\frac{2}{1}$; an unit being subtracted, there remains $\frac{1}{1}$; the half of which is $\frac{1}{2}$; divide this by the assumed number $\frac{1}{2}$, the quotient is the first quantity $\frac{1}{1}$. To half the square of this number add an unit; the result is $\frac{3}{2}$, which is the other quantity. Thus there are produced the two quantities $\frac{1}{1}$ $\frac{3}{2}$.[B] Thus also, if the assumed number is one, the quantities found are $\frac{7}{2}$ $\frac{57}{8}$: if two is the assumed number, they are $\frac{31}{4}$ $\frac{993}{32}$.

According to the second mode, let the assumed number be 1; by the double of which divide an unit, the quotient is $\frac{1}{2}$; and the assumed number being added to this, the result is the first quantity $\frac{3}{2}$. The second quaintity is the unit itself. Thus, also, if two is the number assumed we obtain $\frac{9}{4}$ $\frac{1}{1}$;[C] if three is the number assumed, we obtain $\frac{19}{6}$ $\frac{1}{1}$; if one third is the number assumed we obtain $\frac{11}{6}$ $\frac{1}{1}$.

Rule.—Multiply by eight the biquadrate and also the cube of an assumed number, and add an unit to the first product. The results will be the two quantities. The operation may be performed either by Arithmetic or Algebra.

Let the number assumed be $\frac{1}{2}$; its biquadrate is $\frac{1}{16}$, which being multiplied by eight, the product is $\frac{1}{2}$; add an unit to this, the result is $\frac{3}{2}$, which is the first quantity. Again, the cube of the assumed number is $\frac{1}{8}$, which being multiplied by eight, the product is $\frac{8}{8}$, and this is the other quantity $\frac{1}{1}$. Thus there are obtained the two quantities $\frac{3}{2}$ $\frac{1}{1}$ If one is the assumed number we obtain 9, 8; if two is the as-

---

[A] The original word is *mool*, which signifies root: but here it appears to mean a number whose square root can be extracted, that is, a square number.

[B] $\left(\frac{1}{1}\right)^2 + \left(\frac{3}{2}\right)^2 - 1 = \frac{9}{4}$ $\quad\quad$ $\left(\frac{3}{2}\right)^2 - \left(\frac{1}{1}\right)^2 - 1 = \frac{1}{4}$

[C] $\left(\frac{9}{4}\right)^2 + \left(\frac{1}{1}\right)^2 - 1 = \frac{81}{16}$ $\quad\quad$ $\left(\frac{9}{4}\right)^2 - \left(\frac{1}{1}\right)^2 - 1 = \frac{49}{16}$

sumed number, we obtain 129, 64; if three is the assumed number, we obtain 649, 216.[A]

SECTION V.

OF MULTIPLIER OF THE ROOT.

Def.—The known quantity is what results after multiplying the *square* root of the *required* quantity by the multiplier, and subtracting the product from, or adding it to, the *required* quantity.

Rule.—To the known quantity add the square of half the multiplier, and then add to the *square* root of the sum thus obtained, or subtract from it, half of the multiplier: The square of the result will be the number required.[B]

If the quantity has a negative fraction, subtract the fraction from an unit; if a positive fraction, add it to an unit: By the result divide both the known quantity and the multiplier of the *square* root: Then, from the quotients, find the *required* quantity according to the rule.[C]

[D] When a quantity is observed diminished or augmented by its own *square* root multiplied by a certain multiplier—to that quantity, *so diminished or augmented*, add the square of half the multiplier of the *square* root of the quantity, and to the *square* root of the sum obtained, add half of the multiplier, if the known quantity is the result of subtracting from the *required* quantity the product of the *square* root of the

---

[A] $\overline{129^2 + 64^2 - 1} = 20736$; and $20736^{\frac{1}{2}} = 144$.

$\overline{129^2 - 64^2 - 1} = 12544$; and $12544^{\frac{1}{2}} = 112$.

[B] This is exactly our process for the equation $x \pm a \times x^{\frac{1}{2}} = b$, by completing the square, &c. which gives $x = \overline{\left(\frac{1}{4}a^2 + b\right)^{\frac{1}{2}} \mp \frac{1}{2}a}\,\Big|^2$ Hutton's Tracts, Vol. 2. p.

[C] That is, in our notation, having the equation $x \pm \frac{1}{m}x \pm a \times x^{\frac{1}{2}} = b$: first dividing by $1 + \frac{1}{m}$ gives, $x + \frac{a}{1+\frac{1}{m}} \times x^{\frac{1}{2}} = \pm \frac{b}{1+\frac{1}{m}}$; then proceeding as before

gives $x = \overline{\left(\left(\frac{\frac{1}{2}a}{1+\frac{1}{m}}\right)^2 + \frac{b}{1\pm\frac{1}{m}}\right)^{\frac{1}{2}} \mp \frac{\frac{1}{2}a}{1\pm\frac{1}{m}}}\,\Big|^2$ Hutton's Tracts, Vol. p.

[D] The object of this paragraph is to explain the definition and rule. But instead of affording any elucidation, it has a tendency rather to darken and confuse what is stated with sufficient clearness and precision in the preceding paragraphs. The 'quantity diminished or augmented by its own square root multiplied by a certain multiplier,' signifies the known quantity.

required quantity by the multiplier; but if the known quantity results from adding the said product to the *required* quantity, then subtract half of the multiplier *from the square root of the sum.* The square of the result is the quantity required.

Of the first part, *or definition,* there are two examples.

1.—*Where the known number is what remains after multiplying the square root of the required quantity by the multiplier, and subtracting the product from the required quantity.*

Example.—Half the *square* root of a flock of geese multiplied by seven was observed to march slowly away, and two were seen fighting playfully in the water. Say, what was the number of geese?

Statement.—Multiplier of root is $\frac{7}{2}$; known quantity is 2. Then half of the multiplier is $\frac{7}{4}$, the square of which, $\frac{49}{16}$, being added to the known quantity 2, the sum is $\frac{81}{16}$, the square root of which is $\frac{9}{4}$; this being added to $\frac{7}{4}$, the half of the multiplier, gives $\frac{16}{4}$, the square of which is the whole number of geese 16.

2.—*Where the known quantity is the result obtained after multiplying the square root of the required quantity by the multiplier, and adding the product to the required quantity.*

Example.—What is that number to which the product of its *square* root multiplied by 9 being added, shall be 1240?

Statement.—Multiplier of root is 9; known quantity is 1240. According to the rule the quantity is found to be 961.[A]

Examples of the Rule.

Example.—Ten times the *square* root of a flock of geese seeing the clouds collect, flew to the Manus lake; one eighth *of the whole* flew from the edge of the water amongst a multitude of water-lilies; and three couple were observed playing in the water. Tell me my young girl with beautiful locks, what was the whole number of geese?

Statement.—Multiplier of the root is 10; the fraction is $\frac{1}{8}$; the known quantity is 6. Then according to the rule "if there is a negative fraction," &c. the fraction being subtracted from an unit, there remains $\frac{7}{8}$; by which the multiplier of the root, and also the known quantity being divided, the results are, multiplier of root $\frac{80}{7}$,

[A] Thus, the square of $\frac{9}{2}$ which is half of the multiplier is $\frac{81}{4}$, this added to 1240 the known quantity, the sum is $\frac{5041}{4}$, the root of which is $\frac{71}{2}$; from this subtract half of the multiplier, the remainder is $\frac{62}{2}=31$, the square of which is 961, the quantity required.——Proof:—Root $31 \times 9 + 31^2 = 279 + 961 = 1240$. *Com.*

known quantity $\frac{48}{7}$. Then from these the whole number is found by the rule to be 144. [A]

Example.—The enraged Parthava seized in battle a number of arrows in order to slay Karna; one half he expended in defending himself against the arrows of Karna; four times the *square* root were discharged against the horses; with six arrows he transfixed Shalya the chariotteer; with three arrows he rent the parasol, standard, and bow; and with one arrow he pierced the head of Karna. What number of arrows did Arjun take?

Statement.—Multiplier of root 4; fraction $\frac{1}{2}$; known quantity 10. Then according to the rule "if the fraction is negative or positive," &c. the number of arrows is found to be 100. [B]

Example.—The *square* root of half of a number of bees, and also eight ninths of the whole, alighted on the Jasmins; and a female bee buzzed responsive to the hum of the male inclosed at night in a water-lily. O beautiful damsel, tell me the number of bees?

In this example eight ninths, and also the *square* root of half of the quantity are subtracted from the quantity; and these minus fractions, and the known quantity two, are halved; but as a fraction of the half of a quantity is equal to half the fraction of that quantity, the same fractions are put down. The statement then is, fraction, $\frac{8}{9}$; multiplier of root, $\frac{1}{2}$; known number, 1. From these there is found by the rule,

---

[A] In this example and the two which follow, the fractions are negative.

In this case subtract the fraction $\frac{1}{8}$ from an unit, there remains $\frac{7}{8}$; by this divide 10 the multiplier of the root, and 6 the known quantity; the quotients are $\frac{80}{7}$ $\frac{48}{7}$; that is, multiplier of root $\frac{80}{7}$, known quantity $\frac{48}{7}$. Then from these find the quantity according to the first part of the rule, by adding to the known quantity the square of half the multiplier, and so on. Thus, multiplier of root is $\frac{80}{7}$, half of it is $\frac{40}{7}$, the square of which is $\frac{1600}{49}$; add this to the known quantity $\frac{48}{7}$, and reduce the sum by the common measure seven, the result is $\frac{1936}{49}$, the square root of which is $\frac{44}{7}$; add this to $\frac{40}{7}$ which is half of the multiplier, and reduce the result by the common measure seven, we obtain $\frac{84}{7} = 12$; and $12^2 = 144$ the number required.—*Com.*

[B] In this example subtract the fraction $\frac{1}{2}$ from an unit, there remains $\frac{1}{2}$; dividing by this the known quantity 10, and also the multiplier of the root 4, we obtain $\frac{20}{1}$ $\frac{8}{1}$, which are the known quantity, and the multiplier of the root. The required quantity is then found from these in the manner already directed. Thus, the square of half the multiplier is 16; this added to $\frac{20}{1}$ the known quantity, the result is 36, the square root of which is 6; this added to 4 which is half of $\frac{8}{1}$ the multiplier, the result is 10, the square of which is 100, the number required.——Proof:—Quantity, 100; and $100^{\frac{1}{2}} \times 4 = 40$; half of the quantity is 50; the known quantities are 6, 3, 1. Then $40 + 50 + 6 + 3 + 1 = 100$. *Com.*

the number 36, which being multiplied by 2, the product is the whole number of bees, 72. [A]

Example.—A certain number being added to its own *square* root multiplied by eighteen, and to one third of itself, the result is 1200. What is that number?

Statement.—Multiplier of root 18; fraction $\frac{1}{3}$; known quantity 1200. Then the fraction being added to an unit, the result is $\frac{4}{3}$; and having divided by this the multiplier of the root, and the known quantity, we obtain by the rule already stated, the quantity 576. [B]

[A] In this example the fraction is $\frac{8}{9}$, the multiplier of root is $\frac{1}{2}$, the known quantity is 2. In order to reduce the multiplier of the root by one half, the known quantity is halved; the fractions however remain unchanged:* the statement then is, fraction $\frac{8}{9}$; multiplier $\frac{1}{2}$; known quantity 1. Having subtracted the fraction from an unit, there remains $\frac{1}{9}$; by this divide the known quantity 1, and also the multiplier $\frac{1}{2}$, the quotients obtained are $\frac{9}{1}$ $\frac{9}{2}$. Then from these find the sought quantity according to the first part of the rule. Thus, multiplier $\frac{9}{2}$, known quantity $\frac{9}{1}$; half of the multiplier is $\frac{9}{4}$, the square of which is $\frac{81}{16}$; this added to $\frac{9}{1}$ the known quantity the result is $\frac{225}{16}$, the root of which, $\frac{15}{4}$, being added to $\frac{9}{4}$, which is half of the multiplier, the result is $\frac{24}{4} = 6$: the square of this is 36, which is half of the required number; and $36 \times 2 = 72$, the number required. *Com.*

As this explanation does not seem very correct, we shall add the following. As it is the square root of half the quantity, and $\frac{8}{9}$ of the whole, that are to be subtracted, to leave a remainder of 2, let us find half the quantity, instead of the whole quantity required. Then to preserve the value of $\frac{8}{9}$ of the whole, in terms of the half, we must take it $= \frac{16}{9}$. But as we have supposed the required quantity halved, we must halve all the rest, in order to preserve the conditions of the question; this gives the multiplier of the root $\frac{1}{2}$, the fraction $\frac{8}{9}$, and the known quantity one; then working according to the rule, we get 36 for the half quantity required, and multiplying this by 2, the whole quantity required is 72.

That is, $x - \left(\frac{x}{2}\right)^{\frac{1}{2}} - \frac{8}{9}x = 2$ original statement. But as this involves $\left(\frac{x}{2}\right)^{\frac{1}{2}}$, let us subtitute y for $\frac{x}{2}$ and the equation then becomes

$$2y - y^{\frac{1}{2}} - \frac{16}{9}y = 2$$

Dividing by 2 $\qquad y - \frac{y^{\frac{1}{2}}}{2} - \frac{8}{9}y = 1$ new statement

Then by salving $\qquad y = 36 = \frac{x}{2}$

$$x = 72$$

[B] In this example the fraction added to an unit is $\frac{4}{3}$; by this divide the known quantity 1200, and also the multiplier 18; the quotients are 900, $\frac{54}{4}$. From these the required quantity is found, thus; multiplier $\frac{54}{4}$, half of which is $\frac{54}{8}$; this squared is $\frac{2916}{64}$, which being added to

---

* In consequence of that property of fractions which is mentioned in the text.

SECTION VI.

RULE OF THREE QUANTITIES.

The quantity whose product is given, and the quantity whose product is demanded, must be of the same denomination, and the first and last terms; the given product is of a different denomination and the middle term. [A]

Multiply the middle term by the quantity whose product is demanded, and divide *the product thus obtained* by the first term: the quotient will be the required product.

In inversion operate according to the rule of inversion. [B]

Example.—Two palas and a half of saffron are purchased for three sevenths of a niska: How many will be purchased for nine niskas?

Statement.—$\frac{3}{7}$ $\frac{5}{2}$ $\frac{9}{1}$. Palas of saffron obtained $52\frac{1}{2}$ [C]

Example.—Sixty-three palas of fine camphor produce one hundred and four niskas: What will twelve palas and a quarter produce?

Statement.—63, 104, $\frac{49}{4}$. Produce, niskas 20, drammas 3, panas 8, kakinis 3, waratakas 11, and fraction of a warataka $\frac{2}{9}$.

Example.—One kharika and an eighth of rice are got for two drammas: How many will be got for seventy panas.

In this case the two drammas are reduced to panas, in order that the number whose product is given may be of the same denomination.

Statement.—32, $\frac{9}{8}$, 70. Quantity obtained, kharikas 2, dronas 7, araka 1, prasthas 2.

---

900 the result is $\frac{60516}{64}$, the root of which is $\frac{246}{8}$; subtract this from $\frac{54}{8}$ which is half of the multiplier, there remains $\frac{192}{8} = 24$; and $24^2 = 576$ the quantity required. *Com.*

A The literal translation is, "the given and demanded are of the same class and first and last; the product is of a different class and middle."

B That is, the given product being multiplied by the quantity whose product is given, and the result divided by the quantity whose product is demanded, the quotient is the required product. *Com.*

C The three examples of this rule are too simple to require any illustration from the commentaries.

RULE OF THREE QUANTITIES INVERSE.

If the quantity whose product is demanded increases while its product diminishes; or if the quantity whose product is demanded diminishes, while its product increases; that is, if there is a diminution of its product while the quantity whose product is demanded is increased; or if there is an augmentation of its product while the quantity whose product is demanded is diminished—then those who are skilled in the Rule of Three Quantities call it Inversion. This rule is used in valuing animals according to their age, in weighing gold of a certain colour, and also when there is a diminution of quantities. [A]

Example.—A girl sixteen years old is purchased for thirty-two *niskas*: What will a girl twenty years old cost?

Statement.—16, 32, 20. Product, niskas 25, drammas 9, panas 9, kakinis 2, waratakas 8. [B]

Example.—Bullocks which have ploughed four seasons, [C] cost four *niskas*: What will bullocks which have ploughed twelve seasons cost?

Statement.—2, 4, 6. Product, niska 1, and fraction $\frac{1}{3}$.

Example.—One gadyanaka of gold of ten colour is obtained for one niska: How many of fifteen colour will be obtained?

Statement.—10, 1, 15. Product $\frac{2}{3}$.

Example.—A heap of grain measured by a seven araka measure gives one hundred measures: How many measures will it give measured by a five araka measure?

Statement.—7, 100, 5. Measures obtained 140.

[A] The value of animals whose age is great, is less; of those whose age is less, is great; In like manner the quantity of gold is less when the colour * is greater, and is more when the colour is less. Also the number of measures of a heap of grain measured by a small measure diminishes when measured by a larger measure; and the number of measures of a heap measured by a large measure increases when measured by a smaller measure. *Com.*

[B] It will be recollected that the operation is directed to be performed by the rule of inversion. In the commentaries it is thus exhibited. Multiply the middle term by the quantity whose product is given, the result is 512; divide this by the quantity whose product is demanded, the quotient is niskas 52, &c.

[C] A bullock is put to the plough when six years old, and ploughs for 6 dhu or 12 years, a dhu being equal to 2 years; so that the question is, if bullocks 10 years old cost four, what will bullocks 18 years old cost?

---

* That is, in purchasing gold a quantity of smaller bulk is obtained when its purity is great.

SECTION VII.

RULE OF FIVE, &c. QUANTITIES.

When there are five, seven, nine, &c. quantities, let the products and denominators of one side be mutually carried to the other, and put down; then divide the product of the multiplication of the greater side, [A] by that of the lesser; the quotient is the product.

Example.—One month's interest of one hundred is five: What will be a year's interest of sixteen? Also from the principal and interest required the time? And from the time and interest required the amount of principal?

Statement.—	
1	12 [B]
100	16.
5	0

Quantity, interest $9\frac{3}{5}$ Again, in order to find the time:

[A] That is called the greater side which contains the given product.

[B] Transposed Statement

1	12*
100	16
0	5

The products of the numbers on each side are 100, 960; The product of the greater side being divided by that of the lesser, the quotient is $9\frac{3}{5}$ * which reduced to an improper fraction is $\frac{48}{5}$. Or reduce 100 and 5 by 5; then the statement is

1	12
20	16
0	1

Again reduce 20 and 16 by 4, and the statement is

1	12
5	4
0	1

Then the numbers of the greater side 12, 4, 1, being multiplied together, and the product divided by 5 the product of the lesser side, the quotient is, interest $9\frac{3}{5}$.

In order to find the time, the transposed statement is

1	0
100	16
$\frac{48}{5}$†	5

And the denominator of the fraction being again carried to the other side, is

1	0
100	16
48	5
	5

The product of the greater side, or that containing the ascertained product, is 4800; this being divided by 400 the product of the lesser side, the quotient is 12.

In order to find the amount of principal, the transposed statement is,

1	12
100	5
48	5

The product of the greater side is 4800; this being divided by 300 the product of the lesser, the quotient is 16, the amount of principal. *Com.*

---

* The year reduced to months. † The improper fraction of $9\frac{3}{5}$.

	1	0	
Statement,	100	16	Quotient, months 12. In order to find the amount of prin-
	5	48	
		5	

	1	12	
cipal, the statement is	100	0	Quotient, amount of principal 16.
	5	48	
		5	

Example.—In one month and a third, the interest of one hundred is five and one fifth; In three months and one fifth what will be the interest of sixty-two and a half?

	4	16 [A]	
	3	5	
Statement.—	100	125	Quotient, interest 7 4/5 [B]
	26	2	
	5	0	

Where there are Seven Quantities.

Example.—Eight pieces of cloth each three cubits in breadth and eight in length, are purchased for one hundred: What will one piece three cubits and a half in length and one half in breadth be purchased for?

	3	1	
Statement.—	8	7	Quotient, drammas 14, panas 9, kakini 1, waratakas 6,
	8	2	and fraction of a warataka 1/3. [C]
		1	
	100	2	

[A] It will be observed that all the mixed numbers are reduced to improper fractions.

[B] This example shews the transposition of the denominators. After reducing the mixed numbers to improper fractions, and transposing the denominators, the statement is 4, 5, 100, 2, 5 | 16, 3, 125, 26. The products of the two sides are 20,000, and 15,6000; and the greaters 15,6000, being divided by the lesser, 20,000, the quotient is 7 4/5, having abbreviated the fraction by 4000. The time, principal, &c. may be found as before directed. *Com.*

[C] Original Statement

3	1
1	2
8	7
1	2
8	1
1	1
100	0
1	0

The integers are here converted into fractions by placing an unit under them for a denominator.

Transposed statement

3	1
2	1
8	7
2	1
8	1
1	1
1	100

The product of the greater side divided by that of the lesser, the quotient is 14, 9, 1, 6 1/3. *Com.*

Where there are Nine Quantities.

Example.—Thirty planks each twelve inches thick, sixteen inches broad, and fourteen cubits long, are purchased for one hundred *niskas*: What will fourteen planks each eight inches thick, twelve inches broad, and ten cubits long be purchased for?

Statement.—	
12	8
16	12
14	10
30	14
100	0

Quotient, niskas 16, drammas 10, panas 10, kakinis 2, waratakas 13, and fraction of a warataka $\frac{1}{3}$. [A]

Where there are Eleven Quantities.

Example.—The first mentioned planks were lying at the distance of one league, and to bring them the hire demanded was eight drammas: What will be the hire to bring the second mentioned planks which in length, breadth, and thickness, are less by four, from the distance of six leagues?

Statement.—	
12	8
16	12
14	10
30	14
1	6
8	0

Quotient, hire, drammas 8. [B]

[A] Tranposed statement

12	8
16	12
14	10
30	14
0	100

The product of the greater side is 1344000, that of the less is 80640: The greater divided by the less gives 16 niskas, 10 drammas, 10 panas, 2 kakinis, 13 $\frac{1}{3}$ waratakas. *Com.*

[B] Transposed statement.

12	8
16	12
14	10
30	14
1	6
0	8

SECTION VIII.

OF BARTER.

In Barter after transposing the denominator and value, perform the operation as directed in the Rule of Five, &c. Quantities. [A]

Example.—Three hundred mangoes are purchased for one dramma, and thirty pomegranates for one pana: How many pomegranates will be got in exchange for ten mangoes?

Statement.—

16 [B]	1
300	30
10	0

Pomegranates obtained 16. [C]

[A] Another copy states the rule more accurately thus: "In Barter after transposing the value, perform the operation as directed in the Rule of Five, &c. Quantities" The transposition of the denominator is directed in the Rule of Five, &c. Numbers; the only difference therefore between that rule and the rule of Barter is, that the latter requires also the transposition of the value.

[B] The dramma reduced to panas.

[C] Transposed statement

1	16
300	30
0	10

The products are 300, 4800, and the greater being divided by the less, the quotient is 16.

CHAP. III.

SECTION I.

OF MIXED QUANTITIES.

Multiply by the given time the quantity whose product is given, and multiply the interest by the mixed time: Then multiply by the mixed quantity each of the products put down separately, and divide the result by their sum: The quotients are the principal and interest. or

Find the principal by the Rule of an Assumed Number, and subtract it from the mixed sum; the remainder is the interest.

Example.—If at the monthly interest of five per cent. there is paid in a year the sum of one thousand principal and interest; what will be the separate amount of principal and of interest?

	1	12
Statement.—	100	1000.—
	5	0

The quantity 100 whose product is given, being multiplied by 1 month, the given time, the product obtained is 100; and the interest, 5, multiplied by 12 months, the mixed time, the product is 60. The sum of these products is 160. Then multiply each of the products by 1000, the mixed quantity, and divide the results by the sum of the two products; the quotients are, principal 625, interest 375. [A]

Or, by the rule of Three Numbers. One hundred of principal produces five of interest; then, if an unit is assumed, what will it produce? It produces $\frac{1}{20}$: Then, if $\frac{1}{20}$ is the interest for one month, what will be the interest of an unit for twelve months? Interest of one year is $\frac{3}{5}$.

[A] Write down separately the products 100 and 60, and multiply each of them by the mixed quantity 1000; the results are 100,000, and 60,000; then divide these by 160 the sum of the two products; thus,

$$\frac{100000}{160} = 625 \text{ principal.}$$

$$\frac{60000}{160} = 375 \text{ interest.}$$

Or, according to the Rule of an Assumed Number. Assume the number 1 : Then by the rule of an assumed number, the interest of an unit for one year is found to be $\frac{3}{5}$: this added to an unit, the result is $\frac{8}{5}$; then the known number 1000 being multiplied by an unit, and the product divided by $\frac{8}{5}$, the quotient is, principal sum 625 ; subtract this from the mixed sum, and there remains interest 375.

[A] Rule.—By the number whose interest is given multiply its own time, and divide the product by *each rate of* interest multiplied by the elapsed time : Then multiply the quotients by the mixed number, and divide each product by the sum of the quotients : The results are the separate sums.

Example.—Ninety-four niskas were lent out in three sums ; one sum at five per cent. ; one at three per cent. ; and one at four per cent. ; and each of these sums produced an equal amount of interest in seven, ten, and five months respectively. What was the principal lent at each rate of interest ?

	7	10	5
Statement.—	1	1	1
	100	100	100.
	5	3	4

The sum *of the quotients* is $\frac{235}{21}$: the mixed number is 94. The sums *lent at each rate of interest*, are found to be 24, 28, 42 ; [B] and by the rule of Five Quan-

---

[A] This rule will perhaps be better understand when expressed in the following terms: By the number whose interest is known multiply the time in which this known interest is produced, and divide the product by each rate of interest multiplied by the time in which, at the particular rate of interest, there is produced the equal interest : Then multiply each of the quotients by the mixed number, and divide the products by the sum of the quotients : The results are the principal sums lent at each rate of interest.

[B] In this case, having multiplied 100, the number whose interest is given, by 1, the time in which the interest is produced, the product is 100 : Divide this by 35, which is the interest 5 multiplied by the elapsed time 7 ; and $\frac{100}{35}$ reduced by 5 is $\frac{20}{7}$. Again, divide 100 by 30, which is the interest 3 multiplied by the elapsed time 10 ; and $\frac{100}{30}$ reduced by 5 is $\frac{20}{6}$: In the same manner divide 100 by 20, which is the interest 4 multiplied by the elapsed time ; and $\frac{100}{20}$ reduced by 20 is $\frac{5}{1}$: The sum of the fractions $\frac{20}{7}$ $\frac{20}{6}$ $\frac{5}{1}$, is $\frac{470}{42}$, reduced by 2 is $\frac{235}{21}$. Then multiply $\frac{20}{7}$ by 94, the mixed number, the result is $\frac{1880}{7}$; and divide this by $\frac{235}{21}$ the sum of the fractions, the quotient is $\frac{39480}{1645} = 24$, the first sum. Thus, also, $\frac{20}{6}$ and $\frac{5}{1}$ being multiplied by 94, the products are $\frac{1880}{6}$ $\frac{470}{1}$; divide these by $\frac{235}{21}$, the quotients are the second and third sums 28, 42 ; so that the principal sums lent at each rate of interest are 24, 28, 42. *Com.*

tities, we obtain the equal amount of interest $\frac{42}{5}$.[A]

Rule.—Multiply each of the shares by the mixed number, and divide the products by the sum of the shares: The quotients will be the amount of each share at the division.

Example.—If three shares, fifty-one, sixty-eight, and eighty-five, when increased by the profits of trade make the stock three hundred; what will be the amount of each share at the division?

[A] Thus, if in 1 month 100 gives 5 of interest, in 7 months what will 24 give? After making a similar statement with the two other quantities, transpose according to the rule of five quantities: Also reduce the numbers when it can be done. Then divide the product of the greater side by that of the less; the quotients are the equal amount of interest: Thus,

original statement		transposed statement	
1	7	1	7
100	24	100	24
5	0	0	5

Statement of the numbers reduced.

1	7
5	6
0	1

Then $\frac{7 \times 6 \times 1}{1 \times 5} \ldots\ldots \frac{42}{5}$ interest

The two other quantities also give the same amount; thus,

original statement		transposed statement	
1	10	1	10
100	28	100	28
3	0	0	3

Statement of the numbers reduced.

1	1
10	28
0	3

Then $\frac{1 \times 28 \times 3}{1 \times 10} \ldots\ldots \frac{84}{10} = \frac{42}{5}$ interest

Again,

original statement		transposed statement	
1	5	1	5
100	42	100	42
4	0	0	4

And so on. There is then obtained $\frac{42}{5}$ interest. *Com.*

Statement.—51, 68, 85: mixed number, 300. The sums obtained *at the division* are 75, 100, 125. The original sums subtracted from these, exhibit the profit. [A]

Or, the sum of the original shares being subtracted from the mixed number, the remainder is the whole amount of profit, 96: Then multiply this by each of the shares, and divide the products by the sum of the shares; the results are the separate amounts of profit, 24, 32, 40. [B]

Of the time in which a Pond is filled.

Divide first the denominators by the numerators, and then divide an unit by the sum of the denominators. The quotient will be the time in which the pond is filled.

Example.—A pond is filled by one stream in one day, by a second in half a day, by a third in one third of a day, and by a fourth in one sixth of a day: In what time will it be filled by the four at once?

Statement.—$\frac{1}{1}$ $\frac{1}{2}$ $\frac{1}{3}$ $\frac{1}{6}$. Time in which the pond is filled, fraction of a day $\frac{1}{12}$. [C]

			Sum of the shares				
[A] Thus,	51 × 300	......	15300 ÷ 204	......	75	amount of first share at the division.	
	68 × 300	......	20400 ÷ 204	......	100	do.	do.
	85 × 300	......	25500 ÷ 204	......	125	do.	do.
Then	75 — 51	......	24 profit of first share.				
	100 — 68	......	32 profit of second share.				
	125 — 85	......	40 profit of third share.				
and	300 — 204	......	96 total profit.				

[B] Thus, 300 — 204 = 96 total profit; and

96 × 51 ...... 4896 ÷ 204 ...... 24 profit on first share.
96 × 68 ...... 6528 ÷ 204 ...... 32 profit on second share.
96 × 85 ...... 8160 ÷ 204 ...... 40 profit on third share.

[C] Thus, $\frac{1}{1}$ $\frac{2}{1}$ $\frac{3}{1}$ $\frac{6}{1}$; the denominators divided by the numerators.

$1 + 2 + 3 + 6$ .... 12 sum of denominators.

Then by this sum divide an unit; thus, $\frac{1}{12}$, time in which the pond is filled.

The following question from Diophantus, translated into Latin verse by Bachet, is cited by Montucla, Hist. de Mathematiques:

Totum implere lacum, tubulis è quotuor, uno
Est potis iste die, binis hic, at tribus ille,
Quatuor at quartus: dic quo spatio simul omnes?

A question exactly similar is also found in the Khulasut-ul-Hisab.

SECTION III.

OF BUYING AND SELLING.

Multiply the price of each article by its proportion, and divide *the products respectively by the given quantity of each* article: Then multiply the quotients obtained, and also the proportions by the mixed sum, and divide the products by the sum of the quotients: The results will be the required cost and *quantity of the* article.

Example.—Three maunds and a half of rice are obtained for one dramma, and eight maunds of mug for the same sum; than taking two proportions of rice and one proportion of mug, how much of each sort will be got for thirteen kakinis?

Statement.—

1	1
$\frac{7}{2}$	$\frac{8}{1}$
2	1

Mixed sum, kakinis 13. Then the proportion of each article being multiplied by the price of that article, and the product divided by the *given* quantity of the article, the quotients are $\frac{4}{7}$ $\frac{1}{8}$; the sum of which is $\frac{39}{56}$. Then multiply $\frac{4}{7}$ $\frac{1}{8}$, and also the parts 2, 1, by the mixed sum $\frac{13}{64}$, [A] and divide the products by $\frac{39}{56}$, the sum of the quotients; the results are, price of the rice $\frac{2}{12}$, [B] of the mug $\frac{7}{192}$. [B] Also the *required* quantity of rice is found to be $\frac{14}{24}$; of mug $\frac{7}{24}$. The cost of the rice, therefore, is kakinis 10, waratakas 13, and fraction of a waraka $\frac{1}{3}$. And the cost of the mug is kakinis 2, waratakas 6, fraction of a warataka $\frac{2}{3}$. [C]

The rule in the Lilawati appears only to hold good when the original numerators are all 1; nor do I think that the question from Diophantus can be solved by it. The rule might also be expressed, "Invert the fractions, and divide an unit by the sum of the new fractions." This would serve for the above example, but still it would not be general.

[A] One dramma is equal to 64 kakinis; therefore, by placing 64 as a denominator to 13, there is formed the fraction of a dramma.

[B] Fractions of a dramma.

[C] In the commentaries the operation is thus exhibited:

Statement.—Dramma 1; quantity of rice $\frac{7}{2}$; dramma 1; quantity of mug $\frac{8}{1}$; mixed sum

Example.—One pala of fine camphor costs two niskas, one pala of sandal wood one eighth of a dramma, and half a pala of agaru also costs one eighth of a dramma. Then for one niska bring me one part of camphor, sixteen parts of sandal wood, and eight parts of agaru?

Statement.—			
Drammas [A]	32	$\frac{1}{8}$	$\frac{1}{8}$
palas	1	1	$\frac{1}{2}$
parts	1	16	8

Mixed sum, drammas 16.[B] The camphor, &c. cost *respectively* $14\frac{2}{9}$ $0\frac{8}{9}$ $0\frac{8}{9}$

and the quantity of the different articles in palas is $\frac{4}{9}$ $\frac{64}{9}$ $\frac{32}{9}$.[C]

Rule.—Multiply the gift by the *number of* persons; and after subtracting the product from *each number of* gems, divide an assumed number by the remainders. The quotients are the values.[D]

The product of the remainders multiplied together being divided by these remainders, will give the values in integers.

Example.—Eight rubies, ten sapphires, one hundred pearls, and five diamonds, were the respective property of four merchants, each of whom in friendship gave one

---

$\frac{13}{64}$; proportion of rice 2; proportion of mug 1. The answer is then found, thus;

The price 1 being multiplied by the proportions $\frac{2}{1}$ $\frac{1}{1}$, the products are $\frac{2}{1}$ $\frac{1}{1}$; divide these by the *given* quantities $\frac{7}{2}$ $\frac{8}{1}$, the quotients are $\frac{4}{7}$ $\frac{1}{8}$, the sum of which is $\frac{39}{56}$: Then $\frac{4}{7}$ $\frac{1}{8}$, being multiplied by $\frac{13}{64}$ the mixed sum, the products are $\frac{52}{448}$; $\frac{13}{512}$; and dividing these by $\frac{39}{56}$, the quotients are, cost of rice $\frac{1}{6}$ cost of mug $\frac{7}{192}$. Also the proportions of the rice and mug $\frac{2}{1}$ $\frac{1}{1}$ being multiplied by $\frac{13}{64}$, the products are $\frac{13}{32}$ $\frac{13}{64}$; and dividing these by $\frac{39}{56}$, the quotients are, *required* quantity of rice $\frac{14}{24}$, of mug $\frac{7}{24}$. Then divide the numerator of the fraction $\frac{1}{6}$ by its denominator, and the rice is found to have cost, kakinis 10, waratakas $13\frac{1}{3}$. In the same manner after dividing the numerator of the fraction $\frac{7}{192}$ by its denominator, the mug is found to have cost, kakinis 2, waratakas $6\frac{2}{3}$.

[A] Two niskas reduced to drammas.

[B] One niska reduced to drammas.

[C] Having multiplied the prices $\frac{32}{1}$ $\frac{1}{8}$ $\frac{1}{4}$ respectively by the parts 1, 16, 8, the products are

[D] This rule seems to be very partial.

of his gems to each of the others, by which means the property became equal. Required the values of the gems.

Statement.—Rubies 8; sapphires 10; pearls 100; diamonds 5. The gift being multiplied by the *number of* persons, the product is 4; this subtracted from each number of gems, the remainders are 4 (rubies) 6 (sapphires) 96 (pearls) 1 (diamond). And an assumed number being divided by these, the quotients are the values: but as the values might come out fractions if an indiscriminate number were assumed, the skilful assume such a number as will give *them in* integers: Thus assume 96; the values then found are 24 (rubies) 16 (sapph.) 1 (pearl) 96 (diam.).[A]

Or, the remainders being multiplied together, and the product divided by the remainders separately, the quotients are the values in integers, 576, 384, 24, 2304.[B] The equal property is drammas 5592.

$\frac{32}{2}$ $\frac{2}{1}$ $\frac{2}{1}$; which being divided by the quantities $\frac{1}{2}$ $\frac{1}{1}$ $\frac{1}{1}$, the quotients are $\frac{32}{1}$ $\frac{2}{1}$ $\frac{2}{1}$, the sum of which is the divisor 36. Then multiply the quotients $\frac{32}{1}$ $\frac{2}{1}$ $\frac{2}{1}$ by the mixed sum 16, the products are 512, 32, 32: and divide these by 36 the sum of the quotients, the results are cost of camphor, &c. $14\frac{2}{9}$ $\frac{8}{9}$ $\frac{8}{9}$. Also multiply the parts 1, 16, 8, by the mixed sum 16, and the products are 16, 252, 128; which being divided by 36, the results are palas of camphor, &c. $\frac{4}{9}$ $\frac{64}{9}$ $\frac{32}{9}$. *Com.*

[A] One commentator, and the author of the Udaharna, find the equal property from these values in the following manner:

Each person having given one gem to each of the others, the remainders are, rubies 5, sapphires 7, pearls 97, diamonds 2; Then,

24 the value of each ruby	× 5 =	120	value of the remaining rubies	
16 .... sapphire	× 7 =	112	.... sapphires	
1 .... pearl	× 97 =	97	.... pearls	
96 .... diamond	× 2 =	192	.... diamonds	

The value of the gem given to each person being added to these numbers respectively, the results are the equal property 233; Thus,

120 + 16 + 1 + 96 = 233 equal property by gift added to the value of the rubies
112 + 24 + 1 + 96 = 233 .... sapphires
97 + 24 + 16 + 96 = 233 .... pearls
192 + 24 + 1 + 16 = 233 .... diamonds

[B] These numbers it will be observed are in the same proportion to each other as the preced-

SECTION IV.

OF COMPUTING GOLD.

Multiply *each quantity of* gold by its colour,[A] and divide the sum of the products by the sum of the *quantities of* gold; the quotient will be the colour of the mixed quantity of gold.

The sum of the products *of the gold multiplied by the colour* being divided by the *quantity of* refined gold, gives the colour of the refined gold.

The sum of the products *of the gold multiplied by the colour* being divided by the colour of the refined gold, gives the quantity of the refined gold.

Example.—*Of first rule.*—Ten, four, two, and four mashas of gold of thirteen,[B]

---

ing. They are thus found:

$4 \times 6 \times 96 \times 1 = 2304$ product of remainders

Then $2304 \div 4 = 576$ value of each ruby

$2304 \div 6 = 384$ .... sapphire

$2304 \div 96 = 24$ .... pearl

$2304 \div 1 = 2304$ .... diamond

From these values the equal property is found as before; thus

576 value of each ruby $\times$ 5 = 2880 value of the remaining rubies.

384 .... sapphire $\times$ 7 = 2688 .... sapphires

24 .... pearl $\times$ 97 = 2328 .... pearls

2304 .... diamond $\times$ 2 = 4608 .... diamonds

Then add the value of each gift;

$384 + 24 + 2304 + 2880$ (value of remaining rubies) $= 5592$ equal property by gift added to value of rubies.

The equal property by the gift added to the value of the sapphires, pearls, and diamonds, may be found in the same manner.—It will be observed that the equal property may be any other number or value whatever, according to the value of the assumed number.

[A] The Hindus judge of the purity of gold by the colour.

[B] It is stated in Ayeen Akbery "that the highest degree of purity of gold is twelve degrees, called *barah banny*, but that formerly the old *hun* which is a gold coin current in the Deccan, they reckoned at ten *bannees*." Dr. Heyne also, in his Tracts on India, says that

twelve, eleven, and ten colour, being melted together; what will be the colour of the mixed quantity?

Example.—*Of second rule.*—If during refining, these twenty mashas are reduced to sixteen, what will be their colour?

Example.—*Of third rule.*—If the *above* gold when refined is sixteen colour, how many mashas will be obtained from the twenty mashas?

Statement.—*Of first example.* $\begin{matrix} 13 & 12 & 11 & 10 \\ 10 & 4 & 2 & 4 \end{matrix}$ When the quantities are mixed, the colour is 12.[A]

2.—If, in refining, the twenty mashas are reduced to sixteen, the colour is 15.[B]

3.—If the gold when refined is sixteen colour, the number of mashas obtained is 15.[C]

To find the unknown colour.

By the sum of the quantities of the gold, multiply the colour of the mixed gold; from the product subtract the sum of the products of the *several quantities of* gold multiplied by their colour, and divide the remainder by the quantity of gold of unknown colour. The quotient obtained will be the required colour.

---

pure gold is denoted by the number 12. The examples given in this section must have reference to a higher standard, which probably was 16, this being the highest number mentioned.

[A] $13 \times 10 = 130$
$12 \times 4 = 48$
$11 \times 2 = 22$
$10 \times 4 = 40$

240 sum of the products of the gold multiplied by the colour

$10 + 4 + 2 + 4 = 20$ sum of the quantities of gold

Then $\frac{240}{20} = 12$ colour of mixed quantity of gold

[B] Thus, sum of the products $240 \div 16$ (mashas of refined gold) $= 15$, colour of refined gold.

[C] Thus, sum of the products $240 \div 16$ (colour of refined gold) $= 15$, mashas of refined gold.

Example.—Eight mashas of gold of ten colour, and two mashas of eleven colour, and six mashas whose colour is unknown, when mixed, produce gold of twelve colour. Required the unknown colour?

Statement.— $\begin{matrix} 10 & 11 & 0 \\ 8 & 2 & 6. \end{matrix}$ Colour produced *by mixing the quantities* is 12. The colour which was unknown, is 15.[A]

Rule.—By the sum of the quantities of gold, multiply the colour of the mixed gold; from the result subtract the sum of the products of the *several quantities of* gold multiplied by their colour; then divide the remainder by the difference of the colour of the unknown quantity of gold, and the colour of the mixed gold. The quotient is the quantity of gold which was unknown.

Example.—Three mashas of gold of ten colour, and one masha of fourteen colour, and a certain quantity of sixteen colour, when mixed, produce gold of twelve colour. Required the number of mashas of gold of sixteen colour?

Statement.— $\begin{matrix} 10 & 14 & 16 \\ 3 & 1 & 0. \end{matrix}$ Colour of the mixed gold is 12. Number of mashas *of sixteen colour* is 1.[B]

Rule.—Subtract the colour of the mixed gold from the higher colour, and subtract the lower colour from the colour of the mixed gold; then multiply the remainders by an assumed number; the products are the quantities of high and low colour gold.

[A] Thus, $8 + 2 + 6 =$ 16 sum of the several quantities of gold

$12 \times 16 =$ 192 product obtained by multiplying the colour of the mixed gold by the sum of the quantities

$\overline{8 \times 10} + \overline{2 \times 11} =$ 102 sum of the products of gold multiplied by the colour

Then $192 - 102 = 90$, and $90 \div 6$ (quantity of gold of unknown colour) $= 15$, colour which was unknown.

[B] Thus, $\overline{3 + 1} \times 12 = 48$

$\overline{3 \times 10} + \overline{1 \times 14} = 44$

Then $48 - 44 = 4$, and $4 \div 4$ (difference of colour of unknown and mixed quantity) $= 1$ masha of gold of 16 colour.

Example.—One ball of gold of sixteen colour, and another of ten colour, when mixed, produce gold of twelve colour: Required the quantity of gold in each ball?

Statement.—Colour, 16 10 Colour of mixed gold 12. The required quantities
0 0.
are 2, 4: Or, multiply by an assumed number two, they are 4, 8: or by an assumed number one half, they are 1, 2. [A]

SECTION IV.

OF PERMUTATIONS.

Rule.—By the preceding term multiply the subsequent one, and *multiply* the *next* subsequent by this subsequent, in the series one, &c. increasing by one, and set down in an inverse order, and divide by the same series set down in a direct order. This will give the permutations of one, two, three, &c. [B]

This is a general rule.—To the learned it is useful in reference to the succession of metres; *it is useful also* in ascertaining the permutations in the use of windows, the permutations in the parts of a pile, the permutations in artificers work, and in medicinal preparations. But these will be passed over in a cursory manner in order to avoid prolixity.

Of Permutations in Metres.

Example.—In writing the Gayatri tell me how many permutations may be made *by the long and short syllables contained* in a foot, and how many *by those contained* in a verse?

The Gayatri foot consists of six syllables. Therefore writing one, two, &c. to the last term six, the statement is $\begin{matrix} 6 & 5 & 4 & 3 & 2 & 1. \\ 1 & 2 & 3 & 4 & 5 & 6 \end{matrix}$ Then agreeable to the rule, the permutations with one long syllable [C] are found to be 6; with two long syllables, [C] 15; with three long syllables, 20; with four long syllables, 15; with five long sylla-

---

[A] Thus, 16 (higher colour) — 12 (colour of mixed gold) = 4
12 (colour of mixed gold) — 10 (lower colour) = 2

[B] Tho' the manner of expressing this rule is not very clear, its meaning is made sufficiently manifest by the examples which follow.

[C] That is, when the foot contains one long syllable and five short syllables, two long syllables and four short, and so on.

bles, 6; and with six long syllables, 1 :-also there is one permutation with all the short syllables: *the results then are* 1, 6, 15, 20, 15, 6, 1. The sum of all these is the number of permutations in one foot, 64. [A]

Thus also the number of syllables in four feet being put down as directed, and the permutations with one, &c. long syllables brought out, their sum plus one is the number of permutations in the Gayatri measure, 16777216. [B]

[A] One commentator directs the preceding term 1 to be multiplied by the subsequent term 6, and the product to be divided by the unit below: But another commentator says that the term 6 stands as it is, because it has no preceeding term. Both then proceed thus: "Multiply the subsequent 6 by the preceding 5, and divide the product by 2 in the direct series; then multiply the quotient 15, which is the subsequent, by the preceding term 4, and divide by 3 in the direct series; then multiply the quotient 20, which is the subsequent, by the preceding term 3, and divide the product by 4 in the direct series; then multiply the quotient 15, which is the subsequent, by the preceding term 2, and divide the product by 5 in the direct series; then multiply the quotient 6, which is the subsequent, by the preceding term 1, and divide by 6 in the direct series; the quotient is 1. There is also one permutation with all the short syllables. The sum of the permutations in a foot therefore is 64."

The operation then is, $\frac{6}{1} = 6$, $\frac{6 \times 5}{2} = 15$, $\frac{15 \times 4}{3} = 20$, $\frac{20 \times 3}{4} = 15$, $\frac{15 \times 2}{5} = 6$, $\frac{6 \times 1}{6} = 1$.

And this is the same in principle with that given in our books; viz. $\frac{6 \times 5 \times 4 \times 3 \times 2 \times 1}{1 \times 2 \times 3 \times 4 \times 5 \times 6}$

Dr. Hutton justly remarks that the above "rule is soon comprehended at sight, when expressed in our own convenient mode and notation; as in the present case, $\frac{n}{1} \times \frac{n-1}{2} \times \frac{n-2}{3} \times \frac{n-3}{4}$ &c, denotes the combinations of any number (n) of things, taken two by two, three by three, four by four, &c, the series being continued to as many factors as there are things to be combined."—Hutton's tracts vol. 2 p. 155.

[B] Permutations of 24 syllables:

24	23	22	21	20	19	18	17	16	15	14	13	12	11	10	9	8	7	6	5	4	3	2	1
24	276	2024	10626	42304	134596	346104	735471	1307504	1961256	2496144	2704156	2496144	1961256	1307504	735471	346104	134596	42304	10626	2024	276	24	1
1	2	3	4	5	6	7	8	9	10	11	12	13	14	15	16	17	18	19	20	21	22	23	24

In the same manner the number of permutations may be ascertained as far as the utkrati measure.

Example.—In Mechanics.—A skilful architect constructed eight windows in the king's spacious and beautiful palace: Required the number of permutations in the use of one, two, three, &c. of the windows?

Also, required the permutations which may be made in the six-flavoured condiment, composed of sweet, pungent, astringent, sour, salt, and bitter?

Statement.—*For the windows.* $\begin{matrix}8 & 7 & 6 & 5 & 4 & 3 & 2 & 1\\ 1 & 2 & 3 & 4 & 5 & 6 & 7 & 8.\end{matrix}$ The number of permutations in the use of one, two, three, &c. windows, is $\begin{matrix}8 & 28 & 56 & 70 & 56 & 28 & 8 & 1\\ 1 & 2 & 3 & 4 & 5 & 6 & 7 & 8.\end{matrix}$ Thus the number of permutations in the use of eight windows in the king's palace is 255.

Statement for the permutations in the condiment.— $\begin{matrix}6 & 5 & 4 & 3 & 2 & 1\\ 1 & 2 & 3 & 4 & 5 & 6.\end{matrix}$ The number of permutations with one, &c. in the condiment is $\begin{matrix}6 & 15 & 20 & 15 & 6 & 1\\ 1 & 2 & 3 & 4 & 5 & 6.\end{matrix}$ The sum of which is 63.

CHAP. IV.

OF PROGRESSIONS.

Multiply half the number of terms by the number of terms plus one; this gives the sum of the series one, &c. which is called the summation. Multiply the summation by the number of terms plus two, and divide the product by three; this gives the sum of the summations.

Example.—What are the separate summations of the terms one, &c. as far as nine: And what are the sums of the summations?

Statement.—1, 2, 3, 4, 5, 6, 7, 8, 9.

The summations are 1, 3, 6, 10, 15, 21, 28, 36, 45.

The sums of which are 1, 4, 10, 20, 35, 56, 84, 120, 165. [A]

Rule.—Having multiplied the number of terms by two, and added one to the product, divide the result by three, and multiply the quotient by the summation: The product is the sum of the squares.

Former authors have stated that the sum of the cubes of the terms one, &c. is equal to the square of the summation.

Example.—What is the sum of the squares of the first mentioned series of terms *in the last example*. And also what is the sum of their cubes?

Statement.—1, 2, 3, 4, 5, 6, 7, 8, 9. The sum of the squares is 285. [B] The

---

[A] These rules are, in short, first to find the sum of any number of terms (n) in the series of natural numbers 1, 2, 3, 4, 5, 6, &c; and then to find the sum of any number of the terms arising by the continued additions of the former, being what we call the triangular numbers. Thus,

1, 2, 3, 4, 5, &c, the natural numbers.

1, 3, 6, 10, 15, &c, the triangular numbers.

Our rule for the former series is $\frac{1}{2}n \times (n \times 1) = s$; and for the latter series $\frac{1}{6}n \times (n + 1) \times (n + 2) = s \times \frac{1}{3}(n + 2)$, where the latter form agrees with that given in the Indian rule.

Exam. In the first series; for four terms, $1 + 2 + 3 + 4 = (1 + 4) \times \frac{4}{2} = 10$; for six terms, $(1 + 6) \times \frac{6}{2} = 21$; for nine terms, $(1 + 9) \times \frac{9}{2} = 45$. In the second series; for three terms, $\frac{(3 + 2) \times s}{3} = \frac{(3 + 2) \times (1 + 2 + 3)}{3} = \frac{5 \times 6}{3} = 10$; for four terms, $\frac{(4 + 2) \times s}{3} = \frac{(4 + 2) \times (1 + 2 + 3 + 4)}{3} = \frac{6 \times 10}{3} = 20$; for nine terms, $\frac{(9 + 2) \times s}{3} = \frac{(9 + 2) \times 45}{3} = 165$.—Hutton's tracts vol. 2 p. 156.

[B] The separate summations are thus given in the commentaries:

The number of terms 1 being multiplied by 2, the the product is 2; one added, is 3; this divided by 3, the quotient is 1; this multiplied by 1 the sum of the term, the product is 1, which is the square of the number of terms. Again, the number of terms 2 multiplied by 2, the product is 4, increased by 1 is 5; this divided by 3 is $\frac{5}{3}$, which being mulsum of the cubes is 2025.

Rule.—Multiply the difference by the number of terms minus one, and to the product add the first term; the result is the last term: To the last term add the first term, and halve the result; this gives the mean term: Multiply the mean term by the number of terms; this gives the sum. [A]

Example.—The first day four drammas were given to a brahman, and this sum was increased by five each day. How many drammas were given in fifteen days?

Statement.—First term 4; difference [B] 5; number of terms 15. Here the first term is 4, the mean term is 39, the last term is 74; the sum is 585. [C]

Example.—The first term is seven, the difference is five, and the number of terms is eight. Required the mean term, the last term, and the sum?

Statement.—First term is 7; difference 5; number of terms 8. Here the mean term is $\frac{49}{2}$; the last term is 42; the sum is 196.

---

tiplied by 3 the sum of the number of terms, the result is $\frac{15}{3} = 5$, the sum of the squares of the number of terms. Thus, also, the number of terms 3 multiplied by 2 is 6, one added is 7, this divided by three is $\frac{7}{3}$, which being multiplied by 6 the sum of the number of terms, the product is $\frac{42}{3} = 14$, which is the sum of the squares of the number of terms. And so on. Thus there are obtained 1, 5, 14, 30, 55, 91, 140, 204, 285. *Com.*

This rule is for the summation of series of square and cube numbers, applied to the series 1, 4, 9, 16, 25, &c, and 1, 8, 27, 64, 125, &c. The sum of n terms of the former being $\frac{2n+1}{3} \times s$, and the sum of n terms of the latter s^2, where s denotes the sum of n terms of the natural series 1, 2, 3, 4, &c.—Hutton's tracts vol. 2 p. 156.

[A] This rule and the two or three following rules are for any arithmetical progressions, a being the first term, m the middle term, z the last term, d the common difference, and s the sum; for which the rules, expressed in our algebraical notation, are these: $(n-1)d + a = z$; $\frac{z+a}{2} = m$; $mn = s$; $\frac{s}{n} - (n-1)\frac{d}{2} = a$; $(\frac{s}{n} - a) \div (\frac{n-1}{2}) = d$; $\frac{\sqrt{(2ds + (a - \frac{1}{2}d)^2)} - (a - \frac{1}{2}d)}{d} = n$; where the last form is deduced from the preceding one, by means of the solution of a compound quadratic equation, of a rather complex nature, by the mode of completing the square, and evincing a considerable degree of expertness in the arrangement.—Hutton's tracts vol. 2 p. 156. 157.

[B] What are here called difference, number of terms, and term, are in the original denominated increase, period, and snm, (H. Colebrooke.)

In this example the number of terms is an even number; therefore, in order to find the mean term, add the first and last terms, and halve the result; this gives the mean term.

Rule.—Divide the sum of the progression by the number of terms, and from the quotient subtract the number of terms minus one multiplied by half the difference; the remainder is the first term.

Example.—The sum of the progression is one hundred and five; the number of terms is seven; the difference is three. Required the first term?

Statement.—First term 0; [A] difference 3; number of terms 7; sum of the progression 105. The first term is 6. [B]

Rule.—Divide the sum of the progression by the number of terms; from the quotient subtract the first term, and divide *the remainder* by the number of terms minus one halved: The quotient is the difference.

Example.—A king marched two yojanas the first day, and in order to seize the enemy's elephants he marched eighty yojanas in seven days to the enemy's city. At what rate of increase did he march?

Statement.—First term 2; difference 0; number of terms 7; sum of the progression 80. The difference is found to be $\frac{22}{7}$. [C]

Rule.—Multiply the sum of the progression by the difference, and *the resulting product* by two; *to the last product* add the square of the difference of half the difference and first term; from the *square* root of the result subtract the first term; to the remiander add half the difference, and divide the result by the difference: The quotient is the number of terms.

[A] A cipher denotes that the number is unknown.

[B] The sum of the progression 105 being divided by the number of terms 7, the quotient is 15; the number of terms minus one is 6; multiply this by $\frac{3}{2}$ half the difference, the product is 9, this being subtracted fom 15 there remains 6, which is the first term. *Com.*

[C] The sum of the progression being divided by the number of terms, the result is $\frac{80}{7}$; from this subtract the first term, and there remains $\frac{66}{7}$; divide this by 3, the half of the number of terms minus one, the quotient is $\frac{22}{7}$, which is the difference. Thus, $\left(\frac{80}{7}-\frac{2}{1}\right)\div\frac{3}{1}=\frac{66}{21}=\frac{22}{7}$ *Com.*

Example. Three drammas were given the first day, and each day the difference was two. In how many days were three hundred and sixty drammas given?

Statement.—First term 3; difference 2; number of terms 0; sum of the progression 360. The number of days or *terms* is 18. [A]

Rule.—Add the number of terms to its own square, and by half the result divide the sum of the progression. [B]

Example.—The first term and the difference are unknown; the number of terms is six, and the sum of the progression is also six. Required the first term and the difference?

Statement.—First term 0; difference 0; number of terms 6; sum of the progression 6. The first term is found to be $\frac{2}{7}$, and the difference $\frac{2}{7}$.

Rule.—When the number of terms is uneven, subtract an unit from it, and write down multiplier; when it is even, halve it, and write down square; and thus repeat the operation until the number of terms is exhausted. Then multiply and square beginning at the bottom with the ratio; from the *last* product subtract an unit, and divide the remainder by the ratio minus one. Then multiply the quotient by the first term, and the product will be the sum of the geometrical progression.

Example.—Two waratakas are given the first day, and it is agreed to increase the gift by doubling it each day. How many niskas will be given in a month?

Statement.—First term 2; ratio (or number of increase) 2; number of terms 30. The sum of the geometrical progression is, waratakas 2147483646; equal to niskas

---

[A] Multiply the sum of the progression by the difference, the product is 720; and this being multiplied again by 2, the product is 1440. The difference of half the difference and the first term is 2, the square of which being added to 1440 the result is 1444: from the square root of this, which is 38, subtract the first term, and there remains 35; to this add half the difference; the result is 36. This being divided by the difference, the quotient is 18, which is the number of terms. *Com.*

[B] This rule, which is not contained in the other copies or in the commentaries, appears to be misplaced in the original, as it comes after the following rule. It will be observed also that it is not general, which may be said perhaps of many of the other rules given; but it answers perfectly in the example, and in all arithmetical progressions, whose first term and difference are the same. It is deduced from one of the preceding rules, $\frac{s}{n} - (n-1)\frac{d}{2} = a$; if $a = d$, it becomes $\frac{s}{n} - (n-1)\frac{a}{2} = a$ or $s \div \frac{n^2+n}{2} = a$ as above.

104857, drammas 9, panas 2; kakinis 2; waratakas 6. A

Example.—Two waratakas are given the first day, and each day the gift is tripled. How many waratakas will be given in seven days?

A The explanation of the rule, and also the method of operation, are thus given in the commentaries:

When the number of terms is uneven, subtract an unit from it, and write down the word multiplier*, but do not write down the figures; when the number of terms is even, halve it, and write down the word square†, but do not write the figures. Repeat this operation till the number of terms disappear. Having thus written the words multiplier and square, set down the assumed ratio at the last multiplier place; then square the ratio at the preceding square place, and at the multiplier place multiply the product by the ratio; thus continuing the operation to the first or highest place, where the product is obtained. Subtract an unit from this product, and divide the remainder by the ratio less one, and multiply the quotient by the first term; the product is the sum of the progression.

Example.—First term 2; ratio 2; number of terms 30. In this case the number of terms is an even number, therefore halve it, the result is 15; write down *the word* square; again as 15 is an uneven number, subtract one from it, the remainder is 14; write down *the word* multiplier; half the even number 14 is 7, square; the uneven number 7 less one is 6, multiplier; half the even number 6 is 3, square; the uneven number 3 less one is 2, multiplier; half the even number 2 is 1, square; the uneven number 1 less one, multiplier. Thus, in succession, the statement is,

व:	गु:	व:	गु:
square	multiplier	square	multiplier
व:	गु:	व:	गु:
square	multiplier	square	multiplier

Then set down the ratio at the last multiplier place, and square it at the next square place; the result is 4; multiply this by the ratio, the product is 8; its square is 64; this multiplied by the ratio is 128; its square is 16384; this multiplied by the ratio is 32768; its square is 1073741824, which is the product of multiplying and squaring to the highest place. From this product subtract an unit, and divide the remainder by 1 which is the ratio less one; the result is 1073741823, which being multiplied by 2 the first term, the pro-

---

* As in the example which follows is one.

† As in the present example.

Statement.—First term 2; ratio 3; number of terms 7. The sum of the progression is 2186. A

---

duct is 2147483646 drammas, equal to niskas 104857, &c. The results are thus exhibited:

व : square........ 1073741824
गु : multiplier 32768
व : square........ 16384
गु : multiplier..... 128
व : square........ 64
गु : multiplier 8
व : square 4
गु : multiplier .... 2 *Com.*

It will be observed that multiplier means the ratio. In this example the ratio being *two*, the sum is always doubled at the place of multiplier; in the next example, as the ratio is three, the sum is tripled at the place of multiplier.

The operation then is thus: ratio or multiplier 2; then $2^2 = 4$, $4 \times 2 = 8$, $8^2 = 64$, $64 \times 2 = 128$, $128^2 = 16384$, $16384 \times 2 = 32768$, $32768^2 = 1073741824$, $\frac{1073741824-1}{2-1} \times 2 = 2147483646$.

Dr. Hutton remarks that this comes to the same thing as our own rule, thus expressed, $\frac{r^n - 1}{r - 1} \times a = s$, or $\frac{a^n - 1}{a - 1} \times a = s$, when the ratio r and the first term a are equal.

As a mark of multiplication is directed, in Fyzi's translation, to be placed above the odd number, and a mark of a square above the even number, Dr. Hutton infers that the Hindus had a mark to denote multiplication, and another to denote squaring. The Sanscrit original however does not admit of this supposition. It merely directs the words multiplier and square to be written down to indicate the place for multiplication or squaring. Accordingly these words are some times written at full length in the commentaries, and some times the initial letters only are written, as is seen in the preceding example, where the letters व and गु are the initials of warga (square) and gunaka (multiplier.) I have not observed a mark for multiplication or squaring in any Hindu work.

Thus, as in last example;

7 — 1 = 6 .... multiplier 2187
6 ÷ 2 = 3 .... square 729
3 — 1 = 2 .... multiplier 27
2 ÷ 2 = 1 .... square 9
1 — 1 .... multiplier .... 3 *Com.*

Or thus: Ratio or multiplier 3; then $3^2 = 9$, $9 \times 3 = 27$; $27^2 = 729$, $729 \times 3 = 2187$, $\frac{2187-1}{3-1} \times 2 = 2186$.

Rule.—The number of syllables in the foot being the number of terms, and the multiplier (or ratio) 2; the product then of multiplying and squaring is the number of like metres. Square this product, and also square the square; and from each result subtract its own square root; the remainders are the numbers of half like metres, and of unlike metres respectively.[A]

Example.—What is the number of like metres; the number of half like metres; and the number of unlike metres, in the anashtupa slock or verse?[B]

Statement.—First term 1, ratio 2, number of terms 8. The number of like metres

---

[A] The rule is merely this, that the result of multiplying and squaring gives r^n; but here $r = 2$, therefore 2^n is the rule here given. Now the sum of the series $\frac{n}{1} + \frac{n}{1} \times \frac{n-1}{2} + \frac{n}{1} \times \frac{n-1}{2} \times \frac{n-2}{3}$ &c. to n terms (which expresses the combinations of one, two, three, &c. to n things, out of n things) is $2^n - 1$; but 1 is to be added, for the additional permutation of all the long or all the short syllables taken together, that is $2^n =$ the number of metres.

It may not be unnecessary to remark, that I do not know what word correctly expresses the kind of changes alluded to here and at pages 57 and 58. It is not exactly *combination*, for we count the changes with one thing, which has no combination; nor is it *permutation*, for that would give us a much larger result, as it supposes all things different, instead of only two kinds, long and short. Perhaps, as to this rule, *permutations of metres* may serve to make some distinction; and as the expression *combinations of one, two &c. things*, shews that the changes with one thing are included, it is hoped that no misconception can well take place.

[B] The verse here alluded to consists of four feet, each foot containing eight syllables. Also like metres mean, that all the four feet are like each other; half like metres, that only the first and third are alike, and the second and fourth alike: and unlike metres mean, that all the four feet are different from each other. The numbers of metres therefore, evidently correspond with the permutations of metres, pages 57 and 58, and may be found by the rule there given; that is, the like metres are the permutations of metres in eight syllables (one foot) = 256: the half like metres those in sixteen syllables, (two feet) minus those in the first eight syllables, (as the two succeeding feet must not correspond with each other) viz. 65536 — 256 = 65280: And the number of unlike metres, is that of the permutations of metres in thirty two syllables, (four feet) minus the sum of the numbers of like and half like metres (as no two feet in this metre must be alike) viz. 4294967296 — 65536 = 4294901760.

is found to be 256: of half like metres 65280: and of unlike metres 4294901760.*

---

* The result of the multiplying and squaring is 256; that is 1 more than the permutations of metres in 8 syllables, (or sum of the combinations of one, two, three &c. out of eight things,) which corresponds with the additional permutation, to be added, for that produced by the whole of the long or short syllables taken together. Again in like manner, $256^2 - 256$ (as above noticed) = 65280, the number of half like metres: And 65536^2 (or 256^4) − 65536 = 4294901760, the number of unlike metres. So that this is only a short way of performing particular cases of the former rule page 57.

In reference to the last section and chapter, Dr. Hutton makes this remark.—" It may be doubted, whether some of the rules in these two chapters were known in Europe till after the 16th century. We know that Peletarius, in his algebra, printed in 1558, gave a table of square and cube numbers; and remarked, among other properties of these numbers, that the sum of any number of cubes, taken from the beginning, always makes a square number, the root of which is the sum of the roots of the cubes; which is the same thing as the Lilawatti rule before-mentioned."—Hutton's tracts p. 157-8.

END OF THE ARITHMETIC.

PART II.

CHAP. I.

OF GEOMETRICAL OPERATIONS.[A]

ANY line being supposed the base, the other line which is perpendicular to it is called the side in a triangle or quadrangle.[B]

The root of the sum of the squares of the base and side is equal to the hypothenuse.

The root of the difference of the squares of the base and hypothenuse is equal to the side.

The root of the difference of the squares of the side and hypothenuse is equal to the base.

The square of the difference of the base and side added to twice their product gives the sum of their squares.[C]

The sum of the base and hypothenuse multiplied by their difference gives the difference of their squares. The learned understand this in all cases.

Example.—The side is four, and the base three; required the hypothenuse; the base and hypothenuse being given, required the side; and the side and hypothenuse being given, required the base?

[A] Literally, "of operations concerning fields". The word *kshetra* means a field, or a holy spot; also the body: And in mathematical works it signifies a geometrical figure.

[B] By the definition right angled triangles alone are supposed. And the rules are deduced from the known property of such triangles; viz. that the square of the hypothenuse is equal to the sum of the squares of the base and side.—In a quadrangle, the lower side is termed the base, the side opposite to it, is called *mukha*, which literally means mouth, face, or front; and the two other sides are called the sides.

[C] A figure is given in Hutton's tracts vol. 2. p. 172 which was on the margin of Mr. Strachey's Persian copy, and which beautifully illustrates this proposition. That figure however is not in any of my Shanscrit copies.

Statement.—*To find the hypothenuse.* See Fig. 1.

The base and side being multiplied together and by two, the product is 24; the square of their difference is 1, add this to the product, the result is 25, the root of which is the hypothenuse, 5.

Statement.—*To find the side.* See Fig. 2.

The sum of the base and hypothenuse being multiplied by their difference, the product is 16, the root of which is the side 4.

Statement.—*To find the base.* See Fig. 3.

Thus the base is found to be 3.

Example.—The base is three and one fourth, and the side is the same; required the hypothenuse?

Statement.—Base $\frac{13}{4}$; side, $\frac{13}{4}$; the sum of their squares is $\frac{169}{8}$. As the square root cannot be extracted, the surd number $\left(\frac{169}{8}\right)^{\frac{1}{2}}$ is the hypothenuse.

The nearest root is found by the following method:

Assume a large number, and having multiplied by its square the product of the numerator and denominator, divide the root of the result by the denominator multiplied by the root of the square of the assumed number; the quotient is the nearest root. Thus, hypothenuse $\left(\frac{169}{8}\right)^{\frac{1}{2}}$; the numerator being multiplied by the denominator and by 10,000 [A] the product is 13520000, the nearest *square* root of which is 3677; divide this by the denominator 8 multiplied by 100 the *square* root of the multiplier; thus $\frac{3677}{800}$, the quotient is the nearest root $4\frac{477}{800}$ which is the hypothenuse: [B] This is the process in all cases.

Rule.—A base being supposed, multiply it by the double of an assumed number, and divide the product by the square of the assumed number less one; the quotient is the side; write down the side in a separate place; then multiply it by the assumed

---

[A] That is, the square of the assumed number 100.

[B] The reason of this rule is evident; for if the root of $\frac{x^2}{y^2}$ be required, and n be any assumed number, then $\frac{(n^2x^2y^2)^{\frac{1}{2}}}{ny^2} = \frac{x}{y}$ according to the Rule.

number, and from the product subtract the base; the remainder is the hypothenuse: The triangle thus formed is called *Jatya Tryasra*, or right angled triangle.[A]

Or suppose any number the base; square it, and divide by an assumed number; write down the quotient in two places; in one place subtract, and in the other add, the assumed number; halve each result; the quotients are the side and hypothenuse. Also by knowing the side, the base and hypothenuse are found; and these form a right angled triangle.[B]

Example.—The base being twelve, then according to these two methods what different sides and hypothenuses will be found, such as make a right angled triangle?

Statement.—Base 12; assumed number 2, by the double of which multiply the base, and the product is 48; square of assumed number is 4, less one is 3; and 48 being divided by this number, the quotient is 16, which is the side: Then multiply the side by the assumed number, and subtract the base from the product,

---

[A] To prevent any erroneous inference being drawn, it is necessary to remark here, that in the Indian Geometry plane triangles appear to receive their denominations in relation of their sides only, and not in relation of their angles. The three species are named

Sama Tribhuja—three sides equal—equilateral triangle.
Dwisama Tribhuja—two sides equal—isosceles triangle.
Wisama Tribhuja—three sides unequal—scalene triangle.

The words *jatya tryasra* which I have rendered right angled triangle, properly signify generic triangle, or that species of triangle which comprehends the other sorts, and to which they may be reduced; for by letting fall a perpendicular from the vertex to the base, each of the three kinds of triangles is divided into two right angled triangles.

The *Jyotishis* or astronomers whom I have had an opportunity of conversing with are ignorant of the terms large or small, acute or obtuse angles. These terms are employed perhaps in Hindu astronomical works, tho' I have not observed them in my very limited course of reading.

[B] The truth of these rules is evident; for if $b =$ base, and $\frac{2bn}{n^2-1} =$ side, then will $\left(\left(\frac{2bn}{n^2-1}\right)^2+b^2\right)^{\frac{1}{2}} = \frac{bn^2+b}{n^2+1} = \frac{2bn}{n^2-1} \times n - b =$ hypothenuse according to the rule: Also if $b =$ base, and $\left(\frac{b^2}{n}-n\right) \div 2 = \frac{b^2-n^2}{2n} =$ side; then will $\left(\left(\frac{b^2-n^2}{2n}\right)^2 + b^2\right)^{\frac{1}{2}} = \frac{b^2+n^2}{2n} = \left(\frac{b^2}{n}+n\right) \div 2 =$ hypothenuse according to the rule.

this gives the hypothenuse 20. If three is the assumed number, the side and hypothenuse are 9, 15; if five is the assumed number, they are 5, 13.

Or according to the second method: The supposed base is 12, the square of which is 144; divide this by an assumed number two, the quotient is 72; the assumed number being subtracted from this in one place, and added to it in another, the results are 70, 74; these halved are the side and hypothenuse 35, 37: Or by an assumed number four they are 16, 20; or by an assumed number six they are 9, 15.

Rule.—Multiply twice the value of the hypothenuse by an assumed number, and divide the product by the square of the assumed number plus one; the quotient is the side; put down the side separately, and multiply it by the assumed number; the difference of the product and the hypothenuse will be the base.[A]

Example.—The hypothenuse is eighty-five; required such sides and bases as form a right angled triangle.

Statement.—Hypothenuse 85; this multiplied by two is 170, and this again by an assumed number two, is 340; which being divided by the square of the assumed number plus one gives the side 68; multiply this by the assumed number, the product is 136; then subtract the hypothenuse from it, the remainder is the base 51; or if the assumed number is four we obtain 40, 75.

Rule.—Divide twice the hypothenuse by the square of an assumed number plus one; subtract the quotient from the hypothenuse, the remainder is the side; then multiply the quotient by the assumed number, the product is the base.[B]

Example.—The same as the preceding.

Statement.—Hypothenuse 85, the side and base of which, when the number assumed is two, are 51, 68; or by an assumed number four, are 75, 40.

A That is let h be the hypothenuse; b, the base; and s, the side:

if $\frac{2hn}{n^2+1} = s$; then will $\frac{2hn^2}{n^2+1} - h = b$ according to the rule

for $\overline{h^2 - \left(\frac{2hn}{n^2+1}\right)^2}\Big|^{\frac{1}{2}} = \frac{hn^2 - h}{n^2+1} = \frac{2hn^2}{n^2+1} - h = b$

B If $h - \frac{2h}{n^2+1} = s$; then will $\frac{2h}{n^2+1} \times n = b$

for $\overline{h^2 - \left(h - \frac{2h}{n^2+1}\right)^2}\Big|^{\frac{1}{2}} = \frac{2hn}{n^2+1} = \frac{2h}{n^2+1} \times n = b$

The base and side differ in name only, not in form.

Rule.—Multiply two assumed numbers together and by two; this gives the side; the difference of their squares is the base, and the sum of their squares is the hypothenuse, of a right angled triangle.[A]

Example.—The side, base, and hypothenuse which form a jatya tryasra or right angled triangle are unknown; required these three?

Here by the assumed numbers 1, 2, the base, side, and hypothenuse are found to be 4, 3, 5[B]; or by the assumed numbers 2, 3, they are 12, 5, 13[C]; or by the assumed numbers 2, 4, they are 16, 12, 20[D]. And thus as to any others.

When the sum of the hypothenuse and side is known, and also the base; to find the separate values of the hypothenuse and side.

Rule.—By the staff divide the square of the space between the bottom of the staff and its top[E]; in one place add the quotient to the staff, and in another subtract it from the staff; halve the results; the quotients are respectively the two parts of the staff, or hypothenuse and side.[F]

Example.—If a staff thirty-two cubits high, standing on a level piece of ground, be broken by the violence of the wind, and its top touch the ground sixteen cubits

---

[A] Let m and n be the assumed numbers
then $2mn = s$; $m^2 - n^2 = b$, and $m^2 + n^2 = h$
for $(m^2 + n^2)^2 = (m^2 - n^2)^2 + (2mn)^2$

[B] Thus, $1 \times 2 \times 2 = 4$ the side
$2^2 - 1^2 = 3$ the base
$1^2 + 2^2 = 5$ the hypothenuse

[C] $2 \times 3 \times 2 = 12$ the side
$3^2 - 2^2 = 5$ the base
$2^2 + 3^2 = 13$ the hypothenuse

[D] $2 \times 4 \times 2 = 16$ the side
$4^2 - 2^2 = 12$ the base
$2^2 + 4^2 = 20$ the hypothenuse.

[E] That is, the point where the top of the broken staff touches the ground.

[F] That is, if $h + s = a$; and $b =$ the base; then will

$$\left(a + \frac{b^2}{a}\right) \div 2 = \frac{a^2 + b^2}{2a} = h, \text{ and } \left(a - \frac{b^2}{a}\right) \div 2 = \frac{a^2 - b^2}{2a} = s$$

for $b^2 + s^2 = h^2$; that is, $b^2 + \left(\frac{a^2 - b^2}{2a}\right)^2 = \left(\frac{a^2 + b^2}{2a}\right)^2 = h^2$

from its base; at what height from the bottom is the staff broken?

Statement.—See Fig. 5.

The upper and lower parts are 20. 12,[A]

[B] ***When the sum of the base and hypothenuse is known, and also the side; to find the separate values of the base and hypothenuse.***[C]

Rule.—Square the post, and divide by the distance between the serpent and its hole; from the distance between the serpent and its hole subtract the quotient; half the remainder is the distance in cubits from the serpent's hole where the serpent and the peacock met.

Example.—At the bottom of a post is a serpent's hole; on the top of the post is perched a peacock: the post is nine cubits high, and the peacock descries the serpent running to its hole when distant from it three times the height of the post; the peacock flies down obliquely and seizes the serpent when both have passed over an equal space; at what distance from the serpent's hole did they meet?[D]

Statement.—[E] See Fig. 6.

The place at which they met is distant from the serpent's hole 12.[F]

[A] The example is thus exhibited in the Commentaries:
"Distance between the bottom of the staff and place where the top touches the ground is 16; the square of which is 256; divide this by the staff, the quotient is 8, which being added to 32, the staff, the result is 40, and subtracted from it there remains 24; the results halved are 20, 12, the upper and lower parts of the staff, or the side and hypothenuse. *Com.* See Fig. 5.

[B] Two rules with their examples seem to be transposed at this place in the copy from which I translate. I have followed therefore the arrangement of the other copies and the Commentaries.

[C] The latter part of the enunciation is taken from another copy.

[D] Let $h + b = a$; $s =$ side: then will

$$\left(a - \frac{s^2}{a}\right) \div 2 = \frac{a^2 - s^2}{2a} = b; \text{ and } a - \frac{a^2 - s^2}{2a} = \frac{a^2 + s^2}{2a} = h$$

for $b^2 + s^2 = h^2$; that is $\left(\frac{a^2 - s^2}{2a}\right)^2 + s^2 = \left(\frac{a^2 + s^2}{2a}\right)^2 = h$

[E] Or, as in another copy.—"Post 9, which is the side; distance between the serpent and its hole 27, which is the sum of the base and hypothenuse: Then according to the rule there is found, base 12 cubits; the remainder is the hypothenuse 15."

[F] Thus 81 the square of the post being divided by 27, the quotient is 3; subtract this from the distance 27, the remainder is 24, the half of which is 12. *Com.*

When the difference of the side and hypothenuse is known, and also the base; to find the separate values of the side and hypothenuse.

Rule.—Divide the square of the base by the difference of the side and hypothenuse; write down the quotient in two places, and in one place subtract the difference of the side and hypothenuse, and in the other add the difference; halve the results; the quotients are respectively the side and hypothenuse. The intelligent who understand this rule apply it in all cases. [A]

The distance from the water-lily to where it is immersed in the water is the base; that part of the water-lily which is seen is the difference of the side and hypothenuse; the stalk is the side, and the water is the same depth as the stalk; all this being known, required the depth of the water?

Example.—In a lake the bud of a water-lily was observed one span above the water, and when moved by the gentle breeze it sunk in the water at two cubits distance; required the depth of the water?

Statement.—See Fig. 7.

Depth of the water $\frac{15}{4}$; the measure of the bud added to this is the hypothenuse, $\frac{17}{4}$. [B]

The sum of the hypothenuse and part of the side being known, and also the remainder of the side, [C] *and the base; to find the separate values of the hypothenuse and unknown part of the side.*

[D] Rule.—Multiply the height of the tree by two, and to the product add the dis-

---

[A] The illustration of this rule is exactly the same with the two former, only putting $h - s = a$

[B] Thus, the base is 2, the square of which being divided by $\frac{1}{2}$ (that part of the water-lily which is seen, a span being equal to half a cubit) the difference of the side and hypothenuse, the quotient is 8; $\frac{1}{2}$ subtracted from 8 there remains $\frac{15}{2}$; and $\frac{1}{2}$ added to 8 the result is $\frac{17}{2}$. These numbers being divided by 2, the quotients are, side $\frac{15}{4}$; hypothenuse $\frac{17}{4}$; and the depth of the water is equal to the side. *Com.*

[C] The words in Roman are not in the original.

[D] So partial is this rule that it will only hold good, when the given sum of the hypothenuse and part of the side, is equal to the sum of the remaining part of the side, and the base.

Suppose x = part of the side required

$h + x = a$ the given sum

d = part of the side given

b = the base

$d + x = s$ the side

Then $h^2 = b^2 + s^2 = b^2 + (d + x)^2$

tance between the tree and the pool; by the result divide the height of the tree multiplied by the distance between the tree and the pool; the quotient is the extent of the leap.

Example.—A tree one hundred cubits high is distant from a well two hundred cubits; from this tree one monkey descends and goes to the well; another monkey takes a leap upwards and then descends by the hypothenuse, and both pass over an equal space; required the height of the leap?

Statement.—See Fig. 8.

The leap is found to be 50.

When the sum of the base and side is known, and also the hypothenuse; to find the separate values of the base and side.

Rule.—Multiply the square of the hypothenuse by two, and from the product subtract the square of the sum of the base and side; in one place subtract the root of the remainder from the sum of the base and side, and in another place add it, and halve the results; the quotients are the measures of the base and side. [A]

Example.—The hypothenuse is seventeen, and the sum of the base and side is twenty-three; required the separate values of the base and side?

Statement.—See Fig. 9.

---

now $h = a - x$; therefore

$b^2 + (d + x)^2 = (a - x)^2$

and $x = \frac{a^2 - b^2 - d^2}{2a + 2d}$ the general expression for x

but the rule supposes $h + x = a = b + d$; and substituting this value of a, we have $x = \frac{bd}{2d + b}$, according to the rule. But following the general expression $x = \frac{a^2 - b^2 - d^2}{2a + 2d}$ we have $h = a - \frac{a^2 - b^2 - d^2}{2a + 2d} = \left(a + d + \frac{b^2}{a + d}\right) \div 2$ and $s = d + \frac{a^2 - b^2 - d^2}{2a + 2d} = \left(a + d - \frac{b^2}{a + d}\right) \div 2$; which are the true general values of h and s, and correspond with the rule "by the staff divide," &c.

[A] Let $b + s = a$, $h =$ hypothenuse; then will

$$\frac{a + (2h^2 - a^2)^{\frac{1}{2}}}{2} = b, \text{ and } \frac{a - (2h^2 - a^2)^{\frac{1}{2}}}{2} = s$$

for $(2h^2 - a^2)^{\frac{1}{2}} = (2h^2 - \overline{b + s}^2)^{\frac{1}{2}} = b - s = d$

and $\frac{a + d}{2} = b$ and $\frac{a - d}{2} = s$

Hypothenuse 17; sum of side and base 23: the base and side found, are 8, 15.[A]

When the difference of the base and side is known, and also the hypothenuse; to find the separate values of the base and side.[B]

Rule.—Subtract the square of the difference of the base and side from twice the square of the hypothenuse; find the root of the remainder; put it down in two places, and in one place subtract the difference of the base and side, and in the other place add it; halve the results; the quotients are the separate values of the base and side.

Example.—The difference of the base and side is seven, and the hypothenuse is thirteen; required the base and side separately?

Statement.—Hypothenuse 13; difference of base and side 7; root of difference of the squares 17. The separate values of the base and side are 5, 12.[C]

Rule.—Multiply the two staffs together, and divide the product by the sum of the staffs; the quotient is the perpendicular let fall from the place of intersection of two cords drawn reciprocally from the bottom of one staff to the top of the other; multiply each of the two staffs by an assumed base, and divide the products by the sum of the staffs; the quotients are the segments of the base on each side of the perpendicular.

Example.—One staff is fifteen cubits high, the other is ten cubits high; the base is unknown; required the perpendicular let fall from the intersection of two cords drawn respectively from the bottom of one staff to the top of the other?

Statement.—If the base which is the distance between the staffs is 5, the seg-

---

[A] Square of the hypothenuse is 289; multiply this by 2, the result is 578, from which subtract 529, the square of the sum of the base and side, the remainder is 49, the root of which, 7, being subtracted from the sum of the base and side, there remains 16; and again being added to the said sum, the result is 30; then 16 and 30 halved, are the base and side 8, 15. *Com.*

[B] This problem is not given in any of the other copies. The original also contains an error both in the statement and in the result of the operation.

[C] Thus, $7^2 = 49$

$$2 \times 13^2 - 7^2 = 289 \text{: and } \sqrt{289} = 17$$

$$\frac{17 - 7}{2} = 5 \text{ the base}$$

$$\frac{17 + 7}{2} = 12 \text{ the side}$$

ments of the base are 3, 2; if the base is 10, the segments are 8, 4; if the base is 20, the segments are 12, 8; but in all the perpendicular is the same, 6. [A] Thus, if a base equal to the distance gives sides equal to the staffs respectively, what will the corresponding segments of the base give? [B] And in this manner the result is brought out in each case by the Rule of Three Quantities. The figures are thus represented. See Fig. 10 and 11.

Concerning the form of Figures.

If a person affirm regarding a figure whose sides are straight lines, that the sum of the other sides is less than one of the sides or equal to it, this must be considered an impossible figure. For example, if it be affirmed that a quadrilateral figure has the sides 3, 6, 2, and 12; or that a triangle has the sides 3, 6, 9, such must be considered impossible figures. This will appear by placing a straight staff for the base.

Of the area of Figures.

Rule.—In a triangular figure multiply the sum of the two sides by their differ-

---

[A] The product of the two staffs is 150, which being divided by 25, their sum, the quotient is the perpendicular 6. Then assume the base, or distance between the two staffs, to be 5, and multiply the two staffs by this assumed number; the products are 75, 50; divide these by 25 the sum of the staffs, the quotients are the segments 3, 2. If the distance or base is 10, the segments are 6, 4; if the distance is 15, the segments are 9, 6; if the distance is 20, the segments are 12, 8; but in each case the perpendicular is 6. *Com.*

[B] The following illustration of this rule is given by Strachey in his translation of the Bija Gannita:—Let AB = 10, DC = 15, BD = 20.

By similar triangles BD : BP : : DC : PG,

BD : PD : : BA : PG,

whence BP : PD : : BA : DC,

therefore BD is divided in P in the ratio of DC to BA.

By composition BP + PD : BP : : BA + DC : BA; but BP + PD = BD, therefore BA + DC and BA are in the ratio of BD to BP; whence, by the first proportion, BA + DC : BA : : DC : PG, that is, PG is a fourth proportional to BA + DC, BA, and DC, whatever be the length of BD.—See Plate VI. Fig. 7.

Lucas de Burgo has this proposition, (see his Geometry, p. 56.) where the lengths are 4, 6, and 8; or page 60, where they are 10, 15, and 6. The same is in Fyzi's Lilawati, where the rules are

$$GP = \frac{AB \times CD}{AB + CD},\ PD = \frac{BD \times CD}{AB + CD},\ \text{and } BP = \frac{BD \times AB}{AB + CD}.\text{——Bija Gannita p. 59.}$$

ence, and divide the product by the base; [A] in one place add the quotient to the base, and in another subtract it from the base; halve the results; the quotients are the segments: the root of the difference of the square of each segment and its side is the perpendicular; multiply half the base by the perpendicular; the product is the precise area of the triangular figure.

Example.—The base of a triangular figure is fourteen; one side is thirteen, and the other is fifteen; required the perpendicular, the segments, and the number of the equal spaces [B] which is called the area?

Statement.—See Fig. 12.

The segments are 5, 9, the perpendicular is 12; the area of the figure is 84. [C]

Example.—In a triangular figure one side is ten, the other is seventeen, and the base is nine; required the segment, the perpendicular, and the area?

Statement.—The two sides are 10, 17; the base is 9.

Here by the rule "multiply the sum of the two sides," [D] &c. there is obtained 21. As this cannot be subtracted from the base, the base is subtracted from it, leaving the remainder 12; the half of this is the negative segment. This means that it falls in a contrary direction. The segments then are $\overset{\circ}{6}$, 15; the perpendicular as to both is 8, and the area of the figure is 36. [E] The figure is thus shewn. See Fig. 13.

[A] That is, given a, b, and c the sides of a triangle $b : a+c :: a-c : \frac{\overline{a+c} \times \overline{a-c}}{b}$ = difference of the segments of the base. The rest is the same as has been given before; and the whole corresponds with our own rules.

[B] The Hindus estimate the area of a figure by the number of little squares it contains, these being cubits, or any other measure used, in the same manner as is done in Europe.

[C] The sum of the sides 13, 15, is 28; multiply this by 2, their difference, the product is 56; divide this by the base 14, the quotient is 4; in one place subtract this from the base, and in another add it; the results are 10, 18, the halves of which are the segments. The squares of the segment 5, and side 13, are 25, 169; the difference of the squares is 144, the root of which is 12: Also the squares of the segment 9, and side 15, are 81, 225; the difference of these squares is 144, the root of which is the perpendicular 12. The perpendicular being multiplied by half the base, or 7, the product is 84, the area. *Com.*

[D] See page 76.

[E] Multiply 27, the sum of the sides, by 7 their difference, the product is 189; divide this by 9, the base, the quotient is 21, from which subtract the base, the remainder is 12; also

Rule.—Halve the sum of all the sides; put down the result in four places, and subtract from it the four sides respectively; then multiply the remainders into each other; and the root of the product will be the approximate [A] area in a quadrangular figure, [B] and the precise [C] area in a triangular figure. [D]

Example.—The base is fourteen, the line [E] opposite to it is nine, one of the sides is thirteen, the other is twelve, and the perpendicular is also twelve: Required the area as given by former authors?

Statement —See Fig. 14.

The area found by the above rule, is $\sqrt{19800}$, which has no exact root, the *square* root of it being something less than 141; this is not the true [F] area. But by a rule which shall be afterwards given, viz. "By the perpendicular multiply half the sum of "the base and the line opposite to it [G]"; the true area of the figure is found to be 138. [H]

---

add 21 to the base, the result is 30; these two results halved are 6, 15. In the first case the segment is negative, the base being subtracted from the quotient 21, whereas this quotient should be subtracted from it. Thus we have the negative and positive segments $\overset{\circ}{6}$, 15: Then by the rule "the root of the difference of the squares of each segment and it side, &c." we obtain the perpendicular 8; multiply this by the base, and divide the product by 2; the quotient is 36, which is the area. *Com.*

[A] *Asphuta.*—Not clear, not evident. Fyzi translates it *surhan*, wandering, roaming.

[B] This will give the true area in such a trapezium as can be inscribed in a circle—in other cases it is very vague.

[C] *Sphuta.*—Clear, evident, apparent. Fyzi translates it *durust*,—just, true, right.

[D] This rule might be more distinctly expressed thus: Halve the sum of the sides, and from it subtract the sides respectively; then multiply into each other the four remainders (for the quadrangle); and the three remainders and the half sum (for the triangle): the square root of the result will be the approximate area in the quadrangle, and the precise area in the triangle.

[E] *Mukha.*—The face, or what is opposite.

[F] *Wastava.*—True, proper.

[G] Page 81.

[H] Thus the sum of all the sides 9, 12, 14, 13, is 48, the half of which is 24: Put this down in four places, and subtract the sides, thus $\begin{matrix}24 & 24 & 24 & 24\\ 9 & 12 & 14 & 13\end{matrix}$ the remainders are 15, 12, 10, 11; the product of these multiplied together is 19800, the *square* root of which is some

Also, on making two divisions of the figure, the same area is obtained, 138. See Fig. 15.

By this rule, likewise, we find that the area of a triangle whose sides are 13, 15, and the base 14, is 84.

Reason of the Approximate [A] Area.

As the two diagonals of a quadrangle are not determinate, [B] how can the area of that figure be determinate [C]. Their assumed diagonals which former writers have demonstrated, are not applicable to other *positions of the quadrangle*, because while the sides remain the same, different diagonals may be obtained, and consequently different areas. Thus, by extending the opposite angles of a quadrangle, the diagonal which joins the two angles that go inwards is shortened, but the two other angles being drawn outwards increase their diagonal; therefore it was said that, while the sides remain the same, different diagonals may be obtained. If one of the two

---

what less than 141; This is not the true area. But by a rule which shall be afterwards given "by the perpendicular, &c." the true area is found in this manner: The perpendicular is 12, the base is 14, and the line opposite to it is 9; these two added make 23, the half of which, $\frac{23}{2}$, being multiplied by 12 the perpendicular, the product is 138, which is the true area.

Again, in regard to a triangle, the area is found by the rule "halve the sum of the sides;" &c. Here the sum of the sides 13, 14, 15, is 42, the half of which is 21, which being put down in four places, and the sides subtracted, thus 21 21 21 21, the remainders are 8, 7, 6,
13, 14, 15
21, the product of which is 7056; the *square* root of this is 84, the precise area of the triangle; *Com.*

[A] *Sthula.*—Large.—The words *sthula* and *asphuta* are used in subsequent parts of the work to denote what is inexact, or merely an approximation; and the words *spashta* and *sucshma*, to denote either what is exact and true, or the nearest degree of truth and precision that has been attained.

[B] *Aniyata*—Not unalterable, not unchangeable; formed of the privitive particle *a* and *niyata*, what is fixed, destined, unalterable.

[C] *Niyata.*—Fixed, invariable.

perpendiculars, or of the two diagonals, be not separately given to people, [A] the question is of an indeterminate nature, why then is the determinate area demanded? The person who puts such a question is a demon, and he who pretends to answer it is an arch demon, and both are ignorant of the indeterminate (changeable) position of quadrangular figures. [B]

Rule.—Having assumed one diagonal in a quadrangle whose sides are equal, subtract its square from the square of the side multiplied by four; the root of the remainder is equal to the second diagonal. Multiply the unequal diagonals together, and divide the product by two; the quotient is the precise area of a quadrangle whose sides are equal. [C]

[A] The meaning of this passage is not very clear, and the reading also varies a little in the different copies; in one copy it runs thus, "if one of the two perpendiculars, or of the two diagonals, be not given, how can the other be obtained;" &c. One commentator remarks, that some suppose the reading should be, "if the sum of the two perpendiculars, or the sum of the two diagonals, be not given."

[B] The two diagonals of a quadrangle being indeterminate, how can its area be determinate; for the area of any figure depends on the diagonal. The diagonals of a quadrangle which Bramha Gupta and others assumed and found, were properly assumed, but are not correct, for this reason, that they are not applicable to other *positions of the quadrangle;* because the diagonals found on extending the opposite angles, will not correspond with those put down by these authors, but will be greater or less: Thus diagonals different from those demonstrated are obtained in the given quadrangle. If the diagonal be determinate, then the area of the sides will be determinate; but in consequence of the diagonal being indeterminate, different areas are obtained. *Com.*

In a quadrangle, while the sides remain the same, the area may vary, as it does not depend on the sides; but in a triangle the area does not vary: Therefore it will not answer to assume a diagonal, but a determinate diagonal must be found or demonstrated. It may then be asked, if the diagonals be demonstrated, to what objection are they liable. I reply, that they are not applicable to other cases, for while the sides remain the same, different areas may be obtained; therefore it is said, that if the perpendicular or diagonal be given, the determinate or unchangeable area will be found. Otherwise, as the measure of the diminution or shortning is not known, the perpendicular and diagonal cannot be ascertained. *Udaharana.*

[C] Let any of the sides $= a$; the assumed diagonal $= b$, the unknown diagonal $= x$; then as the sides of the quadrangle are equal, the diagonals bisect each other, and $x = 2\sqrt{(a^2 - \frac{1}{4}b^2)} = \sqrt{(4a^2 - b^2)}$ according to the rule; and $\frac{b \times \frac{1}{2}x}{2} + \frac{b \times \frac{1}{2}x}{2} = \frac{bx}{2} =$ the area.

In a quadrangle of equal sides, and in a parallelogram, when the two diagonals are equal, multiply the side by the base; *this will give the area.* In other quadrangles, if the perpendiculars be equal, then by the perpendicular multiply half the sum of the base and side opposite to it; the product will be the area.

Example.—In a quadrangle whose sides are twenty-five, required the two diagonals; from the diagonals required the area; also, the diagonals being equal, required the area of the above quadrangle; and the area of a parallelogram six in breadth and eight in length, its diagonals likewise being equal.

Statement.—To find the area of the first figure when its diagonals are equal. See Fig. 16.

By the rule "the root of the sum of the squares of the side and base, &c." the two equal diagonals come out an irrational number $\sqrt{1250}$; and the area is 625. [a]

Or, assume one of the diagonals to be 30, the other diagonal will be 40. The construction of the figure then is thus. See Fig. 17.

And the area is 600. [b]

Or, by assuming fourteen for one of the diagonals, then the other diagonal is found to be 48. The construction of the figure is thus. See Fig. 18. And here the area is 336.

---

[a] The diagonal is found by the rule, the "root of the sum of the squares of the base and side is the hypothenuse." In this example the sides are 25, 25, and their squares are 625, 625, the sum of which is 1250; and as the root of this sum cannot be obtained, the irrational number $\sqrt{1250}$ stands for each diagonal: then the area is found by the rule "in a quadrangle of equal sides, and in a parallelogram, when the diagonals are equal," &c. thus: The side is 25, the base is 25; these multiplied together produce 625, which is the area in a quadrangle when the diagonals are equal. *Com.*

[b] If 30 be assumed as one diagonal, the other will be found by the rule, "having assumed one diagonal in a quadrangle whose sides are equal," &c. Thus the square of the side is 625, which being multiplied by 4, the product is 2500: The square of the assumed diagonal is 900; this being subtracted from 2500, the remainder is 1600, the root of which is the second diagonal 40; then the area is found by the rule, "multiply the unequal diagonals by each other;" thus, the product of the diagonals 30, 40 is 1200, which being divided 2, the quotient is 600, the area of the quadrangle of equal sides. *Com.*

The construction of the parallelogram is thus. See Fig. 19. And its area is 48.[A]

Example.—The line opposite the base is eleven; the base is twenty-two; one of the sides is thirteen, and the other is twenty; and the perpendicular is twelve; What is the area?

Statement.—By the rule "halve the sum of all the sides," &c. the approximate area is found to be 250[B]; and according to the rule, "by the perpendicular multiply half the sum of the base and of the line opposite to it," &c. the true area is found to be 198.[C]

In order to make this evident, divide the figure into three parts, and find the separate area of each part; then add the three areas, and observe their sum. The figure is thus represented. See Fig. 20.

And the different parts of the figure are thus exhibited. See Fig. 21, 22, and 23.

By the rule "multiply half the base by the perpendicular," the areas of the right angled triangles are found to be 30, 96[D]; and by the rule "multiply the side and base together," there is found the area of the parallelogram, 72; the sum of these areas is 198, which is the true area.

Example.—The line opposite the base being fifty-one, the base seventy-five, the side on the left hand sixty-eight, and the other side forty; required the area, diagonal, and the perpendicular?

Statement.—See Fig. 24.

A Here the squares of the sides 6, 8, are 36, 48, and the sum of these squares is 100, the root of which is 10; then the area of the parallelogram is obtained by multiplying the base and side; thus, $6 \times 8 = 48$, the area. *Com.*

B The sum of the sides is 66, the half of which being put down in four places, and the sides 11, 13, 22, 20 subtracted, the remainders are 22, 20, 11, 13; these multiplied together produce 62920, the nearest root of which is 250, or the approximate area. *Com.*

C The sum of the base and line opposite to it is 33; the half of which being multiplied by 12 the perpendicular, the product is $\frac{396}{2} = 198$, the precise area. *Com.*

D Each of the triangles being half a parallelogram, their areas are found by multiplying the side by the base, and halving the product, thus, $\frac{5 \times 12}{2} = 30$ area

$\frac{12 \times 16}{2} = 96$ area. *Com.*

Concerning the area, diagonal, and perpendicular.

The perpendicular being known, the diagonal will be obtained; and the diagonal being known, the perpendicular will be obtained, and there also the determinate area will be found; that is, when the diagonal is indeterminate, the perpendicular also is indeterminate.

To find the Perpendicular.

Rule.—In a triangle inscribed in a quadrangle find the perpendicular as before directed.

The two sides form the diagonal and side, and the given base is the base *of the inscribed triangle.*

In order to find the perpendicular, assume a diagonal extending from the top of the left side to the bottom of the right side to be 77, by which also a triangle is formed within the quadrangle; this diagonal is one side of the triangle; the left side is the other side, 68; and the base is the same as stated in the example. The perpendicular and segments are then found in the manner already directed. Thus the sum of the sides is 145; this multiplied by their difference, the product is 1305; this divided by the base 75, the quotient is $\frac{87}{5}$; this quotient being subtracted from the base in one place, and in another added to the base, the results are $\frac{288}{5}$, $\frac{462}{5}$? these halved give the segments $\frac{144}{5}$ $\frac{231}{5}$; and by a rule already given we obtain the perpendicular $\frac{308}{5}$.[b] The figure is thus represented. See Fig. 25.

The perpendicular being known, to find the diagonal.

Rule.—The root of the difference of the squares of the perpendicular and the side which is supported by the perpendicular is called the segment; subtract the segment from the base, and to the square of the remainder add the square of the perpendicular; the *square* root of the result is the diagonal.

---

[a] The following rules in succession give the methods of finding the perpendiculars, diagonals, and the area of the preceding example.

[b] Thus the squares of the segment $\frac{144}{5}$ and of its side 68, reduced to a common denominator, are $\frac{20736}{25}$ $\frac{115600}{25}$; the difference of these squares is $\frac{94864}{25}$, the *square* root of which is the perpendicular $\frac{308}{5}$. *Com.*

Suppose the perpendicular let fall from the top of the left side of the quadrangle to be $\frac{308}{5}$, the segment will be $\frac{144}{5}$: A Then by the rule "subtract the segment from the base, and to the square of the remainder add the square of the perpendicular," &c. we obtain the diagonal 77. B

To find the second diagonal.

Rule.—First assume a diagonal, and in the triangles situated on each side of this diagonal, call the diagonal the base, and the two *other* lines the sides; then find the perpendiculars and segments. Square the distances between the perpendicular situtuated on one side *of the assumed diagonal*, and to this square add the square of the sum of the perpendiculars; the *square* root of the result is the second diagonal. Thus also as to all quadrangular figures. C

D Let a diagonal extending from the top of the left side to the bottom of the right side be assumed equal to 77; in the figure containing this diagonal line, call

---

The commentary also shews the area brought out according to the rule "multiply half the base by the perpendicular," &c. thus, half the base $\frac{75}{2}$ being multiplied by the perpendicular $\frac{308}{5}$, the product is $\frac{23100}{10} = 2310$, the area of the figure.

A The squares of the assumed perpendicular $\frac{308}{5}$, and the side 68 which is supported by it, when reduced to a common denominator, are $\frac{94864}{25}$ $\frac{115600}{25}$, the difference is $\frac{20736}{25}$, the root of which is the *less* segment $\frac{144}{5}$. *Com.*

B Thus, the less segment being subtracted from the base 75, after reducing both to a common denominator, the remainder is $\frac{231}{5}$ the greater segment, the square of which is $\frac{53361}{25}$; this added to $\frac{94864}{25}$ the square of the perpendicular, the result is $\frac{148225}{25}$, the *square* root of which is $\frac{385}{5} = 77$ the diagonal. *Com.*

C See Plate VI. Fig. 1. Let a, and b, be the perpendiculars; d, the distance between the perpendiculars $= w + z$; and let $x + y =$ the second diagonal.

then $x = \sqrt{(a^2 + w^2)}$ $y = \sqrt{(b^2 + z^2)}$; and $x^2 + y^2 = a^2 + w^2 + b^2 + z^2$

$2xy = 2\sqrt{(a^2 b^2 + b^2 w^2 + a^2 z^2 + w^2 z^2)}$

but $a : w :: b : z$; and $a^2 z^2 + b^2 w^2 = 2abwz$

therefore $2xy = 2\sqrt{(a^2 b^2 + 2abwz + w^2 z^2)} = 2ab + 2wz$

then $x^2 + 2xy + y^2 = a^2 + 2ab + b^2 + w^2 + 2wz + z^2$

and $x + y = \sqrt{\left(\overline{a + b}^2 + \overline{w + z}^2\right)} = \sqrt{\left(\overline{a + b}^2 + d^2\right)}$ according to the rule.

D This paragraph is merely intended as an explanation of the rule.

the diagonal the base of the triangles situated on each side of the diagonal, and call the two other lines the sides; then the perpendiculars and segments will be found in the manner already shewn.

Representation of the figure. See Fig. 26.

The square of the difference of the two segments formed by the falling of the perpendiculars is 169; the square of the sum of the perpendiculars is 7056; these two numbers being added together, the result is 7225, the *square* root of which is the *second* diagonal 85.[A] Thus in all cases.

Remarks on assuming a Diagonal.

The sum of the two less sides which fall upon one diagonal being assumed as the base, and the remaining two sides as the sides, find the perpendicular. In this case the one diagonal can never be greater than the base of the figure thus formed, nor the other diagonal less than the perpendicular. Knowing this the intelligent assume a diagonal.

By extending the opposite angles of a quadrangle the *sides* are drawn inwards, and a triangular figure is formed;[B] then the sum of the two less sides which are about one angle being assumed as the base, and the two other sides as the sides, the perpendicular will be found according to the rule already given. The shortened diagonal cannot in any case be less than this perpendicular, nor the other diagonal greater than the two sides assumed as the base. Thus it is in regard to both diagonals. Tho' I have not shewn this, it is understood by those versed in the science.

The sum of the areas of the triangles situated on each side of the diagonal, is the true area *of the figure.*

[A] After finding the segments 32, 42 by the process already exhibited, the perpendiculars are then obtained thus: The squares of the segment 32 and of the side 68 are 1024, 4624, and the difference of these squares is 3600 the *square* root of which is one perpendicular, 60: Also the squares of the segment 32 and of the side 40 are 1024, 1600, and the difference of these squares is 576, the *square* root of which is the other perpendicular, 24. Then the square of 84, the sum of the perpendiculars, is 7056; to this add 169, the square of the difference of the segments, the result is 7225, the *square* root of which is 85, the second diagonal. *Com.*

[B] The triangular figure is exhibited on the margin, still taking the last example, in which the sides of the quadrangle are 75, 68, 51, 40. See Fig 27.

The areas of the triangles in the figure last mentioned are 924, 2310; the sum of these two is the area *of the quadrangle*, 3234.

Rule.—In a quadrangle with equal perpendiculars, assume the base minus its opposite side as the base, and the sides as the sides; then find the segments as in a triangle, and from the segments find the perpendicular; subtract the segment from the base of the quadrangle; the *square* root of the sum of the squares of the remainder and of the perpendicular will be the diagonal.

When the perpendiculars are equal, the sum of the side opposite the base, and the greater of the other two sides, will be less than the sum of the base and the lesser side.

Example.—The two sides are 52 and 39; the side opposite the base is 25, and the base is 60. Preceding authors have said that in this figure the perpendiculars are unequal, and that the two determinate diagonals are fifty-six and sixty-three. I would know two diagonals different from these; also equal perpendiculars, and the diagonal which gives these perpendiculars?

Statement.—See Fig. 28.

Here, if the greater diagonal assumed be 63, the other diagonal found will be 56.[A]

Or, in place of fifty-six, suppose the diagonal thirty-two; there will then be found, by the former rule, two surd parts of the required diagonal $\sqrt{621}$, $\sqrt{2700}$, the sum of the *square* roots of which is the second diagonal, 76 [illegible].[B]

[A] Thus, the two sides are 39, 60, their sum is 99; this multiplied by 21, their difference, the product is 2079, which being divided by 63, the base, the quotient is 33; in one place subtract this from 63, and in another add it; the results are 30, 96, these halved are 15, 48, the segments. The same segments are also found in the other triangle by performing this operation on the sides 25, 52. The perpendicular is then found by the rule "the squares of the segment and side," &c. thus, segment 48, side which falls on it 52, their squares are 2304, 2704, the difference of the squares is 400, the *square* root of which is 20, the perpendicular: Again, segment 15, side which falls on it 39, their squares are 225, 1521; difference of these squares is 1296, the *square* root of which is 36, the second perpendicular; the sum of the perpendiculars 20, 36 is 56, the second diagonal. *Com.*

[B] Or, instead of 56, suppose the diagonal 32; the sides 60, 52 will give the segments 30, 2; then the segment 2, and the side which falls on it 52, squared, are 4, 2704, the dif-

If the figure have equal perpendiculars, then call the base minus its opposite side the base, and in order to find the perpendicular this triangle is assumed. See Fig. 29. Here the segments found are $\frac{3}{5}$ $\frac{172}{5}$; and the perpendicular is the surd number $\sqrt{(\frac{38016}{25})}$, the nearest square root of which, according to the rule, is $38\frac{622}{625}$: This is the common perpendicular of the quadrangle.[A] The sum of the squares of the base minus the less segment, and of the perpendicular is 5049; this is the square for one diagonal: Thus also the sum of the squares of the base minus the greater segment, and of the perpendicular is 2176, which is the square for the other diagonal; and the nearest *square* roots of these numbers are the diagonals $71\frac{3}{50}$ $46\frac{13}{20}$.[B] See Fig. 30.

Thus, in a quadrangle, the sides being still the same, different diagonals are obtained. Notwithstanding their indeterminateness however, two determinate diago-

---

ference of these squares is 2700, the square root of which is $51\frac{24}{25}$ one perpendicular: Again, the other segment is 30, its side is 39, their squares are 900, 1521; the difference of the squares is 621, the *square* root of which is $24\frac{23}{25}$. The two perpendiculars then are $51\frac{24}{25}$, $24\frac{23}{25}$, and their sum is something less than 77, the second diagonal. *Com.*

[A] By the rule "in a triangle the sum of the sides," &c. we obtain the segments $\frac{6}{10}$ $\frac{344}{10}$ $=\frac{3}{5}$ $\frac{172}{5}$. The perpendicular is then found thus; difference of the squares of the side 39, and of the segment $\frac{3}{5}$, is $\frac{38016}{25}$, the square root of which is the surd perpendicular: The nearest *square* root is found in this manner: Multiply 38016 by 25 the denominator, the product is 950400; this multiplied by 625 the square of an assumed number 25, the product is 59400000, the *nearest square* root of which is 24372; divide this by 625, which is the product of 25, the *square* root of the square of the assumed number, and of 25 the denominator, the quotient is $38\frac{622}{625}$; this nearest *square* root is the common perpendicular. *Com.*

[B] Thus the segment $\frac{3}{5}$ being subtracted from the base 60, the remainder is $\frac{297}{5}$, the square of which is $\frac{88209}{25}$; this added to 38016 the square of the perpendicular, the result is $\frac{126225}{25}$ = 5049, which is the sum of the squares, and the square for one diagonal: Thus, also, the greater segment $\frac{172}{5}$ being subtracted from the base, the remainder is $\frac{128}{5}$, the square of which is $\frac{16384}{25}$; this added to 38016 the square of the perpendicular, the result is $\frac{54400}{25}$ = 2176, the square for the other diagonal; the nearest *square* roots of these are the two diagonals, $71\frac{3}{50}$, $46\frac{13}{20}$. *Com.*

nals are found by Bramha Gupta [A] and others by the following rule.

Let the sum of the rectangles of the sides which fall upon the diagonals be reciprocally divided, and multiply the quotients by the sum of the rectangles of the opposite sides; the *square* roots of the results are the diagonals in an irregular figure.

Statement.—See Fig. 31.

The rectangles of the sides which fall upon one diagonal are 2340, 1300, their sum is 3640; the rectangles of the sides which fall upon the other diagonal are 975, 3120, their sum is 4095; divide these reciprocally by each other, thus $\frac{3640}{4095}$ $\frac{4095}{3640}$; or having reduced them by 455, multiply by 3528, the sum of the rectangles of the opposite sides; the results are 3136, 3969, the *square* roots of which are *the diagonals* 56, 63. But as this method of finding the diagonals requires great labour, I shall shew a shorter one.

Rule.—Multiply severally the side and the base of two assumed right angled triangles by the hypothenuse of the other; this will give the sides. Suppose these to form an irregular quadrangle, and then find the diagonals also by the two triangles: Thus, the sum of the rectangles of the bases and of the sides will give one diagonal; and the sum of the rectangles of the side of each *triangle* multiplied respectively by the base of the other will give the other diagonal. As this method is shorter I do not know why the former one was adopted. [B]

Assume the two triangles, Fig. 32, 33. Then multiply severally the side and the base of one *triangle* by the hypothenuse of the other; and call the greatest

---

[A] Bramha Gupta is said to have lived in the 7th century. (As Res. vol. 9. p. 242.) He is still held in high estimation as an astronomer; but I have not had an opportunity of consulting any of his works.

[B] This problem might perhaps be expressed thus: Given two right angled triangles, required a quadrangle, such, that the opposite triangles, formed by the diagonals intersecting at right angles, shall be similar to each other, and to the given triangles respectively. This is performed by the application of the bases and sides of the given triangles, in such a manner, as to obtain proportionate sides and diagonals of a quadrangle. The second case seems merely a variety of the first; by transposing two of the adjacent sides, a quadrangle is formed consisting of two right angled triangles, similar to the two assumed, and having a common hypothenuse, which is a new diagonal.

Bhascara's object seems to be, to construct any quadrangle, in such a manner, that all its parts shall be known, without further calculation.

number the base, and the least the side opposite the base. The figure is thus represented. Fig. 34.

In this case where, according to the former method, the diagonals are found with much labour, multiply respectively the side of one triangle by the base of the other; the products are 36, 20, the sum of which is the diagonal 56: also the rectangle of the bases is 15, and the rectangle of the sides is 48, the sum of which is the other diagonal 63. This is an easy process.

Or, draw the figure with the left side and the side opposite the base, transposed; [A] then the rectangle of the hypothenueses 5, 13 of the two right angled triangles will be the second diagonal 65.

Example.—The base is 300, the side opposite to it is 125; the sides are 260 and 195; one diagonal is 280, the other diagonal is 315; one perpendicular is 189, and the other is 224: Required the lower limbs of the perpendiculars from where the diagonals and perpendiculars intersect; required the perpendicular and segments from the place of intersection of the two diagonals; required the perpendicular, and the segments of the base of the *suchi* [B] formed by the meeting of the two sides produced in their own direction; also required the sides of the *suchi*? I would know all these if thou art skilful in calculation.

Representation of the figure. Fig. 36.

[C] The *square* root of the difference of the squares of the perpendicular and of the side which falls upon it, is called *sandhi*. [D] The base minus the *sandhi* of this per-

---

[A] In one copy the altered figure is thus represented. See Fig. 35.

[B] Literally, a needle; but in mathematical language it signifies a pyramid or cone.

[C] The whole of this part is merely an application of the properties of similar triangles, and seems to require no explanation; but the terms used may perhaps be more clearly understood by referring to Plate VI. Fig. 2; where let ABCD be a quadrangle. Produce AD and BC till they meet in E: let fall the perpendiculars DF, EG, and CH, and draw CI parallel to EA: then will the triangle ABE be the *suchi*; the segments BF and FA, AH and HB are the *pit,h* and *sandhi* respectively, of the perpendiculars DF and CH; HI is the *sama*, and DI the *hara*.

[D] The common signification of this word is union, junction.—A different definition of the *sandhi* is given at this place, viz. "the mean of the perpendicular and of the side which falls upon it is called *sandhi*." This, however, is erroneous and incomprehensible; and

pendicular is called *pit,h*. [A]

Rule.—Having put down in two places the *sandhi* of the perpendicular whose lower limb is sought, multiply it by the other perpendicular and its own diagonal, and divide the products by the other *pit,h*; the quotients are the lower limbs from the place of intersection of the perpendicular and diagonal.

Thus, perpendicular 189, the side which falls upon it is 195; *the square root of the* difference of *the squares* of these *numbers* is the segment, here called *sandhi*, 48; the base minus the *sandhi* is the other segment, which is called *pit,h*, 252: [B] Thus, also, the other perpendicular is 224, the side which falls upon it is 260; the *sandhi obtained* is 132, and the *pit,h* is 168: [C]

The lower limb of the first perpendicular 189 is thus found; its *sandhi* is 48, this being multiplied by the other perpendicular 224, and by the diagonal 280, separately, and the products divided by the other *pit,h* 168, the quotients are, lower limb of the perpendicular 64, and lower limb of the diagonal 80. [D]

---

disagrees not only with the other copies, but also with the definition of the same word which follows, apparently out of place, at the end of the succeeding paragraph, and is the one which is here adopted.

[A] Literally, a chair or stool.

[B] The perpendicular is 189, the side which falls upon it is 195; the *sandhi* is then found by the rule, "the *square* root of the difference of the side and hypothenuse is equal to the base," thus, the difference of the squares of the numbers 189 and 195, is 2304, the *square* root of which is the *sandhi*, 48; this being subtracted from the base, the remainder is the *pit,h* 252. *Com.*

[C] The other *sandhi* is also found thus: The second perpendicular is 224, the side which falls upon it is 260, "the difference of the squares of these numbers is 17424, the *square* root of which is the *sandhi* 132; subtract this from the base 300, the remainder is the *pit,h*, 168. *Com.*

[D] The lower limb of the first perpendicular 189, and the lower limb of the diagonal from where the hypothenuse and perpendicular intersect, are thus found: The *sandhi* of this perpendicular is 48; put this down in two places, and multiply it by the other perpendicular 224, and by its diagonal 280, the products are 10752, 13440; divide this by 168 the *pit,h* of the other *sandhi*, the quotients are, lower limb of the perpendicular 64, and lower limb of the diagonal 80. *Com.*

Thus, also, the second perpendicular is 224; its *sandhi* is 132, which being multiplied by the other perpendicular 189, and its diagonal 315, separately, and the products divided by the other *pit,h* 252, the quotients are, lower limb of the perpendicular 99, and lower limb of the diagonal 165. [A]

To find the lower perpendicular from the place of intersection of the two diagonals.

Rule.—Multiply both the perpendiculars by the base, and divide each by its own *pit,h*; the quotients are the two staffs; then by these staffs are found the perpendicular and segments of the base from the intersection of the two diagonals, according to the rule formerly given.

In this manner we obtain the staffs 225, 400; then, according to the rule "from the intersection of a cord drawn from the base of the one to the top of the other," &c. the lower perpendicular from the place of intersection of the diagonals is found by these staffs to be 144, and the segments 108, 192. [B]

To find the perpendicular, segments, and sides of the suchi (triangle formed by two sides of the quadrangle produced.)

Def.—The *sandhi* of one perpendicular being multiplied by the other perpen-

---

At this place there is given the following definition of the *sandhi*: "The *square* root of the difference of the squares of the side and hypothenuse is the *sandhi*."

[A] Thus, also, the *sandhi* of the second perpendicular 224 is 132; this being put down in two places and multiplied by the other perpendicular 189, and by its diagonal 315, the products are 24948, 41580; these divided by 252 the *pit,h* of the other *sandhi* 48, the quotients are, lower limb of the perpendicular 99, lower limb of the diagonal 165. *Com.*

[B] The perpendiculars 189, 224, being multiplied by 300 the base, the products are 56700, 67200, divide these respectively by their own *pit,h* 252, 168, the quotients are the two staffs 225, 400; multiply these two staffs together, the product is 90000, divide this by 625, the sum of the two staffs, the quotient is the perpendicular let fall from the place of intersection of the diagonals, 144: Also the two segments are found by the rule "multiply the staffs by the base, &c." Thus, multiply the staffs 225, 400 by the base 300, the products are 675000, 120000, divide these by 625 the sum of the two staffs, the quotients are the segments on each side of the perpendicular, 108, 192. *Com.*

dicular, and the product divided by its own perpendicular, the quotient is called *sama* [A]. The sum of the *sama* and of the other *sandhi* is called *hara* [B].

Rule.—Multiply separately the *sama* and the other *sandhi* by the base, and divide the products by the *hara*; the quotients are the segments of the *suchi*. The product of the other perpendicular multiplied by the base, being divided by the *hara*, the quotient is the perpendicular of the *suchi*. Multiply each of the two sides by the perpendicular of the *suchi*, and divide the product of each side by the perpendicular *of that side*; the quotients are the sides of the *suchi*.

The skilful perform the whole operation by the rule of Three Quantities.

Here one perpendicular is 224; its *sandhi* is 132; multiply this by the other perpendicular 189, and divide the product by its own perpendicular 224, the quotient is $\frac{891}{8}$, which is called the *sama*; the sum of this and of the other *sandhi* 48, is $\frac{1275}{8}$; this is called the *hara*. [C] The *sama* and this other *sandhi* being severally multiplied by the base 300, and the products divided by the *hara*, the quotients are the segments of the base of the *suchi*, $\frac{1536}{17}$ $\frac{3564}{17}$. [D] The other perpendicular 189 being multiplied by the base, and the product divided by the *hara*, will give the perpendicular of the *suchi*, $\frac{6048}{17}$. [E] The two sides 195, 260 being multiplied by the perpendicular of the *suchi*, and the products divided respectively by their own perpendi-

---

A Literally, equal.

B Divisor.

C Thus, multiply the *sandhi* 132 by 189, the perpendicular let fall from the other angle, the product is 24948; divide this by 224, the perpendicular which falls upon the *sandhi* 132, the quotient is $\frac{24948}{224}$, or reduced by 28 is $\frac{891}{8}$; this is called the *sama*: add together the other *sandhi* 48, and the *sama* $\frac{891}{8}$, the result is $\frac{1275}{8}$; this is called the *hara* or divisor. *Com.*

D The *sama* $\frac{891}{8}$, and the other *sandhi* 48, being multiplied by 300 the base, the products are 267300, 14400; divide these by $\frac{1275}{8}$ the *hara* or divisor, the quotients are $\frac{2138400}{1275}$, $\frac{115200}{1275}$; the first reduced by 8 is $\frac{267300}{1275}$, and this again reduced by 75 is $\frac{3564}{17}$, which is one segment of the *suchi*: Also $\frac{115200}{1275}$ reduced by 75 is $\frac{1536}{17}$, which is the other segment of the *suchi*. *Com.*

E The perpendicular of the *suchi* is found in this manner: Multiply the perpendicular 189 by 300 the base, the product is 56700; divide this by $\frac{1275}{8}$ the *hara* or divisor, and reduce the quotient by 75, the result is $\frac{6048}{17}$, which is the perpendicular of the *suchi*. *Com.*

culars 189, 224, the quotients are the two sides of the *suchi* which is formed by two sides *of the trapezium* produced in their own direction, $\frac{6240}{17}$. $\frac{7020}{17}$. A

Thus here, and in every instance, by assuming to any particular sum of divison or of multiplication, such a quotient or divisor, as may be proper, the intelligent consider it an operation by the Rule of Three Quantities. B

A The two sides of the *suchi* are found thus: Multiply the two sides 195, 260 of the original figure by $\frac{6048}{17}$, the perpendicular of the *suchi*, the products are $\frac{1179360}{17}$ $\frac{1572480}{17}$; divide these by their own perpendiculars 189, 224, the quotients are $\frac{6240}{17}$ $\frac{7020}{17}$, the sides of the *suchi*. *Com.*

B In the original the first part of this paragraph is very obscure, and I doubt whether it be here rightly translated. The meaning however, evidently is, that the preceding operations can be performed by the rule of proportion.

CHAP. II.

SECTION I.

OF CIRCLES.

Rule.—Multiply the diameter by 3927, and divide the product by 1250; this gives the more precise [A] circumference;

Or, multiply the diameter by 22, and divide the product by 7; this gives the approximate circumference, which answers for common operations.

Example.—The diameter being 7, what is the circumference? the circumference being 22, what is the diameter?

Statement.—See Fig. 37.

The *more precise* circumference is $\begin{matrix}21\\1239\\1250\end{matrix}$; or the approximate circumference is 22.

By making the multiplier the divisor, and the divisor the multiplier, the *more precise* diameter is found to be $\begin{matrix}7\\11\\3927\end{matrix}$; or the approximate diameter is 7.

Rule.—The fourth of the diameter multiplied by the circumference gives the area of the circle; this area multiplied by four gives the area of the convex superficies of the sphere which is like the net work of a ball; the superficial area multiplied by the diameter, and the product divided by 6, gives the cubic content of the sphere.

Example.—The diameter being 7, what is the area of the circle; also the diameter of a sphere being 7, what is the area of the convex superficies which resem-

---

[A] *Sukshma.*—Literally, small, minute. In note [A] page 79, it is mentioned that this word is employed to denote either what is exact or true, or the nearest degree of truth that has been attained. The original does not contain the words which are printed in Italics in the example. The astronomers whom I have consulted, suppose that the number $21\frac{1239}{1250}$ is the precise circumference; but it is not probable that such a mathematician as Bhascara should have considered these excellent approximations as the exact truth.

bles the net work of a ball; and what is the cubic content of the sphere? Answer these three questions if thou understandest the Lilawati well.

Statement.—The area of the circle is $38\frac{2423}{5000}$; the convex superficies of the sphere is $153\frac{1173}{1250}$; the cubic content of the sphere is $179\frac{1487}{2500}$.

Rule.—Multiply the square of the diameter by 3927, and divide the product by 5000; this gives the more precise area of the circle: Or, multiply the square of the diameter by 11, and divide the product by 14; this gives the approximate area, which is sufficient for common operations. To half the cube of the diameter add its own one and twentieth part; the result is the cubic content of the sphere.

The more precise area is $38\frac{2423}{5000}$; the approximate area is $38\frac{1}{2}$; the approximate cubic content is $179\frac{2}{3}$.

Rule.—Multiply together the sum and difference of the chord [A] (of double the arc) and the diameter, and from the diameter subtract the *square* root of the product; half the remainder is the versed sine. [B] Subtract the versed sine from the diameter, and multiply the remainder by the versed sine; the *square* root of the product multiplied by two is the chord (of double the arc). Divide the square of half the chord (of double the arc) by the versed sine, and add the versed sine to the quotient; the result is the diameter of the circle.

Example.—The diameter is ten, and the chord (of double the arc) is six; required the versed sine; from the versed sine required the chord (of double the arc); and from the chord (of double the arc) and the versed sine, required the diameter?

Statement.—See Fig. 38.

The versed sine is 1; by knowing the versed sine we obtain the chord (of dou-

---

[A] *Jya.*—The string of the bow, or the chord of double the arc.—In astronomical works *jya* always means *ardha jya*, half the chord of double the arc, or the sine. See Phil. Trans. vol. 4. p. 86. As. Res. vol. 2. p. 245, et seq.

[B] *Shara.*—An arrow.

ble the arc) 6; by knowing the chord (of double the arc) and versed sine, we obtain the diameter 10.

Rule.—Multiply the diameter by 103923, by 84853, by 70534, by 60000, by 52055,[A] by 45922, by 41031;[A] and divide each product by 120000; the quotients will be the sides inscribed in a circle, from a trigon to a nonagon.

Example.—In a circle whose diameter is 2000, required a trigon, tetragon, pentagon, &c. of equal sides?

The diameter is 2000; the value of the sides of the trigon is $1732\frac{3}{60}$; of the tetragon is $1414\frac{13}{60}$; of the pentagon is $1175\frac{34}{60}$; of the hexagon is 1000; of the heptagon is $867\frac{35}{60}$; of the octagon is $765\frac{22}{60}$; of the nonagon is $683\frac{51}{60}$: Also different chords are obtained by assuming different diameters. These are mentioned in treatises on circles.—See Fig. 39, 40, 41, 42, 43, 44, 45.

Short method of finding the approximate Chord.

Def.—The circumference minus the arc being multiplied by the arc, the product is called *prathama*.[B]

Rule.—Multiply by five the fourth part of the square of the circumference, and having subtracted the product from the *prathama*,[C] by the remainder divide the

---

[A] Dr. Hutton, in his mathematical tracts, mentions that the number 52055 for the heptagon, and the number 41031 for the nonagon, are erroneous, and ought to be 52070 and 4.042, and he suggests that the error has probably arisen from miscopyings. But as the text contains the words which are symbolical of these numbers, as well as the numbers themselves, it is probable that there may have been an error in the original calculations. The number for the trigon which is given wrong in Fyzi's translation is here correctly put down.

[B] This word literally signifies first, but here it seems to be used in a technical sense.

[C] *Adya* is the word which occurs in the original, but as it has the same signification as *prathama*, we shall retain only the latter, in order to lessen the perplexity which arises from the use of foreign terms.

prathama multiplied by four times the diameter; the quotient will be the chord.

Example.—The eighteenth part of a circle multiplied separately by one, &c. gives similar arcs; required the chord of each arc in a circle the semidiameter of which is one hundred and twenty?

Statement.—See Fig. 46.

The diameter is 240; hence the circumference is 754; the eighteenth part of which being multiplied separately by one, &c. similar arcs are obtained, the chords of which are required to be found. The nearest arcs *in integral numbers* are 42, 84, 126, 168, 210, 252, 293, 335, 377. The arcs are eighteen, but the tenth, &c. being the same as the eighth, &c. in an inverse order, nine only are put down.[a] The operation is then performed according to the rule, thus: circumference 754, minus the arc, is 712; this multiplied by the arc is 29904 the *prathama*; square of the circumference is 568516, the fourth of which, 142129, being multiplied by 5, the product is 710645, this minus the *prathama* is 680741, the divisor; the diameter multiplied by 4 is 960; by this multiply the *prathama*, the product is 28707840, which being divided by the divisor, we obtain the chord 42: And in this manner the following chords are obtained, 82, 120, 154, 184, 208, 226, 236, 240. In the same manner in regard to all arcs.

Or, to shorten the operation, reduce the circumference and the arcs by 42, which is the eighteenth part of the circumference; the same chords will then be found as before. Thus reduced, the statement is, circumference 18; arcs 1, 2, 3, 4, 5, 6, 7, 8, 9: The circumference minus the arc 1 is 17, this multiplied by the arc, the product is 17, which is called the *prathama*: the square of the circumference is 324, the fourth part of which is 81; multiply this by 5, the product is 405; and this minus 17, the *prathama*, is 388, which is the divisor. The diameter 240 multiplied by 4 is 960, this multiplied by the *prathama* is 16320, which being divided by the divisor 388, the quotient is the chord. Thus, by repeating the ope-

---

[a] Notwithstanding this remark, 18 arcs are put down increasing in the same ratio; thus, 42, 84, 126, 168, 210, 252, 293, 335, 377, 419, 461, 503, 545, 586, 628, 670, 712, 754. The other copies, however, contain only the first nine.

ration in succession, the same chords as before are obtained 42, 82, 120, 154, 184, 208, 226, 236, 240. The same process answers for any diameter.

Rule.—Multiply the square of the circumference by five times one fourth of the chord, and divide the product by the chord added to four times the diameter; subtract the quotient from one fourth of the square of the circumference; and subtract the *square* root of the remainder from half the diameter: this last remainder is the arc.

Example.—Required the arcs of the chords which have just been mentioned?

Statement.—Chords 42, 82, 120, 154, 184, 208, 226, 236, 240. The reduced circumference is 18; the diameter multiplied by 4 is 960; add 42 the chord, the result is 1002; the square of the circumference is 324, this multiplied by a fourth of 42 the chord, is 3402, and this multiplied by 5 is 17010; which being divided by 1002, the quotient is 17; subtract this from 81 the fourth of the square of the circumference, the remainder is 64, the *square* root of which is 8; subtract this from the circumference, the remainder is 1, which is the arc. In this manner there are found the arcs 1, 2 3, 4, 5, 6, 7, 8, 9,; these multiplied by the eighteenth part of the circumference give the former arcs. A

A The rules contained in this section are so fully illustrated by Dr. Hutton, that I deem it sufficient to quote his words, without any other commentary.

"To find the circumference of a circle, multiply the diameter by 3927, and divide the product by 1250; or multiply the diameter by 22, and divide by 7.

"In this precept we find two approximations; one of them, 7 to 22, the same ratio as had been the result of one of the labours of the prince of the ancient mathematicians, Archimedes; and the other 1250 to 3927, the very same as 1 to 3·1416, nearer than those of any of the Europeans before the labours of Vieta.

"Among other rules in mensuration, they have the following: D being the diameter, and C the circumference; then $\frac{1}{4}$DC = area of the circle; also DC = surface of the sphere, and $\frac{1}{6}D^2C$ = its solidity.—Other rules are, $\frac{3927}{5000}D^2$ = area, which is exactly equivalent to our $\cdot7854D^2$, and shows that it is derived from the ratio above-mentioned, 1250 to 3927. Another rule for the same is, $\frac{11}{14}D^2$ = area, which is another of our approximations, and derived from the ratio 7 to 22.—Another rule given for the solidity of the sphere in terms

SECTION II.

OF PONDS. [A]

Rule.—After measuring the breadth in several places, add together the different breadths, and divide by a figure equal to the number of places measured; perform the same operation in regard to the length and depth. Then multiply the area of the pond by the depth; the product is the cubic content of the pond.

Example.—In consequence of the sides being unequal, the length in three places

---

of the diameter, is $\frac{D}{2} + \frac{D^3}{\frac{2}{21}}$ = the solidity of the sphere, which must be wrong printed in various respects.* Having endeavoured to restore this form to some probability, I have imagined it might be intended to mean the same as $\frac{D}{2} \times \frac{D^2}{\frac{20}{21}}$, which reduces to $\frac{D}{2} \times \frac{21}{20}D^2 = \frac{21}{40}D^3 = \cdot525D^3$, and is very nearly the same as our own approximation $\cdot5236D^3$.—Again, D being the diameter, c the chord,† and v the versed sine of an arch a, then $\frac{1}{2}D - \frac{1}{2}\surd(D^2 - c^2) = v$, a theorem geometrically correct: from which is derived $2\surd(Dv - v^2) = c$, which is correct also.‡—But the two following are only approximations, where C = the circumference, viz, $\frac{4aD(C-a)}{\frac{1}{4}C^2-(C-a)a} = c$, which gives the chord c rather too great, by about the 58th part in an arc of two degrees, and about the 166th part in an arc of thirty degrees, being true to the 4th place of figures in the former case, and to the 3d place in the latter; but it does not appear how they have got this rule. From this however they have derived the following rule, by resolving a compound quadratic equation, viz, $\frac{C}{2} - \surd(\frac{C^2}{4} - \frac{\frac{1}{4}C^2c}{4D+c}) = a$.——Hutton's tracts, vol. 2. p. 158-9.

[A] The diagrams of the ponds in this section, and of the wall and cut timber in the two next sections, have been omitted, as they afford no kind of illustration.

---

* The true expression given by Bhascara is $\frac{D^3}{2} + \frac{1}{2} \times \frac{D^3}{21} = \frac{22}{42}D^3 = .5238D^3$ which is much nearer the truth than Dr. Hutton's conjecture.

† In these two cases, c must mean the chord of double the arc.

‡ Bhascara has also given $D = \frac{c^2}{4v} + v$

is 10, 11, 12; in three places the breadth is 6, 5, 7; and the depth is 2, 3, 4: Required the cubic content of the pond?

According to the rule for finding the mean measure, the *mean* breadth in cubits is found to be 6, the length 11, the depth 3; and the cubic content is 198.

Rule.—Divide by six the sum of the several areas of the top, of the bottom, and of the bottom added to the top; the quotient will be the mean area of the figure; the mean area multiplied by the depth gives the exact cubic content. [A]

The third part of the *cubic* content of the pond is the *cubic* content of the *suchi* (pyramid or cone.) [B]

Example.—The top is ten cubits in breadth and twelve in length; the bottom is one half of these numbers; and the depth is seven cubits: Required the *cubic* content of the pond?

Statement.—Area of the top of the pond is 120, of the bottom is 30, of the bottom added to the top is 270; the sum of the whole is 420; and the *cubic* content of the pond is 490.

Example.—Each of the four sides of a pond is 12, and the depth is 9: Required

---

[A] That is, let a^2 and b^2 be the length and breadth of the top
and c^2 d^2 the length and breadth of the bottom
then $a^2 : b^2 :: c^2 : d^2$
and $a^2 d^2 = b^2 c^2 = abcd$

Now by our rules $\dfrac{a^2b^2 + c^2d^2 + abcd}{3}$ = solid content of the pond or frustum of a pyramid; but $abcd = \dfrac{a^2d^2 + b^2c^2}{2}$ therefore

$$\frac{a^2b^2+c^2d^2+\dfrac{a^2d^2+b^2c^2}{2}}{3} = \frac{2a^2b^2+2c^2d^2+a^2d^2+b^2c^2}{6} = \frac{a^2b^2+c^2d^2+\overline{a^2+c^2}\times\overline{b^2+d^2}}{6}$$

solid content of the pond according to the rule.

[B] The *suchi* here means a pyramid or cone, having the same altitude or depth, as the pond, and the area of its base equal to the mean area of the pond; therefore as a pyramid or cone, is one third of a prism or cylinder, of equal base and altitude, the cubic content of the *suchi* is one third that of the pond.

the *cubic* content; also required the *cubic* content of a circular pond the diameter of which is 10, and the depth 5; required likewise the *cubic* content of the *suchi* of these two ponds?

Statement. *For the square pond.*—Sides 12, depth 9. The *cubic* content of the square pond is 1296; the *cubic* content of the *suchi* is 432.

Statement for the circular pond.—Diameter 10, depth 5. Here the *cubic* content is $\frac{3927}{10}$; *cubic* content of the *suchi* is $\frac{1309}{10}$; approximate *cubic* content is $\frac{2750}{7}$; approximate *cubic* content of the *suchi* is $\frac{2750}{21}$.

SECTION III.

OF THE BRICKS OR STONES IN A WALL.

The area of the top (or horizontal section) multiplied by the height gives the cubic content. The cubic content of the wall divided by the cubic content of a brick, gives the number of the bricks. The height of the wall divided by the height of a brick gives the number of layers of bricks.

The operation is the same when the wall is built of stones.

Example.—The bricks are 18 inches long, 12 inches broad, and 3 inches thick; and the wall is 5 cubits broad, 8 cubits long, and 3 cubits high: Required the *cubic* content of the wall and of a brick; also required the number of bricks it contains, and the number of layers of bricks?

The cubic content of a brick is $\frac{3}{64}$, of the wall is 120; the number of bricks is 2560; the number of layers is 24. In the same manner if the wall is built of stones.

SECTION IV.

OF CUTTING TIMBERS, &c.

Rule.—By the length multiply half the sum (or the mean) of the thickness of the apex and base expressed in inches; multiply the product by the number of directions in whichthe wood is cut, [A] and divide this last product by 576; this will give the cubits. [B]

Example.—The thickness at the base is 20 inches, at the apex 16 inches, and the length is 100 inches: Required in cubits the measure of this wood cut in four directions?

Directions 4; half the sum (or the mean) of the thickness is 18; this multiplied by the length,the product is 1800, and this multiplied by the directions, the product is 7200, which divided by 576 gives the cubits $\begin{matrix}12\\1\\2\end{matrix}$.

Rule.—If the wood is cut in a transverse direction, then, according to the preceding rule, the thickness multiplied by the breadth will give the product.

The cost of brick or stone walls, of making ponds, sawing wood, &c. is determined by professional knowledge, and the hardness or softness of the materials.

Example.—If the breadth is 32 inches, and the thickness 16 inches, what will be the product, in cubits, of the plank cut in nine directions?

Breadth 32; thickness 16; directions 9. The product in cubits is 8.

SECTION V.

OF HEAPS.

In a heap of large grain the tenth part of the circumference is the depth; in a heap of small grain the eleventh part, and in a heap of grain with the husk the ninth part, of the circumference is the depth. [C]

[A] Here the wood is supposed to be cut longitudinally.

[B] The division by 576 is merely to reduce the square inches to cubits. The result both of this and the following rule gives the sum of the areas of the vertical sections of the wood, and as this sum expresses the space thro' which the saw passes in cutting, the object seems to be to determine the expence of sawing wood.

[C] That is, if the diameter and circumference of the base be 1 and 3.1416, the depths will be .31416, .2856, .349 respectively.

Rule.—By the depth multiply the square of the sixth part of the circumference; the product is the number of solid cubit measures, which are the kharya of the Magadha country. [A]

Example.—On an even piece of ground there is a heap of large grain, the circumference of which is sixty: Required the number of kharyas in the heap? Also the number of kharyas in an equal quantity of small grain, and of grain with the husk?

Statement.—Circumference 60. The depth of the large grain is 6; the number of kharyas obtained is 600. The circumference of the heap of small grain also is 60, the depth is $\frac{60}{11}$, and the product in kharyas is $545\frac{5}{11}$. Also the circumference of the grain in husk is 60, the depth is $\frac{10}{3}$, and the number of kharyas obtained is $\frac{1000}{3}$.

Rule.—Multiply respectively by two, four, one and one third, the circumference of a heap of grain lying against a wall, at the inside corner, and at the outside corner; then find the cubic product according to the preceding rule, and divide it by the sum by which each heap was multiplied; the quotients will be the cubic quantity of each heap. [B]

Example.—The circumference of the quantity lying against the wall is 30 cubits; of that placed at the inside corner is 15 cubits; and of that at the outside corner is 45 cubits: Required the cubic content of each of the quantities?

Statement.—The product of the circumference of the first heap multiplied by two is 60; of the second multiplied by four is 60; of the third multiplied by one and one third is 60. We then obtain the common product 600; this being divided by each of the multipliers, we obtain the separate quotients 300, 150, 450.

[A] That is, if c be the circumference, and d the depth, as above; then will $\left(\frac{c}{6}\right)^2 \times d = .083\,c^2 \times \frac{d}{3}$ be the content; for which our more accurate rule is $.07958\,c^2 \times \frac{d}{3}$

[B] These are evidently $\frac{1}{2}$, $\frac{1}{4}$, and $\frac{3}{4}$ of the entire heap or cone.

SECTION VI.

OF SHADOWS.

Rule.—Square the difference of the two shadows and the difference of the two hypothenuses; and by the difference of these two squares divide the number 576; [A] add an unit to the quotient, and find the *square* root of the result; then by this *square* root multiply the difference of the hypothenuses, and in one place subtract the difference of the shadows from the product, and in another place add it; the results halved are the two shadows. [B]

Example.—The difference of the two shadows is 19 and the difference of the two hypothenuses is 13. I reckon him who can tell the shadows, a proficient both in arithmetic and algebra.

[A] The number 576 is the square of twice the gnomon (which is always understood in these rules to be 12); and the shadow is caused by a lamp placed at different distances.

[B] See Plate VI. Fig. 3.

That is given the gnomon $= a = 12$

$$4a^2 = 576$$

$2b =$ difference of the shadows

$2c =$ difference of the hypothenuse

Let $2x =$ sum of the shadows

$2y =$ sum of the hypothenuses

Then $x + b$ and $x - b$ are the two shadows

and $y + c$ and $y - c$ are the two hypothenuses

We have then $a^2 = (y + c)^2 - (x + b)^2 = (y - c)^2 - (x - b)^2$

hence $cy = bx$, and $x^2 = \frac{c^2y^2}{b^2}$

also $a^2 = y^2 + c^2 - x^2 - b^2$

Statement.—Here the difference of the shadows is 19, the difference of the hypothenuses is 13; and the number 576 being divided by 192, the difference of the two squares, the quotient is 3, plus one is 4, the *square* root of which is 2; by this *square* root multiply the difference of the hypothenuses, the product is 26; from which the difference of the shadows being subtracted in one place, and added in another, and the results halved, we obtain the shadows $\begin{matrix}3\\1\\2\end{matrix}$ $\begin{matrix}22\\1\\2\end{matrix}$.

In this example call the gnomon 12 the side, and the shadows the bases; then the *square* roots of the sum of their squares will be the hypothenuses $\begin{matrix}12\\1\\2\end{matrix}$ $\begin{matrix}25\\1\\2\end{matrix}$.

Rule.—Multiply the gnomon by the space between the foot of the lamp and the bottom of the gnomon, and divide the product by the height of the lamp minus the

---

or $x^2 = y^2 + c^2 - a^2 - b^2 = \frac{c^2y^2}{b^2}$

$$\frac{b^2y^2 - c^2y^2}{b^2} = b^2 - c^2 + a^2$$

$$y^2 = \frac{b^2 - c^2 + a^2}{b^2 - c^2} \times b^2$$

$$y = b\sqrt{\left(1 + \frac{a^2}{b^2 - c^2}\right)}$$

but $x = \frac{cy}{b} = c\sqrt{\left(1 + \frac{a^2}{b^2 - c^2}\right)}$

therefore $x + b = c\sqrt{\left(1 + \frac{a^2}{b^2 - c^2}\right)} + b = \frac{\sqrt{\frac{4a^2}{4b^2 - 4c^2} + 1} \times 2c + 2b}{2}$

and $x - b = c\sqrt{\left(1 + \frac{a^2}{b^2 - c^2}\right)} - b = \frac{\sqrt{\frac{4a^2}{4b^2 - 4c^2} + 1} \times 2c - 2b}{2}$

The two shadows according to the rule

by varying the transpositions we might also get

$c\sqrt{1 - \frac{a^2}{c^2 - b^2}} + b$, and $c\sqrt{1 - \frac{a^2}{c^2 - b^2}} - b$ for the values of the two shadows

height of the gnomon; the quotient is the shadow.[A]

Example.—The space between the gnomon and the lamp is 3 cubits, and the height of the lamp is $3\begin{smallmatrix}1\\2\end{smallmatrix}$ cubits: Required the shadow of a gnomon 12 inches in height?

Statement.—Gnomon $\begin{smallmatrix}1\\2\end{smallmatrix}$;[B] distance between the foot of the lamp and the bottom of the gnomon 3; this multiplied by the gnomon, the product is $\begin{smallmatrix}3\\2\end{smallmatrix}$; this being divided by 3, the height of the lamp minus the gnomon, the quotient in inches is 12. See Fig. 49, 50.[C]

Rule.—Multiply the gnomon by the space between it and the lamp; divide the product by the shadow, and to the quotient add the gnomon; the sum is the height of the lamp.

Example.—The space between the lamp and the gnomon is 3 cubits, and the shadow is 16 inches: Required the height of the lamp; and the height of the lamp being known, required the distance between the lamp and the gnomon?

Statement.—Space between the lamp and the gnomon 3 *cubits*; gnomon 12 *inches*; shadow 16 inches. The height of the lamp is found to be cubits $\begin{smallmatrix}2\\3\\4\end{smallmatrix}$.

Rule.—Multiply the shadow by the height of the lamp minus the gnomon, and divide the product by the gnomon; the quotient is the space between the lamp and the gnomon.

Thus take the numbers from the foregoing example: The height of the lamp is $\begin{smallmatrix}2\\3\\4\end{smallmatrix}$ *cubits*; the shadow in inches is 16; the gnomon in inches is 12. The distance be-

---

[A] See Plate VI. Fig. 4

Let a be the gnomon

$b =$ the space between the foot of the lamp and the bottom of the gnomon

$x =$ the shadow

then $a - c : b :: c : x = \frac{bc}{a-c}$ according to the rule.

[B] This is half a cubit or 12 inches.

[C] The lamp is placed on the top of a long brass rod, which is represented here by a straight line.

tween the gnomon and lamp is found to be cubits 3. [A]

Rule.—Multiply the two shadows, severally, by the space between the ends of the shadows, and divide the two products by the difference of the lengths of the shadows; the quotients are the respective spaces *between the bottom of the lamp, and the ends of the shadows*; multiply either of these spaces, and the gnomon, together; and divide the product, by the corresponding shadow; the quotient is the height of the lamp.

All these operations may be performed by the Rule of Three Numbers, which pervades all calculations, as Hari, by his own portions, pervades all thing.

Example.—A gnomon of 12 inches was observed to throw a shadow of 8 inches; the gnomon being placed two cubits forward opposite the point of this shadow, was observed to throw a shadow of 12 inches: Required the space between the lamp and the gnomon, [B] and also the height of the lamp? See Fig. 51, 52, 53.

[A] See Plate VI. Fig. 5.

Let $a =$ gnomon

b and $c =$ the two shadows

$d =$ the space between the ends of the two shadows

$x =$ the space between the bottom of the lamp and the end of the first shadow

$y =$ the height of the lamp, then

$b : a :: x : y$

and $c : a :: x + d : y$

therefore $b : c :: x : x + d$

$$\left.\begin{array}{l} \text{and } c - b : d :: b : x = \dfrac{bd}{c-b} \\ c - b : d :: c : x + d = \dfrac{cd}{c-b} \\ \text{also } y = \dfrac{ax}{b} = \dfrac{ax + ad}{c} \end{array}\right\} \text{according to the rule}$$

[B] All the copies have this reading; but from the subsequent operation, the question appears to be, "required the space between the lamp and ends of the shadows." If, however, the shadows be subtracted from this space, the remainder will be the distance between the lamp and gnomon; and this perhaps is the object of the question.

Here the space between the ends of the shadows is $\frac{13}{6}$;[a] the shadows are $\frac{1}{3}$, $\frac{1}{2}$;[a] the first of these $\frac{1}{3}$ being multiplied by $\frac{13}{6}$, and the product divided by the space between the ends of the shadows, the quotient is the measure of the space $\frac{13}{3}$: this is the space between the bottom of the lamp and the end of the first shadow. Thus, also, the measure of the space between the bottom of the lamp and the end of the second shadow is $\frac{13}{2}$. Then either space and the gnomon being multiplied together, and the product divided by the corresponding shadow, the height of the lamp is, in both instances, found to be the same, $\frac{13}{2}$.

Or, the measurement of shadows may be made by the Rule of Three Numbers, thus:

If by the excess of one shadow above the other, a space is found equal to the distance between the ends of the shadows, what will each shadow give? In this manner we obtain the respective distances between the end of each shadow and the bottom of the lamp. There is then another statement by the Rule of Three, thus,

If the gnomon is the side, the base being the shadow; what will be the side corresponding to a base equal to the space between the end of the shadow and the bottom of the lamp?

Thus the height of the lamp is found to be the same in both cases.

In the same manner all the operations for 5, 7, 9, &c. numbers, may be performed by two, three, &c. statements of the Rule of Three Numbers.

As Vishnu the comforter, the one seed from which all things spring, pervades the whole world, mountains, rivers, gods, demons, cities, &c. which are only distinctions of himself, so the Rule of Three Numbers runs thro' all arithmetical ope-

---

[a] These are fractions of a cubit. In two copies the reading is thus; "The distance in inches between the ends of the shadows is 52 inches; the shadows are 8, 12."

The distance between the ends of the shadows is found in the following manner: The gnomon is carried 2 cubits or 48 inches forward from its first position; from this number subtract 8 inches, the length of the first shadow, there remains 40; to this add 12, the length of the other shadow, the sum is 52, which is the space between the ends of the two shadows.

rations. It may then be asked, why has so much been written? The answer is, that tho' the calculations made in arithmetic and algebra by means of the processes of multiplication and division, are merely cases of the Rule of Three Numbers, yet this is perceived only by those who have acute minds; but to assist those who, like me, are of slow understanding, the skilful in the science have made easy, by different modes of operation, the various ways in which the Rule of Three Numbers may by performed. [A]

---

[a] The results in arithmetic, algebra, and in calculating the motions of the heavenly bodies, which are usually obtained by the processes of multiplication and division, are produced also by the Rule of Three Quantities; but operations for the square, &c. do not proceed from this rule. *Com.*

It is stated in the Bija Gannita, that with the exception of the square and square root, cube and cube root, all operations may be done by the Rule of Three Quantities.

PART III.

SECTION I.

OF THE KUTAKA.[A]

PREPARATORY to finding the *Kutaka* (required multiplier) reduce first by some number, if it can be done, the dividend,[B] divisor, and augment. If the number which divides the dividend and divisor, do not divide the augment, the question is not solvable.[C]

The common measure[D] of the dividend and divisor is the last divisor which is obtained by their reciprocal division. The dividend and divisor when divided by this

---

[A] A known quantity being multiplied by an unknown multiplier, and a given augment added to the product, or subtracted from it, and the result divided by a given divisor, if no remainder be left, the multiplier in this case has been named by former authors *kutaka*. *Kutaka*, therefore, means the particular or individual multiplier. The number multiplied is called dividend. The dividend, divisor, and augment must be reduced by a common divisor when it can be done; and for this purpose find any common divisor, except an unit or a fraction. After this reduction of the dividend and divisor, they are called *drada* or condensed, as they cannot be farther reduced. *Com.*

[B] *Dushta.* Literally, ill, bad.

[C] *Apawartanam.* Abbreviation.

[D] The word *shesham* which, in the translation, is rendered last divisor, usually signifies remainder. According to this sense, a literal translation of the passage would run thus: "The remainder of the two (dividend and divisor) reciprocally divided is the abbreviation, by which abbreviation the dividend and divisor being divided, are called *drada*." The ambigui-

common divisor are reduced to their lowest proportionals.[A]

Divide the reduced dividend and divisor reciprocally till the remainder in the dividend is an unit. Place the quotients under each other in succession; below these set down the augment, and below the augment a cipher. Then having multiplied by the last figure but one, the figure immediately above it, add the last figure to the product, and then throw out the last figure.[B] Repeating the operation in this manner two quantities are found. Divide the upper quantity by the reduced dividend, and call the remainder the quotient; then divide the other, *or lower* quantity, by the reduced divisor, and call the remainder the multiplier. If the number of quotients is an even number, the results *of these two divisions*, are the quotient and multiplier. But if the number of quotients is an odd number, then the quotient and multiplier thus found being subtracted from their respective divisors,[C] *the remainders* are the quotient and multiplier.

Example.—What is that number by which when 221 is multiplied, and 65 added to the product, and the result divided by 195, there shall no remainder?

Statement.—Dividend 221; augment 65: divisor 195.

The last divisor, after the reciprocal division of the dividend and divisor, is 13. The dividend, divisor, and augment, when divided by this number, are the reduced dividend 17, divisor 15, augment 5. The quotients which result from the reciprocal division of the reduced dividend and reduced divisor, being placed under each other, and

---

ty, however, is removed by the subsequent example, in which it is stated that 13 is the last, or remainder, after what is termed the mutual division of 221 and 195. Now, if 221 be divided by 195, and this last number by the remainder, and so on, the last divisor will be 13.

A *Drada.* Hard, solid, firm, excessive. Here it signifies what cannot be farther reduced or divided.

B Something seems wanting here; the insertion of the following paragraph would perhaps supply the deficiency. "And by the result multiply the number next above in the line, and to the product add the last remaining number as before."

C *Takshana.* The operation of rejecting the quotient and taking the remainder is called *tashta*: Thus 56 being divided by 17, the quotient is 3, and the remainder is 5: This remainder is the number taken. The number or divisor by which the remainder is obtained is called its *takshana.* Thus 17 is the *takshana* of 5, because the remainder 5 results from the

the reduced augment set down below them, and a cipher below the augment, the line is

1
7
5
0

Then according to the rule "by the last figure but one multiply the figure immediately above it, &c." there are found the two quantities 40, 35. Having divided *the first quantity* by the reduced dividend 17, and the *other quantity* by the reduced divisor 15, the remainders are the quotient 6, and multiplier 5.

Or, to each of these add its own divisor multiplied by an assumed number[A]; we then obtain the quotient and multiplier 23, 20: Or 40, 35.[B]

---

division of 56 by 17. By divisors, therefore, of the remainders, (termed quotient and multiplier) we are not to understand numbers by which they are divided, but numbers from which, when used as divisors, these remainders result.

[A] If the number assumed is one, the quotient and multiplier are 23, 20: if the assumed number is two, they are 40, 35.

[B] In the commentaries the whole operation is thus exhibited. "Divide the dividend by the divisor, the remainder is 26, by this divide the divisor, the remainder is 13, which is the common measure. Divide the dividend, divisor, and augment by this common measure; the results are, reduced dividend 17, reduced augment 5, reduced divisor 15. Then divide the reduced dividend by the reduced divisor, the quotient is 1, and there remains 2; by this remainder divide the divisor, the quotient is 7, and the remainder is 1. Having thus divided the two quantities till an unit is the remainder, place the quotients below each other in succession, thus 1
7
and below these set down the reduced augment, and below the augment a cipher. The line then is

1
7
5
0

Multiply by the last figure but one the figure immediately above it, the product is 35; and by this number multiply 1 the next upper figure, the product is 35; to this add the augment 5, the result is 40: Then throwing out the last figure in the line there remain the two

After reducing the augment and dividend, find the multiplier according to the preceding operation :[A] Or,

After reducing the augment and divisor, find a multiplier, and multiply it by their common divisor ; the product is the multiplier.

Example.—What is that number by which when 100 is multiplied, and 90 added to the product ; or that number by which when 100 is multiplied, and 90 subtracted from the product—and the result divided by 63, there shall be no remainder.

Statement.—Dividend 100; augment 90; divisor 63. Then, according to the preceding operation, we obtain the quotient and multiplier 30, 18.[B] Or,

---

quantities $\begin{matrix}40\\35.\end{matrix}$ Divide the uppermost quantity 40 by the reduced dividend 17, the remainder is 6, which is called the quotient: Also divide the other quantity 35 by the reduced divisor, the remainder is 5, and is called multiplier. Thus, then, the quotient is 6, and the multiplier is 5."

For $\frac{221 \times 5 + 65}{195} = 6$

[A] This gives a true multiplier, but a wrong quotient.

[B] Thus,

```
63) 100 (1
    63
    --
    37) 63 (1
        37
        --
        26) 37 (1
            26
            --
            11) 26 (2
                22
                --
                 4) 11 (2
                     8
                    --
                     3) 4 (1
                        3
                        -
                        1
```

The quotients are then put down below each other in succession, and below them is set

Reduce the dividend and augment by ten. The statement then is, dividend 10; augment 9; divisor 63. Divide reciprocally the dividend and divisor, and place the quotients below each other, the augment below the quotients, and a cipher below the augment; thus,

0
6
3
9
0

Then, according to the former operation, we obtain the multiplier 45; but this must not be taken; for the number of quotients being an odd number, the multiplier 45 must be subtracted from its own divisor; the remainder is the multiplier

---

down the augment, and below the augment a cipher, and the multiplication is performed as follows

Line

1 × 1530 + 900 = 2430
1 × 900 + 630 = 1530
1 × 630 + 270 = 900
2 × 270 + 90 = 630
2 × 90 + 90 = 270
1 × 90 + 0 = 90
90
0

Divide the uppermost quantity 2430 by the dividend 100:

100) 2430 (24
200
———
430
400
———
30 remainder, called the quotient

Divide the other quotient 1530 by the divisor 63:

63) 1530 (24
126
———
270
252
———
18 remainder, called the multiplier.

18. Then multiply the dividend by this number, and having added the augment to the product, divide the result by the divisor; the quotient is 30. Or,

Reduce the divisor and augment by nine. The statement then is, dividend 100; augment 10; divisor 7. The line is

14
3
10
0

and the multiplier obtained is 2. This being multiplied by 9, the common measure of the divisor and augment, the same multiplier is found as before, 18. Multiply the dividend by this number; add the augment to the product, and divide the result by the divisor; the quotient obtained is 30. [A]

Thus when the augment 90 is affirmative, the number required is 18. For

$$\frac{100 \times 18 + 90}{63} = 30$$

[A] One Commentator also gives the following method:

"First, reduce the dividend and augment by 10. We have dividend 10, augment 9.

Again, reduce this reduced augment, and also the divisor, by 9. We have augment 1; divisor 7.

Divide the reduced dividend 10 by the reduced divisor 7:

```
7) 10 (1
   7
   --
   3) 7 (2
      6
      --
      1
```

The line and the two quantities then obtained agreeably to the rule, are

Line
1 × 2 + 1 = 3 quotient
2 × 1 + 0 = 2 multiplier
1
0

These two quantities being less than the reduced dividend, and the reduced divisor, stand as they are, being called quotient and multiplier.

Or, Add to the multiplier and quotient their respective divisors multiplied by any assumed number: *if one is the number assumed,* the multiplier and quotient obtained are 81, 130: if two, they are 144, 230; and so on.

Rule.—The multiplier and quotient being subtracted from their respective divisors, are the multiplier and quotient which result if the augment is negative.

Take the last example. When the augment 90 is affirmative, the quotient and multiplier obtained are 30, 18. These being subtracted from their respective divisors, or numbers by which they were obtained, viz. 100, 63, the remainders 70, 45, are equal to the quotient and multiplier which result when the augment 90 is negative.[A]

To this multiplier and quotient add their respective divisors multiplied by any assumed number. *If one is the number assumed,* the multiplier and quotient obtained are 170, 108: *if two,* they are 270, 171.

Example.—What number is that by which when 60 is multiplied, and 16 added to the product; or that number by which when 60 is multiplied, and 16 subtracted from the product—and the result divided by 13, there shall be no remainder.

Statement.—Dividend 60; augment 16; divisor 13. According to the process stated before, there are found multiplier and quotient 2, 8. The number of quotients is an odd number; therefore the multiplier and quotient must be subtracted from their respective divisors 13, 60; the remainders are 11, 52, which are the multiplier and quotient produced by an affirmative augment 16.[B] These being subtracted from their respective divisors 13, 60, the remainders are 2, 8, which are the multiplier and quotient produced by a negative augment 16.[C]

Then multiply the multiplier 2 by 9, the number by which the augment and divisor were reduced; the product is 18, which is the true multiplier.

And multiply the quotient 3 by 10, the number by which the dividend and augment were reduced, the product is 30, which is the true quotient.

A Thus, $\frac{100 \times 45 - 90}{63} = 70$

B Thus, $\frac{60 \times 11 + 16}{13} = 52$

C Thus, $\frac{60 \times 2 - 16}{13} = 8$

Rule.—In dividing the two quantities take the same result, or quotient, as to both the multiplier and quotient. [A]

If an affirmative augment be divided by the divisor, then by the rule formerly given, find the multiplier and quotient, and to this quotient, add the quotient obtained by dividing the augment; the result is the true quotient. If a negative augment be divided by the divisor, then subtract the number called quotient, from the quotient obtained by dividing the augment; and the result will be the *true* quotient.

Example.—What number is that by which when 5 is multiplied, and 23 added to the product; or that number by which when 5 is multiplied, and 23 subtracted from the product—and the result divided by 3, there shall be no remainder.

Statement.—Dividend 6; augment 23; divisor 3. The *valli* or line is

1
1
23
0

and the two quantities obtained are 46, 23. Then divide these two quantities severally

---

[A] The commentaries give the following explanation of this part of the rule: "In dividing the uppermost quantity by the dividend, and the other quantity by the divisor, with a view to find the multiplier and quotient, take the same quotient in the division of both quantities. That is, in dividing the two quantities take the least quotient obtained, for the quotient in both cases of division."

It will be observed that, in the preceding examples, the upper and lower quantities, when divided respectively by the dividend and divisor, have always given equal quotients. If however, unequal quotients result, then instead of multiplying each divisor by its own quotient, one of the two quotients must be taken as a common quotient number. The two divisors being multiplied by this common quotient, and the products subtracted from the two dividends, the remainders are the required multiplier and quotient. Thus, in the following example, having divided the uppermost quantity 46 by the dividend 5, the quotient is 9; and having divided the lower quantity 23 by the divisor 3, the quotient is 7. But 7, which is the least quotient, is taken in both cases, and 5, which is the divisor of 46, instead of being multiplied by 9, is multiplied by 7, and the product 35 being subtracted from 46, the remainder is called the quotient, 11. In the same manner 3 multiplied by 7 is 21; this being subtracted from 23, the remainder is 2, which is called the multiplier.

by the dividend and divisor, calling the remainders multiplier and quotient, Thus, dividing the lower quantity by the divisor 3, the quotient is 7; and dividing the uppermost quantity by the dividend 5, the quotient is 9, which however must not be taken; for, agreeably to the rule, the skilful take the same result, or quotient, in order to find both the *remainders called* multiplier and quotient; therefore 7 is taken. Thus, then, there are obtained multiplier and quotient 2, 11.[A] And the multiplier and quotient produced by an affirmative augment, being subtracted from their own divisors, the remainders are the multiplier and quotient produced when the agument is negative; in this case they are 1, $\overset{\circ}{6}$. Increase each of these by its own divisor multiplied by an assumed number; here, each divisor being multiplied by two, and the product added to the multiplier and *negative* quotient, this quotient becomes affirmative, and the multiplier and quotient then are 7, 4.[B] And so on in every case.

If the augment be divided by the divisor, &c. the statement for this method is, dividend 5; augment 2; divisor 3. When the augment is affirmative, the multiplier and quotient obtained according to a former rule, are 2, 4. These being subtracted from their own divisors, the remainders 1, 1, are the multiplier and quotient which result when the augment is negative. The quotient obtained in dividing the augment being added to the quotient 4, the multiplier and quotient obtained when the augment is affirmative, are 2, 11.[B] When the augment is negative, subtract the quotient 1 from the quotient obtained in dividing the augment; the multiplier and quotient then are 1, $\overset{\circ}{6}$: In order to obtain a plus quotient, add to the multiplier and quotient the product of their respective divisors multiplied by 2; the multiplier and quotient then obtained are 7, 4.[C]

[A] Thus, $\frac{5 \times 2 + 23}{3} = 11$

[B] Thus, $\frac{5 \times 7 - 23}{3} = 4$

[C] This second method shews how the multiplier and quotient are obtained, after dividing or reducing the augment by the divisor. The number which remains upon this division is

Rule.—If the augment be a cipher, or if the augment when divided by the divisor leave no remainder, then the multiplier shall be a cipher; and in the *latter* case the quotient which results from dividing the augment by the divisor, is the quotient.

Example.—What number is that by which when 5 is multiplied, and either a cipher or 65 added to the product, and the result divided by 13, no remainder shall be left.

Statement. A—Dividend 5; augment 65; divisor 13. The augment being divided by the divisor, no remainder is left; therefore the multiplier is cipher: and the

---

called the augment; thus,

augment
divisor 3) 23 (7
21
———
2 remainder, called augment

The statement then is, dividend 5, augment 2, divisor 3.

Then divide the dividend by the divisor, &c. and place the quotients below each other, and below them the augment, and below the augment a cipher; and find two quantities according to the former rule:

$$1 \times 2 + 2 = 4$$
$$1 \times 2 + 0 = 2$$
$$2$$
$$0$$

The two numbers 2, 4, being less than the dividend and divisor, are the multiplier and quotient. When the augment 23 is affirmative, add this quotient 4 to the quotient 7 obtained in dividing the augment; the result is 11, which is the true quotient.

Again, the two numbers 2, 4 being subtracted from their own divisors (dividend and divisor) the remainders 1, 1 are the multiplier and quotient when the augment is negative. Subtract this quotient 1 from the quotient 7 obtained in dividing the augment; the remainder 6 is the true quotient, which in this case is minus. To obtain a plus quotient multiply by an assumed number 2. The multiplier and quotient found are 7, 4.

A The copy from which I have translated does not give an example where a cipher is the augment. But in another copy it is stated thus: "Dividend 5; divisor 13; augment 0. As the augment is a cipher, the multiplier and quotient are 0, 5."

There is a mistake however in stating the quotient to be 5. This will appear by the following operation:

quotient which results from the division of the augment by the divisor, is the quotient. Thus the multiplier and quotient obtained are 0, 5:[A] or, *by an assumed number* 1, are 13, 10. And so on.

Having divided the dividend by the divisor, and so on, the quotients which result are 0, 2, 1, 1. Put down these below each other, and below them put the augment which is a cipher, and below the augment write a cipher: Then beginning with the last figure but one, multiply upwards, according to the rule formerly given:

Line

$$
\begin{array}{l}
0 \times 0 + 0 = 0 \\
2 \times 0 + 0 = 0 \\
1 \times 0 + 0 = 0 \\
1 \times 0 + 0 = 0 \\
0 \\
0
\end{array}
$$

The two quantities which result from multiplying the figures in the line, being ciphers, both the multiplier and quotient also are ciphers. When a cipher, therefore, is the augment, the number required is 0. For

$$\frac{5 \times 0 + 0}{13} = 0$$

Or, to the numbers 0, 0, add the product of their own divisors multiplied by an assumed number 1; thus,

$$
\begin{array}{l}
13 \times 1 + 0 = 13 \text{ multiplier} \\
5 \times 1 + 0 = 5 \text{ quotient}
\end{array}
$$

For $\frac{5 \times 13 + 0}{13} = 5.$

[A] In this example the *walli* or line is 0, 2, 1, 1, 65, 0. Then multiplying by the last figure but one, and so on, the two quantities found are 130, 325; thus,

Line

$$
\begin{array}{l}
0 \times 325 + 130 = 130 \\
2 \times 130 + 65 = 325 \\
1 \times 65 + 65 = 130 \\
1 \times 65 + 0 = 65 \\
65 \\
0
\end{array}
$$

To obtain different multipliers and quotients.

Rule.—Increase the multiplier and quotient, each by the product of its own respective divisor multiplied by any assumed number; the result will be different multipliers and quotients. The method has been already shewn.

SECTION II.

OF THE STHIRA OR FIXED KUTUKA.

Rule.—The multiplier and quotient obtained when an affirmative augment is an

---

Divide the uppermost quantity 130 by the dividend 5;

```
5) 130 (26
   10
   --
    30
    30
   --
     0  the multiplier
```

And divide the augment by the divisor,

```
13) 65 (5  the quotient
    65
    --
```

Thus when 65 is the augment, the number required is also 0. For

$$\frac{5 \times 0 + 65}{13} = 5$$

Or, to the numbers 0, 5 add the product of their own divisors multiplied by an assumed number 1:

$$13 \times 1 + 0 = 13 \text{ multiplier}$$
$$5 \times 1 + 5 = 10 \text{ quotient}$$

The multiplier and quotient in this case are 13, 10. For

$$\frac{5 \times 13 + 65}{13} = 10$$

unit, or when a negative augment is an unit, being multiplied respectively by an assumed affirmative augment, or by an assumed negative augment, and each product divided by its own divisor, we obtain the multiplier and quotient of the assumed augment.

Example.—Take the first example given of the reduced dividend, divisor, and augment.

Statement.—Dividend 17 ; affirmative augment 1 ; divisor 15. In this case the multiplier and quotient obtained are 7, 8. These being multiplied by an assumed augment 5, and the products divided by their own divisors, the remainders are 5, 6.

Or, when a negative augment is an unit, the multiplier and quotient found, are 8, 9. These being multiplied by an assumed augment 5, and divided by their own divisors, the remainders are 10, 11. And thus in any case.[A]

[A] In this example the *walli* or line is 1, 7, 1, 0; after multiplying by the last figure but one, &c. the two quantities obtained are 8, 7: thus,

```
15) 17 (1
    15
    --
     2) 15 (7
        14
        --
         1
```

Line: 1, 7, 1, 0

$1 \times 7 + 1 = 8$
$7 \times 1 + 0 = 7$

These two quantities being less than the dividend and divisor, are not divided; the multiplier then is 7, and the quotient is 8.

Multiply these by an assumed augment 5:

$$7 \times 5 = 35$$
$$8 \times 5 = 40$$

Divide each of the numbers 35, 40 by its own divisor, calling the respective remainders multiplier and quotient:

```
15) 35 (2
    30
    --
     5 remainder, called multiplier
```

This operation is of great use in astronomical operations, as I shall now briefly shew.

Suppose the remainder or numerator of the fraction of a second to be the negative augment; 60 [A] the dividend; and the *kudina* [B] the divisor. The quotient obtained

---

17) 40 (2
34
—
6 remainder, called quotient

Or, subtract the multiplier and quotient 7, 8 from their own divisors; the remainders are the multiplier and quotient when the augment is negative; thus,

15 — 7 = 8 multiplier, when the augment is negative

17 — 8 = 9 quotient, when the augment is negative.

Multiply these by an assumed number 5:

$8 \times 5 = 40$

$9 \times 5 = 45$

Divide each of the numbers 40, 45 by its own divisor, calling the remainders respectively multiplier and quotient:

15) 40 (2
30
—
10 remainder, called multiplier

17) 45 (2
34
—
11 remainder, called quotient.

Thus the multiplier and quotient when the augment is negative, are 10 11.

[A] The number of seconds in a minute.

[B] The space included in a day of Bramha;—a fixed period from which eclipses are calculated, as the beginning of a *kalpa* or *yuga*. Eclipses are now generally calculated from the period of the GRAHA LAGHOWA, which was composed about 100 years ago.

is seconds, and the multiplier is the numerator of the fraction of a minute.[A] From this multiplier and quotient, find the minutes and the fraction of a degree. Then, from the intercalary month,[B] and from the fraction of lost days,[C] find in the same manner the number of solar and lunar days.

Example.—From a fraction of the second of a planet, to find the planet and *ahargana.*[D]

Call 60 the dividend; the *kudina* the divisor; and the numerator of the fraction of a second the negative augment. Then the quotient number found will be seconds, and the multiplier will be the numerator of the fraction of a minute. Thus also, calling the numerator of the fraction of a minute the negative augment; the quotient obtained will be minutes; and the multiplier will be the numerator of the fraction of a degree. Call this numerator of the fraction of a degree the negative augment; the *kudina* the divisor; and 30[E] the dividend. The quotient number obtained will be degrees; and the multiplier will be the numerator of the fraction of a sign. Then call 12[F] the dividend; the *kudina* the divisor; and the numerator of the fraction of a degree the negative augment: the quotient number obtained will be signs;[G] and the multiplier will be the numerator of the fraction of a revolution.[H] Then call the revolutions in the *kalpa* the dividend; the *kudina* the divisor; and the

---

[A] *Vikalla.*

[B] *Adi.*

[C] *Kshya.*

[D] The time or number of days elapsed from the commencement of Bramha's day;—or from the beginning of a *kalpa*;—or from an assumed period.

The definitions of *kudina* and *ahargana* are given merely upon verbal explanations which I have received; it is possible, therefore, that they may not be perfectly correct.—See, also, Bailly, Traité de L' astronomie Indienne, p. 392.

[E] The number of degrees in a sign.

[F] The number of signs in the zodiac.

[G] *Bhag*; also *ansa.*

[H] *Bhagana.*

numerator of the fraction of a revolution the negative augment. The quotient number obtained will be the revolutions passed; and the multiplier will be the *ahargana.*[a]

The examples in illustration are contained in the *Prashna Adya* of the SIROMANI.

---

[a] The illustration of the preceding example is thus given in the Commentaries:

" Let the *kalpa kudina* be 13;* the *kalpa bhagana* 11;* the *ahargana* 2.* Then if *kalpa kudina* 13 give *kalpa bhagana* 11, what will an assumed *kudina* 2 give?

$$13 : 11 :: 2 : 1\tfrac{9}{13}$$

Multiply the remainder 9, which is the numerator of the fraction of a bhagana or revolution, by 12 the number of signs in a revolution, and divide the product by 13 the denominator; the quotient is signs $8\tfrac{4}{13}$. Multiply the remainder or numerator of the fraction 4 by 30, the number of degrees in a sign, and divide the product by 13; the quotient is degrees $9\tfrac{3}{13}$. Multiply the remainder or numerator of the fraction 3 by 60, the number of minutes in a degree, and divide the product by 13; the quotient is minutes $13\tfrac{11}{13}$. Multiply the remainder or numerator of the traction 11 by 60, the number of seconds in a minute, and divide the product by 13; the quotient is seconds $50\tfrac{10}{13}$. The result then is, 1 rev. 8 signs, $9^\circ\ 13'\ 50''\ \tfrac{10}{13}$.

Then from this numerator of the fraction of a second 10, to find the planet and the ahargana:

The dividend is 60;† the numerator of the fraction of a second is the negative augment 10; the kudina is the divisor 13.

In this case, according to the rule for dividing the dividend by the divisor, and the divisor by the remainder, &c. the line obtained, and the two quantities which result from multipliying the numbers in the line, are

Line								
	4	×	50	+	30	=	230
	1	×	30	+	20	=	50
	1	×	20	+	10	=	30
	1	×	10	+	10	=	20
	1	×	10	+	0	=	10
	10						
	0						

The quotient obtained from these two quantities 230, 50, is 50, and the multiplier is 11. But as the number of quotients in the line is odd, the multiplier and quotient must be subtracted from their respective divisors 60, 13; the results are multiplier 10, quotient 2. These,

---

* These small assumed numbers are taken to shorten the calculations.

† The number of seconds in a minute.

In the same manner, call the adi or intercalary months in the kalpa, the dividend, the solar days the divisor; and the numerator of the fraction of an intercalary month, the negative augment. The quotient obtained in this case is the number of intercalary months expired; and the multiplier is the number of solar days expired.

In the same manner call the thrown out days in the kalpa the dividend; the lunar days the divisor; and the numerator of the fraction of thrown out days, the negative

---

however, are the multiplier and quotient when the augment is positive; but here the augment being negative, they must be subtracted from their respective divisors 60, 13; the results are, quotient 50, multiplier 11; the quotient number 50 is seconds; the multiplier 11 is the numerator of the fraction of a minute.

Call the numerator of the fraction of a minute the negative augment 11; the dividend 60;* the divisor 13.

By dividing the dividend by the divisors, &c. the line obtained, and the two quantities which result from multiplying the numbers in the line, are

Line								
	4	×	55	+	33	=	253
	1	×	33	+	22	=	55
	1	×	22	+	11	=	33
	1	×	11	+	11	=	22
	1	×	11	+	0	=	11
11							
0							

The quotient obtained from these two quantities is 13, and the multiplier is 3. But as the number of quotients in the line is odd, the multiplier and quotient must be subtracted from their respective divisors 60, 13; the remainders are, quotient 47, multiplier 10, when the augment is affirmative. But here the augment is negative; therefore these must again be subtracted from their respective divisors 60, 13; the remainders are, quotient 13, multiplier 3, when the augment is negative. The quotient 13 is minutes, and the multiplier 3 is the numerator of the fraction of a degree.

Call the dividend 30†; the numerator of the fraction of a degree the negative augment 3; and the divisor 13.

---

* the number of minutes in a degree.

† The number of degrees in a sign.

augment. The quotient then obtained will be the number of thrown out days expired, and the multiplier will be the number of lunar days expired.

The line and the two quantities which result, are

Line
2 × 9 + 3 = 21
3 × 3 + 0 = 9
3
0

As the two quantities 21, 9, cannot be reduced by their respestive divisors 30, 13, they are called quotient 21, and multiplier 9. These being subtracted from their own divisors 30, 13, the remainders are quotient 9, multiplier 4, when the augment is negative. The quotient 9 is degrees, the multiplier 4 is the numerator of the fraction of a sign.

Call 12* the dividend; this numerator of the fraction of a sign the negative augment 4; and the divisor 13.

Here the line and the two quantities are

Line
0 × 4 + 4 = 4
1 × 4 + 0 = 4
4
0

These two quantities being less than their disivors, are the quotient and multiplier: And subtracting them from their respective divisors 12, 13, the remainders are, quotient 8, multiplier 9, when the augment is negative. The quotient 8 is signs; the multiplier is the numerator of the fraction of a *bhagana* or revolution.

Call the dividend 11†; the numerator of the fraetion of a revolution the negative augment 9; and the divisor 13.

The line and the two quantities are

Line
0 × 54 + 45 = 45
1 × 45 + 9 = 54
5 × 9 + 0 = 45
9
0

The numbers 45, 54 being divided by their respective divisors 11, 19, we obtain the remainder 1, 2, which are called quotient and multiplier. But as the number of quotients in the line is odd, the quotient and multiplier must be subtracted from their respective divisors

---

* The number of signs in the zodiac.

† The number of *kalpa bhagana* assumed in the example.

SECTION III.

OF THE SANSLISTA KUTAKA.

Rule.—If there be one divisor, and several multiplicands, call the sum of the multiplicands the dividend; and call the sum of the remainders the negative augment. This manner of performing the kutaka is called sanslista kutaka.

Example.—What is the number by which when 5 is multiplied, and the product divided by 63, leaves the remainder 7; and by which when 10 is multiplied, and the product divided by 63, leaves the remainder 14.

In this example call the sum of the multiplicands the dividend; and the sum of the remainders the negative augment. The statement then is, dividend 15, augment 21, divisor 63. According to the former rule, the multiplier obtained is 14.*

11, 13; the remainders are, quotient 10, multiplier 11, when the augment is positive: And these being again subtracted from their divisors 11, 13, the remainders are, quotient 1, multiplier 2, when the augment is negative. The quotient 1 is the number of revolutions, and the multiplier 2 is the Ahargana.

Thus, then, there are obtained 1 rev. 8 signs, 9°, 13′, 50″. And the Ahargana are 2."

* Thus, dividend 15; divisor 63; augment 21. Reduce the dividend, divisor, and augment by 3. The statement then is: Reduced dividend 5; reduced divisor 21; reduced augment 7. The line and the two quantities obtained are

Line
0 × 28 + 7 = 7
4 × 7 + 0 = 28
7
0

Divide the uppermost quantity 7 by the reduced dividend 5; the remainder is 2, which is called quotient

5) 7 (1
5
—
2 remainder, called quotient

NOTE CONTINUED.

And divide the lower quantity 28 by the reduced divisor 21; the remainder is 7, which is called multiplier

21) 28 (1
21

—

7 remainder, called multiplier

Thus, when the augment is affirmative, the quotient is 2, and the multiplier is 7. Subtract these from their own divisors, 5, 21; the remainders are, quotient 3, multiplier 14, when the augment is negative. Reject the quotient; and the multiplier 14 is the required number. For

5	10
14	14
63) 70 (1	63) 140 (2
63	126
7 remainder	14 remainder

The whole of the *kutaka* corresponds with our method for the solution of indeterminate problems of the first degree. the same rules are given in Strachey's Bija Ganita, pages 29 and following. The process will also be found in Euler's Algebra, vol. 2. p. 17 &c. with which Bhascara's may be compared. It may not, however, be uninteresting to solve one of the examples according to our method, to shew how the rules of the *kutaka* correspond with ours.

$$\frac{100x + 90}{63} = y \qquad y = x + \frac{37x + 90}{63} = x + p$$

$$x = \frac{63p - 90}{37} = p + \frac{26p - 90}{37} = p + q$$

$$p = \frac{37q + 90}{26} = q + \frac{11q + 90}{26} = q + r$$

$$q = \frac{26r - 90}{11} = 2r + \frac{4r - 90}{11} = 2r + s$$

$$r = \frac{11s + 90}{4} = 2s + \frac{3s + 90}{4} = 2s + t$$

$$s = \frac{4t - 90}{3} = t + \frac{t - 90}{3} = t + u$$

$$t = 3u + 90$$

NOTE CONTINUED.

then putting $u = 0$, we have

$$\begin{array}{llll}
u = & 0 & = 0 & = 0 \\
t = & 3u + 90 & = 3 \times 0 + 90 & = 90 \\
s = & \left\{\begin{matrix} t + u \\ 4u + 90 \end{matrix}\right\} & = 1 \times 90 + 0 & = 90 \\
r = & \left\{\begin{matrix} 2s + t \\ 11u + 270 \end{matrix}\right\} & = 2 \times 90 + 90 & = 270 \\
q = & \left\{\begin{matrix} 2r + s \\ 26u + 630 \end{matrix}\right\} & = 2 \times 270 + 90 & = 630 \\
p = & \left\{\begin{matrix} q + r \\ 37u + 900 \end{matrix}\right\} & = 1 \times 630 + 270 & = 900 \\
x = & \left\{\begin{matrix} p + q \\ 63u + 1530 \end{matrix}\right\} & = 1 \times 900 + 630 & = 1530 \\
y = & \left\{\begin{matrix} x + p \\ 100u + 2430 \end{matrix}\right\} & = 1 \times 1530 + 900 & = 2430
\end{array}$$

Comparing these columns with note [a] p. 111, we can evidentlytrace Bhascara's rule. And these are true values of x and y; but as we have not rejected all the whole numbers in the course of the above operation, they will admit of being reduced to lower terms; repeating therefore the solution, and rejecting all the whole numbers we have,

$$\begin{array}{lll}
u = & 0 & = 0 \\
t = & 3u + 1 & = 1 \\
s = & t + u & = 1 \\
r = & 2s + t & = 3 \\
q = & 2r + s & = 7 \\
p = & q + r + 1 & = 11 \\
x = & p + q & = 18 \\
y = & x + p + 1 & = 30
\end{array} \left.\vphantom{\begin{matrix} a \\ b \end{matrix}}\right\} \text{according to Bhascara}$$

or by reducing $\dfrac{100 \times 1530 + 90}{63} = 2430$

we have $\dfrac{100 \times 18 + 90}{63} = 30$

that is $x = 18$, and $y = 30$

It also appears, that in our solution, we have one equation more than Bhascara gives quo-

NOTE CONTINUED.

tients; and it is evident, that while the augment is positive, an odd number of equations (corresponding with an even number of quotients) will give a positive sign to the augment in the last equation, and an even number of equations (or an odd number of quotients) a negative sign; which has exactly the same effect as a negative or positive augment at first; so that an even number of quotients answers to a positive augment, and an odd number, to a negative augment: and therefore in the negative case, we subtract the remainders, that is the new quotient and multiplier, from their respective divisors, in order to obtain positive values in their lowest terms, thus

$$\frac{100x - 90}{63} = y \text{ gives } \begin{matrix} x = -1530 \text{ or } -11 \\ y = -2430 \text{ or } -30 \end{matrix}$$

to make these positive put $u = 1$, and we have

$$x = 63u - 18 = 45$$

$$y = 100u - 30 = 70$$

or according to Bhascara (calling the remainders positive) subtract them from their respective divisors, $x = 63 - 18 = 45$ $y = 100 - 30 = 70$

The *Sthira Kutaka* appears to be merely an application of the foregoing Rules; for instance, suppose that in a certain period of years, (*Kalpa Kudina*, 13) a planet performs a certain number of revolutions, (*Kalpa Bhagana*, 11). Now in a certain period of years unknown, this planet has performed a certain unknown number of revolutions, signs, degrees, minutes, seconds and $\frac{10}{13}$ of a second; then from this fraction $\frac{10}{13}$, to find the required period, and number of revolutions &c. which is done as follows:

$$\frac{10}{13} = \text{fraction of a second}$$

$$\frac{60x - 10}{13} = y = \text{whole number of seconds passed over}$$

$$y = 50'' \text{ passed over}: x = 11; \frac{11}{13} = \text{fraction of a minute}$$

$$\frac{60x' - 11}{13} = y' = \text{whole number of minutes passed over}$$

$$y' = 13' \text{ passed over}: x' = 3, \frac{3}{13} = \text{fraction of a degree}$$

$$\frac{30x'' - 3}{13} = y'' = \text{whole number of degrees passed over}$$

NOTE CONTINUED.

$y'' = 9^s$ passed over : $x'' = 4$, $\frac{4}{13}$ = fraction of a sign.

$\frac{12x''' - 4}{13} = y'''$ = whole number of signs passed over

$y''' = 8$ signs passed over : $x''' = 9$, $\frac{9}{13}$ = fraction of a revolution

$\frac{11x'''' - 9}{13} = y''''$ = whole number of revolutions passed over

$y'''' = 1$ Revolution passed over : $x'''' = 2$, period or *Ahargana* required; and collecting all the results we have 1 Rev. 8 signs, 9°, 13', 50'' $\frac{10}{13}$ as before given.

The *Sanslista Kutaka* may be solved as follows.

$$\frac{5x}{63} = w + \frac{7}{63}$$

and $\frac{10x}{63} = y + \frac{14}{63}$

by addition $\frac{15x}{63} = w + y + \frac{21}{63}$

hence $\frac{15x - 21}{63} = w + y$ = a whole number, from which the solution follows as before.

END OF THE KUTAKA.

PART IV.

OF TRANSPOSITIONS.

Where particular figures are given.

THE series of figures one, &c. increasing by one, being multiplied to the last place, the product is the number of transpositions.[A] When particular figures are given, multiply this product by the sum *of the values* of the figures; and having divided this last product by the number of the figures, set down the quotient as many times as there are figures, *advancing it one place forward each time,* and then add up the whole; the result is the sum *of the values* of the figures *set down according to the number of transpositions.*[B]

Example.—What number of transpositions may be made by 2, 8; by 3, 9, 8; and by a continued series from 2 to 9: Also, what is the sum *of the values* of the figures *set down according to the number of transpositions.*

Statement.—*For first example.*—2, 8. Here the number of places is 2. Multiply one, &c. increasing by one, to the last place, the product is 2. Thus the number of transpositions is 2. Multiply this product by 10 the sum of the figures; the product is 20, which being divided by 2, the number of figures, the quotient is 10. This quotient being set down as many times as there are figures, advancing it forward one place each time, and the whole added up, the result is 110,

---

[A] That is, the natural series of figures being multiplied continually together up to the given number of places, the product is the number of transpositions.

[B] This method of finding the sum of the figures set down according to the number of transpositions, does not appear to be contained in any of our arithmetical books.

the sum of the transposed figures. [A]

Statement.—*For second example.*—3, 9, 8. Multiply the figures one, &c. increasing by one, to the last place; the product is 6, the number of transpositions. Multiply this product by 20, which is the sum of the figures; the product is 120, which being divided by 3, the number of places, the quotient is 40. This quotient being set down as many times as there are figures, advancing it forward one place each time, and the whole added up, the result is 4440, the sum of the transposed figures. [B]

Statement.—*For third example.*—2, 3, 4, 5, 6, 7, 8, 9. In this example the number of transpositions is 40320. The sum of the transposed figures is 2463999975360. [C]

Example.—The net, hook, serpent, drum, cranium, trident, bedstead foot, spear, arrow, and bow, *which are held in the ten hands of Mahadev*, being changed successively from one hand to another, how many changes will take place in the

---

A 10 } quotient set down as many times as there are figures, and advanced forward one
10 } place each time

110 sum of the transposed figures. For

2 8 } number of transpositions
8 2 }

110 sum of the transposed figures.

B 40 } quotient set down as many times as there are figures, and advanced forward one
40 } place each time
40 }

4440 sum of the transposed figures. For

389 }
839 }
938 } number of transpositions
398 }
893 }
983 }

4440 sum of the transposed figures.

C The number of places is 8, and $1 \times 2 \times 3 \times 4 \times 5 \times 6 \times 7 \times 8 = 40320$. Then the number of transpositions, 40320, being multiplied by $2 + 3 + 4 + 5 + 6 + 7 + 8 + 9 = 44$, the product is 1774080, which being divided by 8, the number of figures,

appearance of the image; also how many changes are produced by the club, discus, lotos, and shell of Vishnu?

Statement.—*For first example.*—The places are 10. The number of changes produced in the appearance of the image of Mahadev is 3628800. *Statement for second example.—The places are 4.* The number of changes produced in the image of Vishnu is 24.

Rule.—Divide the number of transpositions which result from all the figures, by the sum of the transpositions which result from the like figures; the quotient is the number of transpositions which can be made by the mixed figures.[a] Then find the sum of the transposed figures according to the former rule.

Example.—Required the number of transpositions which result from two, two, one, one; and the sum of these figures when transposed? Also, required the number of transpositions which result from four, eight, five, five, five; and the sum of these figures when transposed?

---

and the quotient put down as many times are there are figures, advancing it forward one place each time, and the whole added up, the result is the sum of the transposed figures; thus,

```
221760
 221760
  221760
   221760
    221760
     221760
      221760
       221760
-------------
2463999975360
```

(221760 …) quotient set down as many times as there are figures in the example, and advanced one place forward each time.

2463999975360 sum of the transposed figures

[a] *Any Number of Things being given; of which there are several given Things of one Sort; and several of another, &c; To find how many Changes can be made out of them all.*

Rule.—Take the series $1 \times 2 \times 3 \times 4$, &c, up to the number of things given, and find the product of all the terms.

Take the series $1 \times 2 \times 3 \times 4$, &c, up to the number of given things of the first sort, and the series $1 \times 2 \times 3 \times 4$, &c, up to the number of given things of the second sort, &c.

Divide the product of all the terms of the first series by the joint product of all the terms of the remaining ones, and the quotient will be the answer required.

Hutton's Mathematics, vol. I, p. 128.

Statement.—*For first example.*—2211. The number of transpositions *of four figures* is 24. Then the rule is, " divide the number of tranpositions which result from all the figures, by the sum of the transpositions which result from the like figures." Thus the number of transpositions of the two first like figures is 2; again, the number of transpositions of the two other like figures is 2. Then the number of transpositions, 24, being divided by 4, the sum of the transpositions of the like figures, the quotient is 6, the number of transpositions which can be made by the mixed figures: viz. 2211, 2112, 1221, 1212, 1122, 2121. According to the former rule the sum of these figures, thus transposed, is found to be 9999.

Statement.—*For second example.*—48555. The number of transpositions which result from the number of figures is 120. The number of transpositions of three places is 6. The former number, 120, being divided by this, the quotient is 20, the number of transpositions *of the mixed figures*:[a] thus, 48555, 84555, 58455, 55485, 55845, 55548, 55584, 45855, 54855, 85455, 54585, 58545, 55458, 55854, 45585, 85545, 54558, 58554, 45558, 85554. The sum of the figures, thus transposed, is 1199988.[b]

Where the particular figures are not given, and where they are also unlike.

The *natural series of* figures decreasing from the last place by one, *to the num-*

---

[a] The whole number of figures is 5: Then $1 \times 2 \times 3 \times 4 \times 5 = 120$.

The number of like figures is 3; Then $\frac{120}{1 \times 2 \times 3} = 20$ number of transpositions of the mixed figures.

[b] Thus, $4 + 8 + 5 + 5 + 5 = 27$ (sum of figures) $\times\ 20$ (number of transpositions) $= 540 \div 5$ (number of figures) $= 108$

```
108          ⎫ quotient put down
 108         ⎪ as many times as
  108        ⎬ there are figures,
   108       ⎪ and one place for-
    108      ⎭ ward, &c.
-------
1199988        sum of transposed figures.
```

For 48555 ÷ 84555 + 58455 + 55485 + 55845 + 55548 + 55584 + 45855 + 54855 + 85455 + 54585 + 58545 + 55458 + 55854 + 45585 + 85545 + 54558 + 58554 + 45558 + 85554 = 1199988

ber of figures taken, being multiplied together, the product is the number of changes of unlike figures. [A]

Example.—What number of changes can be made by six places of figures, the same figure not being put down twice?

The last figure is 9. And the figures when put down in six places, decreasing by one, are 9, 8, 7, 6, 5, 4. These being multiplied into each other, the product is the number of changes, 60480.

Rule.—Subtract an unit from the sum of the figures, and having set down the remainder, decreasing by one, in as many places less one as the example contains places, divide by one, &c. and multiply the quotients together; the product will be the number of transpositions.

This rule is applicable only when the number of places does not exceed nine.

To avoid prolixity this is treated in a brief manner; for the science of calculation is an ocean without bounds.

Example.—By figures the sum of which is 13, placed in five places, what number of changes will result? [B]

In this case an unit being subtracted from the sum of the figures, the remainder is 12. Set this down decreasing by one in as many places less one, as there are places given, and divide by one, &c. thus $\begin{matrix} 12, & 11, & 10, & 9 \\ 1, & 2, & 3, & 4 \end{matrix}$. The product of the figures in the upper line being divided by that of the figures in the lower line, the quotient is the number of transpositions, 495.

Though neither multiplier, divisor, square, nor cube, has been demanded, yet this specimen of *anka pasha* (transpositions,) will suffice to humble the most proud.

[A] *Any Number of different Things being given; to find how many Changes can be made out of them, by taking a Given Number of Quantities.*

Rule.—Take a series of numbers, beginning at the number of things given, and decreasing by 1 to the number of quantities to be taken at a time, and the product of all the terms will be the answer required." Hutton's mathematics, vol. 1 p. 127.

[B] This is a literal translation; but the following will perhaps be a more clear enunciation of the example.—Required the number of transpositions that can be made with any five, out of the nine digits, such that their sum shall be always 13?—That is the transpositions of
1 + 1 + 1 + 1 + 9
2 + 2 + 2 + 2 + 5 &c. &c. to as many forms as can be made amounting to the sum 13. This, according to our rules, may be done by summing up all the transpositions that can be made in each of all the forms.

The happiness and wealth of him will increase who thoroughly understands the Lilawati, the rules of which are excellent, and its operations free from error; which shews the method of multiplying and squaring, and in a familiar way illustrates by examples.

End of the LILAWATI which was composed by Bhascara Acharya.[a]

Changes				
1 + 1 + 1 + 1 + 9 = 13 gives	$\frac{120}{24}$	=	5	Number of Changes in the Form
2 + 2 + 2 + 2 + 5	$\frac{120}{24}$	..	5	....
3 + 3 + 3 + 3 + 1	$\frac{120}{24}$	..	5	....
1 + 1 + 1 + 2 + 8	$\frac{120}{6}$	..	20	....
1 + 1 + 1 + 3 + 7	$\frac{120}{6}$	..	20	....
1 + 1 + 1 + 4 + 6	$\frac{120}{6}$	..	20	....
1 + 1 + 1 + 5 + 5	$\frac{120}{12}$	..	10	....
2 + 2 + 2 + 1 + 6	$\frac{120}{6}$	..	20	....
2 + 2 + 2 + 3 + 4	$\frac{120}{6}$	..	20	....
3 + 3 + 3 + 2 + 2	$\frac{120}{12}$	..	10	....
1 + 1 + 2 + 3 + 6	$\frac{120}{2}$	..	60	....
1 + 1 + 2 + 4 + 5	$\frac{120}{2}$	..	60	....
1 + 1 + 2 + 2 + 7	$\frac{120}{4}$	..	30	....
1 + 1 + 3 + 3 + 5	$\frac{120}{4}$	..	30	....
2 + 2 + 1 + 3 + 5	$\frac{120}{2}$	..	60	....
2 + 2 + 1 + 4 + 4	$\frac{120}{4}$	..	30	....
1 + 1 + 3 + 4 + 4	$\frac{120}{4}$	..	30	....
3 + 3 + 1 + 2 + 4	$\frac{120}{2}$	..	60	....
			495	sum of the transpositions

Out of these eighteen forms there are three, each of which gives five transpositions .. 15

two	ten	20
five	twenty	100
four	thirty	120
four	sixty	240
	Total	495

which corresponds with the result of Bhascara's rule $\frac{12}{1} \times \frac{11}{2} \times \frac{10}{3} \times \frac{9}{4} = 495.$

[a] The copy from which I have translated concludes with the following intimation:

"The writing of this copy of the Lilawati was finished on Thursday 15th Kartika Suda, in the Samvata year 1729.—May prosperity attend it."

The present Samvata or Vicramadita year is 1872, so that this copy was written 143 years ago, or in the year 1673 of our era.

APPENDIX.

APPENDIX.

SHORT ACCOUNT OF THE PRESENT MODE OF TEACHING ARITHMETIC IN HINDU SCHOOLS.

ARITHMETICAL science, as taught in the Lilawati, is confined exclusively to the Jyotishis or astronomers. At school children are taught little beyond the four elementary rules of addition, subtraction, multiplication, and division, together with one or two examples of the rule of three, and of interest. In the method of teaching these rules, however, there is something peculiar, an account of which may be not altogether uninteresting to those who are fond of observing the various modes of calculation practised in different countries.

As the instruction received at Hindu Schools is almost entirely confined to arithmetic, a few additional remarks will be sufficient to convey a general and pretty accurate idea of the education afforded to Hindu children. The following account being founded chiefly upon information received from natives of the Mahratta country and of Guzerat, and on observations made during visits to schools kept by inhabitants of those countries, must be regarded in some measure as local. At the same time, the conversations which I have had with people from different and remote parts both of Hindustan and the Peninsula, leave little doubt that, in the general features, it will be found to correspond with the plan adopted throughout the whole of India.

On joining the school the young pupil performs the *pati puja*, or worship of the writing board, in the following manner. The board is first covered with gulal, on which is drawn the figure of Saraswati the goddess of learning; it is then covered with perfume, rice, flowers, sugar, beetle-nut and leaf, cocoanut, &c. and near it are placed a lighted taper of incense, and also a burning lamp scented with camphor, all of which are presented to the master along with a small sum of money and a turband, or some similar present, suitable to the condition of the parent or relation of the child. The rice, flowers, beetle-nut, &c. are distributed by the master among the children of the school. Trifling presents are also made to such brahmans as may attend upon the occasion. The scholar then prostrates himself before the writing board, which is supposed to represent the goddess Saraswati, and the master writes the words " Shri Ganesayanama"—reverence to Ganesa, the god of wisdom;—" Om"—the mystic name of god; after which he puts a reed pen into the scholar's hand, and directs it a few times over the forms of the letters.

Having performed these preliminary ceremonies, which are supposed to have a mighty influence over his future progress, the scholar proceeds to learn first the vowels, then the consonants, and finally the combinations of the vowels and consonants. Five or six vowels being written down on the board, he retraces their forms by drawing his pen over the characters which have been written in the sand, until the forms of the letters given in the lesson have become so familar that he can write them without a copy, and pronounce their names. In the next lesson five or six letters more are put down, which the scholar learns to write in the same manner as before; and thus he proceeds until he have learned to write and read the whole number of vowels and consonants, and the combinations of these letters, in the Devanagari alphabet, which, in this part of India, is called Balbodh.

After learning the letters of the alphabet, the scholar proceeds to the numeral figures. A copy of these being written down on the board, together with their names, he retraces their forms, and at the same time pronounces audibly the name of each figure, according as was done in learning the letters of the alphabet. The lesson is thus put down on the board:

1 ek .... one
2 don .... two
3 tin .... three
4 char .... four
5 panch .... five
6 saha .... six
7 sath .... seven
8 ath .... eight
9 now .... nine
10 daha .... ten

After writing these figures, and repeating their names, until he is able to write them even when no written lesson is placed in his view, the scholar is then taught to put down and read the figures as far as one hundred, in the following manner:

11 one before one is eleven
12 one before two is twelve
and so on to nine, when the first numeral is changed; thus,
20 two before cipher is twenty
21 two before one is twenty-one
22 two before two is twenty-two, &c.

30 three before cipher is thirty
31 three before one is thirty-one
32 three before two is thirty-two, &c.

40 four before cipher is forty
41 four before one is forty-one
42 four before one is forty-two
and so on to 100.

This species of enumeration being acquired, the scholar proceeds to the multiplication table called *Pare*. In the Mahratta schools, this table consists in multiplying ten numbers as far as thirty, and in Guzeratti schools, in multiplying ten numbers as far as one hundred: thus,

which the scholar also writes down, repeating audibly

1 one time one is one
2 one time two is two
3 one time three is three
4 one time four is four
5 one time five is five
6 one time six is six
7 one time seven is seven
8 one time eight is eight
9 one time nine is nine
10 one time ten is ten

2 two times one are two
4 two times two are four
6 two times three are six, &c.

3 three times one are three
6 three times two are six
9 three times three are nine, &c.

4 four times one are four
8 four times two are eight
12 four times three are twelve, &c.

And so on to 30, according to the Mahratta table, or to 100, according to the Guzeratti one.

The Mahratta table may be exibited in this manner:

TABLE NAMED PARE.

1	2	3	4	5	6	7	8	9	10	11	12	13	14	15	16	17	18	19	20	21	22	23	24	25	26	27	28	29	30
2	4	6	8	10	12	14	16	18	20	22	24	26	28	30	32	34	36	38	40	42	44	46	48	50	52	54	56	58	60
3	6	9	12	15	18	21	24	27	30	33	36	39	42	45	48	51	54	57	60	63	66	69	72	75	78	81	84	87	90
4	8	12	16	20	24	28	32	36	40	44	48	52	56	60	64	68	72	76	80	84	88	92	96	100	104	108	112	116	120
5	10	15	20	25	30	35	40	45	50	55	60	65	70	75	80	85	90	95	100	105	110	115	120	125	130	135	140	145	150
6	12	18	24	30	36	42	48	54	60	66	72	78	84	90	96	1.2	108	114	120	126	132	138	144	150	156	162	168	174	180
7	14	21	28	35	42	49	56	63	70	77	84	91	98	105	112	119	126	133	140	147	154	161	168	175	182	189	196	203	210
8	16	24	32	40	48	56	64	72	80	88	96	104	112	120	128	136	144	152	160	168	176	184	192	200	208	216	224	232	240
9	18	27	36	45	54	63	72	81	90	99	108	117	126	135	144	153	162	171	180	189	198	207	216	225	234	243	252	261	270
10	20	30	40	50	60	70	80	90	100	110	120	130	140	150	160	170	180	190	200	210	220	230	240	250	260	270	280	290	300

After this, the scholar is taught three tables, in which fractional parts are multiplied by whole numbers.

The first table of this sort is called *Pouke*, or Table of Quarters.

(which the scholar writes down, repeating audibly)

one time one quarter is one quarter

$\frac{1}{2}$ two times one quarter are one half

$\frac{3}{4}$ three times one quarter are three quarters,

and so on to 30 or 100 times.

The second table is the *Nimke*, or Table of Halves.

$\frac{1}{2}$ one time one half is one half

1 two times one half are one

$1\frac{1}{2}$ three times one half are one and a half

and so on to 30 or 100.

The third table is the *Pounke*, or Table of Three Quarters,

$\frac{3}{4}$ one time three quarters is three quarters

$1\frac{1}{2}$ two times three quarters are one and a half

$2\frac{1}{4}$ three times three quarters are two and a quarter

and so on to 30 or 100.

The next tables are those in which the fractions $\frac{1}{4}$ $\frac{1}{2}$ $\frac{3}{4}$ are joined with whole numbers:

The first table of this sort is called *Sawake*, or One and a Quarter Table.

$1\frac{1}{4}$ one time one and a quarter is one and a quarter.

$2\frac{1}{2}$ two times one and a quarter are two and a half

$3\frac{3}{4}$ three times one and a quarter are three and three quarters

and so on to 30 or 100 times.

The second is called *Dirke*, or One and a Half Table.

$1\frac{1}{2}$ one time one and a half is one and a half

3 two times one and a half are three

$4\frac{1}{2}$ three times one and a half are four and a half

and so on to 30 or 100 times.

The third is called *Arizke*, or Two and a Half Table.

$2\frac{1}{2}$ one time two and a half is two and a half

5 two times two and a half are five

$7\frac{1}{2}$ three times two and a half are seven and a half

add so on to 30 or 100.

Another table called *Outke*, or Three and a Half Table, is also committed to memory.

$3\frac{1}{2}$ one time three and a half is three and a half

7 two times three and a half are seven
$10\frac{1}{2}$ three times three and a half are ten and a half
and so on to 30 or 100.

Two other tables then follow which exhibit the multiplication of whole numbers. The first, which is called *Akarke*, or Eleven Table, exhibits the multiplication of the numbers from 11 to 20 into one another.

121 eleven times eleven are one hundred and twenty-one
132 eleven times twelve are one hundred and thirty-two
143 eleven times thirteen are one hundred and forty-three

132 twelve times eleven are one hundred and thirty-two
144 twelve times twelve are one hundred and forty-four
156 twelve times thirteen are one hundred and fifty-six

144 thirteen times eleven are one hundred and forty-three
156 thirteen times twelve are one hundred and fifty-six
169 thirteen times thirteen are one hundred and sixty-nine and so on.

Or, reduced to a tabular form it would be thus:

TABLE NAMED *AKARKE.*

	11	12	13	14	15	16	17	18	19	20
11	121	132	143	154	165	176	187	198	209	220
12	132	144	156	168	180	192	204	216	228	240
13	143	156	169	182	195	208	221	234	247	260
14	154	168	182	196	210	224	238	252	266	280
15	165	180	195	210	225	240	255	270	285	300
16	176	192	208	224	240	256	272	288	304	320
17	187	204	221	238	255	272	289	306	323	340
18	198	216	234	252	270	288	306	324	342	360
19	209	228	247	266	285	304	323	342	361	380
20	220	240	260	280	300	320	340	360	380	400

The other table is called *Ekotri*, or Table of Squares. It contains the multiplication of each figure into itself, or the square of each figure, from 1 up to 100: thus;

$$1 \times 1 = 1$$
$$2 \times 2 = 4$$
$$3 \times 3 = 9 \quad \text{and so on to}$$
$$100 \times 100 = 10000$$

After learning to multiply in this manner, the scholar proceeds to the tables of weights and measures. The following tables will be sufficient to shew the order and method adopted in the schools, and to render intelligible the examples which occur in subsequent parts of these remarks.

TABLE OF MONEY.

1 reas	quarter dugani
2 reas	half dugani
4 reas	1 dugani
8 reas	1 faddea
25 reas or $6\frac{1}{4}$ dugani	1 anna
4 anna	quarter rupee
8 anna	half rupee
16 anna	1 rupee

TABLE OF WEIGHTS.

10 walla	quarter tola
or, according to the Poona table	
3 masa	quarter tola
40 walla	1 tola
24 tola	1 sir
10 sir	quarter man
40 sir	1 man
5 man	quarter khandi
20 man	1 khandi

GRAIN MEASURE.

2 tepri	1 sir
4 sir	1 adoli
16 adoli	1 phata

8 phara .... 1 khandi
25 phara .... mora

Having committed to memory the multiplication tables, and also the tables of weights and measures, which are the ground work of his future arithmetical practice, the scholar next proceeds to what is termed *miloune*, which signifies adding. It is exhibited in the following manner:

Write down the successive multiples as far as 10, of the numbers from 1 to 30, and, draw a perpendicular line along the right hand side of these multiples, when they contain only one place, or a perpendicular line on each side, when they contain two or three places. Also draw a horizontal line under the series of multiples.

Then, beginning at the top, add the units of the uppermost row to the units in the second row, and after putting down the sum opposite to the second row, add it to the units in the third row, and put down the result opposite to the third row. Having proceeded in this manner through all the rows, set down under the horizontal line the number of tens obtained, and, on drawing another horizontal line, set down the units below it.

Carry the tens obtained to the tens in the next column, beginning at the bottom, and having put down the sum opposite to the lowermost row, add this sum to the tens in the next upper row, and opposite to it put down the sum. Proceed in this manner through all the rows to the uppermost row. Then set down the hundreds obtained below the first horizontal line, and the tens below the second, and, carrying the hundreds to the column of hundreds, add up this column, and put down the sum under the second horizontal line. The number which stands under this line is the sum of the multiples. The three following examples will be sufficient to shew the nature of this operation.

EXAMPLES.

1		43	17		49	29	
2	3	42	34		47	58	17
3	6	39	51	11	42	87	24
4	10	34	68	12	34	116	36
5	15	28	85	20	33	145	35
6	21		102	25	29	174	39
7	28	20	119	27		203	42
8	36	19	136	36	22	232	44
9	45	16	153	42	19	261	45
10		11	170	45	13	290	
4			44			44	
55			935			1595	

The scholar is next taught what is called *waza baki beriz,* that is, ADDITION and SUBTRAC-

TION, these two operations being taught at the same time, and by the same examples, in the following manner:

EXAMPLE.

546283	
621436	
953785	
1921704	
546283	subtract
1375421	remainder
621436	subtract
953785	remainder

In the mode of performing addition nothing peculiar occurs. Subtraction, likewise, is frequently done in the manner practised in Europe; but the most common method is by a process of addition, according to the following rule:

When the figure in the minuend line is greater than the corresponding subtrahend figure, add to the subtrahend a number such as shall make it equal to the minuend; and set down below the subtrahend the number thus added. When the figure of the minuend is less than the corresponding one of the subtrahend, add ten to the minuend, and also add to the subtrahend a number such as shall make it equal to the minuend thus increased. Then put down under the subtrahend, as before, the number added to it, and carry one to the next subtrahend figure.

EXAMPLE.

2435675
1321692
1113983

Thus say, 3 and 2 are 5; put down 3; 9 and 8 are 17; put down 8, and 1 is obtained; 1 and 6 are 7, 7 and 9 are 16; put down 9, and 1 is obtained; 1 and 1 are 2, 2 and 3 are 5; put down 3; 1 and 2 are 3; put down 1; 1 and 3 are 4; put down 1; 1 and 1 are 2; put down 1. Therefore 1113983 is the remainder.

The following is an example of compound addition and subtraction.

EXAMPLE.

	qrs.	annas*	
684395421 ..	3 ..	2	
435862643 ..	2 ..	3	
6345219 ..	1 ..	1	
1126603284 ..	3 ..	2	
684395421 ..	3 ..	2	subtract
442207863 ..	0 ..	0	remainder
435862643 ..	2 ..	3	subtract
6345219 ..	1 ..	1	remainder

GUNAKAR BHAGAKAR, or MULTIPLICATION and DIVISION, are also taught together, as in the case of addition and subtraction. In looking at the following example, it should be recollected, that the Mahratta multiplication table extends to 30, and the Guzeratti one to 100; hence, as they can multiply by any number below 30, without separating the figures of the multiplier into their places, the result of the operation is exhibited in one line. It will be observed that the multiplier is put down indiscriminately any where below the multiplicand.

EXAMPLE.

12345678910	
15	multiplier
185185183650	product
15	divisor
12345678910	quotient

When the multiplier is a high number, the operation is performed in the same way as in Europe, putting a mark, however, above each figure in the multiplicand when it is multiplied, and writing down the tens which result on one side of the board towards the right, as in the example given at the end of the next paragraph.

DIVISION is performed in this manner: Write the divisor any where below the dividend, and draw a line; then find how often the divisor is contained in as many places of the dividend as are just necessary, and, having set down these places on one side of the board, multiply the divisor by this number, and subtract the product from these places; to the remainder bring down the next figure of the dividend, and repeat the former process. The quotients are set down in a line under the divisor. This, in reality, is precisely our own method.

* An anna is the 4th part of a quarter, or 16th part of a rupee.

EXAMPLE OF MULTIPLICATION AND DIVISION.

```
                 . . . . . . . . .
multiplicand     1 2 3 4 5 6 7 8        7        3
                 . . . . . . . .        7        3
multiplier           3 4 9              6        3
                 ---------------        5        2
                     111111102          4        2
                     49382712           3        1
                   37037034             1    2   1
                 ---------------             2
                 . . . . . . . . .           1
                   4308641622   dividend     1
                        349     divisor      1
                 ---------------             1
                   12345678     quotient
```

```
430
349
----
 818
 698
----
1206
1047
----
1594 and so on.
```

Each figure in the multiplicand, when multiplied, being marked with a dot, there occur, in this instance, three rows of dots, two of which are above, and one below, the multiplicand. The three lines of figures on the right hand are the tens obtained during the multiplication, and are put down in this manner to assist the memory. The product of the multiplication being afterwards taken as a dividend, and the former multiplier put down any where below it as a divisor, the dividend figures are marked successively with a dot when multiplied by the quotient.

In the case of fractional numbers, the mode of multiplication is as follows, the multiplier being 14 rupees, 3 quarters, and 3¼ annas.

EXAMPLE.

```
   123456789
   14..3..3¼
------------------
1728395046   qrs.
  61728394 .. 2
  30864197 .. 1   annas
  15432098 .. 2 .. 2
   7716049 .. 1 .. 1
   3858024 .. 2 .. 2¼
   1929012 .. 1 .. 1¼
------------------
1849922822 .. 2 .. 2¼  product
        14 .. 3 .. 3¼  divisor
------------------
 123456789  quotient
```

The operation in regard to the fractional parts is termed *nimki*, or halving, and is founded on the regular quadrate division of the tables of money, weights, and measures. Thus the multiplicand being halved affords 2 qrs. out of the 3 qrs.

	qrs.
61728394 ..	2

This again is halved, because the remaining 1 qr. is the half of one half

30864197 .. 1

This being once more halved affords 2 annas out of the 3

		annas
15432098 ..	2 ..	2

Which is again halved, because the remaining anna is half of two annas

7716049 .. 1 .. 1

This again being halved yields half an anna out of the 3 qrs. of an anna

3858024 .. 2 .. $2\frac{1}{2}$

And this is halved, because one quarter anna is half of half an anna

1929021 .. 1 .. $1\frac{1}{4}$

The fractional parts being divisible into fourth parts of the whole, and of each other, this mode of operation is both the most expeditious and least liable to error; as it saves the trouble of multiplying by the fractional parts, and dividing by a large divisor.

Compound Division is performed in this manner:

Write the divisor any where below the dividend, and draw a line; then find how often the divisor is contained in as many places of the dividend as are just necessary, and, having set down these places on one side of the board, multiply the divisor by this number, and subtract the product from these places; to the remainder bring down the next figure of the dividend; also, if the remainder contain fractions, that is quarters, annas, or fractions of an anna, multiply them by ten, and add the product to the number formed by bringing down the figure; then divide this number so increased, in the same manner as before, placing the quotient under a horizontal line drawn below the divisor; and proceed in this manner till all the figures in the dividend are used.

EXAMPLE.

		qr.	annas
dividend	1849922822 ..	2 ..	$2\frac{1}{4}$
divisor	14 ..	3 ..	$3\frac{1}{4}$
quotient	123456789		

operation

	18
14 .. 3 .. $3\frac{1}{4}$ × 1	14 .. 3 .. $3\frac{1}{4}$
	3 .. .. $\frac{1}{4}$
4 brought down is	34
anna remainder $\frac{1}{4}$ × 10	$2\frac{1}{2}$
	34 .. .. $2\frac{1}{2}$
14 × 2	28
qrs 3 × 2	1 .. 2
annas 3 × 2	1 .. 2
anna $\frac{1}{4}$ × 2	$1\frac{1}{2}$
	29 .. 3 .. $3\frac{1}{2}$
	34 .. .. $2\frac{1}{2}$
	29 .. 3 .. $3\frac{1}{2}$
	4 3
9 brought down is	49
annas remainder 3 × 10	1 .. 3 .. 2
	50 .. 3 . 2
14 × 3	42
qrs 3 × 3	2 .. 1
annas 3 × 3	2 .. 1
anna $\frac{1}{4}$ × 3	$2\frac{1}{4}$
	44 .. 3 .. $3\frac{1}{4}$
	50 .. 3 .. 2
	44 .. 3 .. $3\frac{1}{4}$
	5 .. 3 .. $2\frac{3}{4}$ and so on thro' all the figures of the dividend.

When these fundamental rules are thoroughly understood, the instructor gives a few examples of the Rule of Three, and of Interest.

No special rule of proportion is given; but any question, for instance, what is the amount of wages for 4 months and 10 days, at 15 rupees per month? is answered in this manner: The wages of 4 months are 60;—then to find the amount for the fraction of the month;—the wages for 15 days, or half a month, are the half of 15, or $7\frac{1}{2}$; then for 10 days, which are two thirds of half a month, the wages are $\frac{2}{3}$ of $7\frac{1}{2}$, or 5 rupees. Or they would say at once, the wages for one month being 15, the wages for 10 days or $\frac{1}{3}$ of a month are $\frac{1}{3}$ of 15, or 5.

One school-master, however, gave me the following rule of proportion, which he was pleased to call a Lilawati rule.

Having multiplied the time by the wages, halve the product, and divide the remainder by fifteen. If there be any remainder after this division, reckon it annas. [A]

Example.—What will 12 days wages amount to at the rate of 10 rupees per month?

```
 12   time
 10   wages
----
120
halved
 60
 15   divisor
----
  4   quotient
```

Altogether, the wages for 12 days amount to 4 rupees.

[A] I do not know why the remainder is reckoned annas. Besides, it does not bring out the answer exactly. In the question, what will 11 days wages amount to at 7 rupees per month, the answer is not 2 .. $8\frac{1}{2}$, but 2 .. $9\frac{1}{15}$. For

```
30 : 11 : 7
      7
   -----
30) 77 (2
    60
   -----
    17
    16   qrs in a rupee
   -----
30) 272 (9 1/15
    270
   -----
      2
```

The person who gave me the rule stated very gravely that this difference was of no consequence, it being the practice of the Mahratta karkuns, or clerks, to pay those employed by their masters in whole numbers only, and to retain the fractions in their own pockets.

Example.—At the rate of 7 rupees per month, what will 11 days wages amount to?

11 days
7 monthly wages
—
77
halved
38 .. 2
15 divisor
—
2 .. 8½ annas quotient

Altogether, two rupees, 8 annas and a half.

RULE OF INTEREST.

Multiply the sum by the time, and after throwing out the last figure of the product, take the third part of the remainder, [A] and call it *kache*.

Example.—If the sum of 120 rupees be lent at ¼ per cent. monthly interest; what will the interest amount to in 4 months and 10 days.

130 time
120 principal sum
—
15600
520 third part of 1560

The money being at ¼ per cent. the interest of 500 rupees is five quarters; and that of 20 days is four fifths of an anna:—for if 100 give 1 qr. monthly interest

then 50 .... 2 annas do.
25 .... 1 ....
20 .... ⅘ [B] ......

Having gone thro' these different rules, the scholar proceeds to learn the method of keeping books of accounts, and also to read letters and papers written in the common Mahratta or Guzeratti character.

In books of accounts they employ marks for addition and subtraction. These marks consist of placing at the left hand end of a line drawn beneath the sum to be added or subtracted, the first letter of the word which signifies addition or subtraction; thus,

23456
34567
a———

denotes that these two numbers are to be added; and

[A] This is the same as dividing by 30 the number of days of the month.

[B] The native schoolmaster stated ¾ of an anna as the interest of 20 days. If the result be true within one fourth of an anna, they do not seem to aim at a more minute degree of accuracy.

34567
23456
s———

denotes that these numbers are to be subtracted.

They also employ a mark for *wasul*, or receipt, which consists of two straight lines united in the middle by a curve.—It has been already remarked in the introduction, that a circle is used to denote obliteration; thus,

2 Pounds of split pease .... (1)

o 6 Pounds of rice 1

The circle around the number 1, in the first case, and the circle placed opposite the number 6, in the second, shew that the item has been discharged.

No branch of MENSURATION is taught in the schools, tho' one schoolmaster furnished me with two examples of the measurement of fields. In order to understand them it is necessary to recollect the following table :

5	breadths of the hand	1	cubit
6	cubits	1	kati
20	kati	1	pand
20	pand	1	bigah

Example 1.—Required the area of a field 20 *kati* in breadth and 30 *kati* in length ?

30
20
———
600 *kati*
20 divisor—*kati*
———
30 quotient—*pand*
20 divisor—*pand*
———
1½ quotient—*bigah*

In this example, which is a regular figure, the area is found by multiplying the length by the breadth.

Example 2.—The breadths of an irregular figure, *at three equidistant places,** being 6, 10, 8 *kati*, and the whole length 25 *kati* ; required the area ?

10
8
6
———
24 sum of the different breadths ; and $24 \div 3 = 8$, mean breadth

* The words in Italics are supplied to render the example more intelligible.

25	length
8	mean breadth
200	*kati*
20	divisor—*kati*
10	quotient—*pand*, or $\frac{1}{2}$ bigah

This example is done by adding all the perpendicular breadths together, and dividing their sum by the number of them for the mean breadth, by which is multiplied the length. The product in this case tho' not exact, is a near approximation to the truth.

Something like what, in the Lilawati, is called the rule of assumed number, is also occasionally taught as a kind of arithmetical riddle. The scholar is desired to think of, or assume any number, then multiply it by three, and after halving the product, reject the fraction, if there be one, and multiply the whole number by 3; then taking half the product, and rejecting the fraction if there be one, divide the whole number by 9. From the quotient the number thought of, or assumed, will be told.

It has been already remarked, that in going thro' all these operations the scholar speaks in a loud singing tone. An European would naturally suppose that this practice must produce great confusion, and distract the mind of each scholar. In the Hindu schools, however, it does not seen to have this effect; but, on the contrary, this audible repetition appears to keep up the scholar's attention, and to fix his mind firmly on the subject about which he is employed. It also affords the teacher means of observing when any one is idle or inattentive to his leson; and by connecting the sound with the thing signified, the calculator may perform the operation by a kind of mechanical process. Besides, it takes away the idea of mental exertion, and converts the exercises at school into a kind of play and amusement.

Before the scholars are dissmissed in the evening, it is usual to repeat the different multiplication tables in the following manner:

All the scholars stand up, when one of them, by directions of the master, takes his station in front, and goes thro' the different tables with a loud voice, all the other scholars repeating after him at once. The boy who is the greatest proficient is generally chosen to take the lead; but at other times the master selects one of the younger boys, in order to ascertain whether he be able to go thro' the tables with accuracy. This proves no small incentive to each boy to make himself master of these tables, as any failure in this conspicuous situation is accompanied with great disgrace.

The multiplication tables being thus daily repeated are fixed indelibly on the mind of the scholar; and in this way he acquires a facility of performing arithmetical operations off hand, which frequently astonishes an European observer. For instance, I have often heard a series of pretty intricate questions, involving fractions and the Rule of Three, put to half a dozen of boys, one question being put to the first boy, another to the second, and so on in succession ; and by the time that a question had been given to the last boy, the first boy would answer the one which had been put to him, immediately after which the second boy would answer his question ; and thus it went thro' the whole ; so that in the course of two minutes, six different questions would be put to as many boys, and answered by them with the utmost correctness.

The children learn to write and cipher on a board covered with sand or brick dust, and the letters or figures are traced with a reed, or small wooden style, which the scholar is permitted to hold in whatever manner he finds most convenient. In the more advanced stages, however, and when the arithmetical operations extend to some length, I have observed in the schools here, that they paint the board with a black ground, and then write upon it with a mixture of chalk and water. This occupies much less room than in writing upon sand, is less liable to obliteration, and at the same time shews the figures in a plain and distinct form.

In the system of education thus briefly detailed, several very judicious arrangements will be noticed, both in regard to economy, and as to saving of time.

First, by writing upon a board covered with sand, there is saved the expence of paper, ink, and pens.

Secondly, writing and reading are taught together, instead of being made different branches of instruction. While tracing the forms of the letters or figures, the scholar at the same time repeats their names, a practice which is followed also when he proceeds to ciphering.

Thirdly, the scholar is taught the effect of placing one or more figures before another, and thus learns to distinguish between the nature of this position and the result of adding numbers together, a distinction which often puzzles beginners to whom it has not been carefully pointed out.

But what chiefly distinguishes the Hindu schools is the PLAN OF INSTRUCTION BY THE SCHOLARS THEMSELVES. When a boy joins the school, he is immediately put under the tuition and care of one who is more advanced in knowledge, and whose duty it is to give lessons to his young pupil, to assist him in learning, and to report his behaviour and progress to the master. The scholars are not classed as with us, but are generally paired off, each pair consisting of an instructor and a pupil. These pairs are so arranged that a boy less advanced may sit next to one who has made greater progress, and from whom he receives assistance and instruction. When, however, several of the elder boys have made considerable and nearly equal progress, they are seated together in one line, and receive their instructions directly from the master.

This plan of getting the older boys, and those who are more advanced, to assist those who are less advanced and younger, greatly lessens the burden imposed upon the master, whose duty, according to this system, is not to furnish instruction to each individual scholar, but to superintend the whole, and see that every one does his duty. If the younger boy does not learn his lessons with sufficient promptitude and exactness, his instructor reports him to the master, who enquires into the case, orders the pupil to repeat before him what he has learnt, and punishes him if he has been idle or negligent. As the master usually gives lessons to the elder scholars only, he has sufficient leisure to exercise a vigilant superintendance over the whole school, and by casting his eyes about continually, or walking up and down, and enquiring into the progress made by each pupil under his instructor, he maintains strict discipline, and keeps every one upon the alert thro' expectation of being called upon to repeat his lesson.

The arithmetical lessons are written down at full length. Thus in giving a case of addition, subtraction, multiplication, division, or the rule of three, the whole process is set down in figures, and the scholar goes over it on another part of the board, repeating the different steps in a loud voice as has been already noticed. After each lesson has been gone over till it be committed to memory, it is rubbed out, and then written down by the scholar himself without any assistance.

FINIS.